AVOID FINES!
BRING BOOKS BACK ON TIME

HILLINGDON
LONDON

NORTHWOOD HILLS
01923 824505

1 6 JUL 2009

1 7 AUG 2011

3 1 OCT 2012

0 4 OCT 2014

3 0 MAR 2015

- 9 JUL 2015

2 1 OCT 202

3 0 MAR 2024

Adult readers will be fined for items kept beyond the latest date stamped above. If not reserved by another reader, this item may be renewed by telephone or in person. When renewing, quote the barcode number or your ticket number.

PS 717

CALU 1

PEOPLE FROM THE OTHER SIDE

THE ENIGMATIC FOX SISTERS

AND THE HISTORY OF VICTORIAN SPIRITUALISM

MAURICE LEONARD

The
History
Press

First published 2008

The History Press Ltd
The Mill, Brimscombe Port
Stroud, Gloucestershire, GL5 2QG
www.thehistorypress.co.uk

British Library Cataloguing in Publication Data.
A catalogue record for this book is available from the British Library.

ISBN 978 1 84588 637 0

Typesetting and origination by The History Press Ltd
Printed in Great Britain

CONTENTS

Acknowledgements   7

Introduction   9

Chapter 1   17

Chapter 2   31

Chapter 3   55

Chapter 4   79

Chapter 5   111

Chapter 6   129

Chapter 7   145

Chapter 8   173

Chapter 9   193

Epilogue   205

Notes   209

Bibliography   215

Index   219

ACKNOWLEDGEMENTS

Thanks are due to many sources and people; without co-operation no biographical work would ever get written. Research, of course, started with the Fox sisters themselves who, between them, wrote quite a bit about their lives and opinions. Since I began this book, two other biographies have been published: *Talking to the Dead* by Barbara Weisberg, which concentrates on Kate and Maggie, and *The Reluctant Spiritualist*, a life of Maggie by Nancy Rubin Stuart.

I have tried to acknowledge help I received in the relevant pages, but among those due special thanks are: Nellie and Tony Liddell; Christina Hatt; Kevin Hubbard; Alan Woodhouse; Sarah Warre; Richard Wiseman, Professor of the Public Understanding of Psychology at the University of Hertfordshire; Peter Katin; John Lill; Earle E. Spamer of the American Philosophical Society; The Leslie Flint Educational Trust; The Theosophical Society; websites of the Elisha Kent Kane Historical Society; the Literary Network website; survivalafterdeath.org; all those colourful mediums who so enriched my youth; and, most particularly, the willing and able help of the magnificent British Library: so many exotic secrets buried in its archives.

INTRODUCTION

My early childhood was spent propped up on cushions, on a chair, sitting round a table in a room full of women, each of whom had one finger on an upturned glass frantically trying to hold on to it as it whizzed around, spelling out messages from letters cut out of newspapers, or else hand-written, which had been placed around the edge of the table.

The sound of the Cossor radio, buzzing away in the background, was often drowned by the noise of the glass, as it skidded over the wood before jerking to rest in front of whatever letter it wanted. Someone had a pencil and paper and would jot down the letter, then the glass would whiz off again until a message was written.

This was a normal evening during those blitz-ridden nights in London's war-scarred Tooting Broadway.

There was not much else to do. All places of entertainment were closed, due to the fear of air raids. Not that there were many places of entertainment to close, apart from the cinema.

As with Mrs Gaskell's *Cranford*, Tooting Broadway was a society 'in possession of the Amazons'; that is, there were no men about, just kids and old-timers. All able-bodied men were away defending us against the Nazis.

We could make our homes cosy, but outside it was pretty unwelcoming. Unless there was a moon, it was Stygian gloom; there were no streetlights, or lights from windows, due to black-out restrictions, and there was virtually no traffic. It was not a neighbourhood where many possessed cars, and with the majority of drivers being men, they were all away anyway.

What few cars did venture into the neighbourhood, and I seem to remember a battered Austin Seven with a discoloured windscreen that caused great excitement, had to crawl along with dim pin-point lights so as not to be visible to enemy planes overhead.

If people were walking at night – visiting relatives usually, as there was nowhere else to go – and bumped into each other (literally, as they couldn't see), they linked arms to avoid smashing into lamp posts – my grandmother suffered a bleeding nose through this – or twisting ankles by stumbling down kerbs. If the moon came out that was a bonus. God was on our side.

There was a great deal of laughter, and sometimes we'd sing songs as we blundered about in the dark, unable to see street names.

Enemy planes used to liven the place up as, when they approached, there would be dog-fights as they were repelled by our fighters, the sky lacerated with searchlights which appeared by magic. Spotlit, the two planes would fight to the death, the battle heralded by the ululating sirens. If a Nazi plane was shot down, plunging to the earth in a ball of fire, we cheered. If a British plane caught it, that was a terrible sadness; another brave man gone, another barrier less between Nazi domination and us.

People were killed all the time. Those at home never knew if their loved ones, who were at war, were dead or alive. We never knew if we'd survive the night. Only the spirits knew these things, but they would tell us.

It's not surprising that séances were popular. They were as routine as being woken up, under the protection of the cage-like, indoor Morrison shelter, by the crash of the plywood which had been nailed to the window frames in lieu of glass, as it was smashed against the wall opposite by bomb blasts. The glass had gone ages ago and there was none on sale to replace it, not that anyone would have bought it if there had been. That would have been a waste of time and, worse, a waste of money.

Spirits were a part of our lives, invariably friends, and we contacted them daily. We were warned by them that dark forces existed, that there were 'possessions' out there, lost souls killed in the mayhem who didn't know they were dead, and that there were also evil and frightened entities waiting to pounce on the unprotected (us) and live vicariously through us. But, providing we said prayers before the séances and ensured our guides were guarding us, then we would be safe. And for those who weren't safe, all was not lost, for there were 'rescue' mediums about, those who specialised in releasing possessions and putting them on the path to redemption. These 'rescue' circles could be pretty scary, with mediums threshing about and moaning before their guides achieved control of the possession. Only the strongest sitters joined forces with the 'possession' mediums, to help them in their Godly work.

My mother heard voices. Not all the time and not often, but when they came they were always accurate, although not always welcome. Once, my Aunt Ethel brought round for us to see a stray puppy she'd adopted. Homes were bombed all the time so there were plenty of lost, traumatised pets roaming the sites. You could hear the dogs whimpering at night, but seldom cats – they were too self-sufficient for that. Everyone in Tooting seemed to love animals and no matter how mean the rations, or short the money, there was always enough to scrape together some scraps to feed a dog and cat.

We all hugged the puppy but mother told me, after my aunt had left with the tail-wagger, that she'd gone cold when she held it. The voices had come: 'He won't live,' something horrid had whispered in her ear. The poor thing was soon run over by a 94 bus.

One of my grandmothers had died during the war and she and my mother had had words before she went. Upsets were not unusual and had that quarrel been put right another would undoubtedly have taken its place, but my mother was sad. At one of the table sessions the whizzing glass spelled out, 'I understand … Mother.' With that it turned on us all, knocked every letter off the table and refused to move again for the night. Always the spirits were capricious.

My Aunt Win was a medium, a tubby (but not jolly, rather sour if anything) lady who had never been young, with wiry auburn curls – her best feature everyone said – little piggy green eyes behind specs and an unkind tongue. She had been pushed out of her home at fourteen, as there was no place for her to sleep when her brothers came along, and was sent 'into service', starting off as a scullery maid and becoming a cook for a rich household.

She was well treated and enjoyed the camaraderie. But the war changed the circumstances of many. There was a great levelling of society; when peace came few houses could afford staff and Win lost her job. She became a school cook instead which, somehow, did not have the same cachet, even though she could sometimes nobble a bit of extra margarine or the like, which made her a useful contact.

She had never met a man who could love her. She had never 'known' a man in her lonely life: the archetypal Old Maid. This, coupled with her plain face, thick ankles attached to little feet always jammed into low-heeled court shoes, high blood pressure and a dodgy heart, gave her – understandably – a grudge against the world. She hated most people, but loved me. It was reciprocal: I adored her far more than my parents, and spent hours sitting with her. The spirits were her best friends.

She rented two rooms at the top of a house from a nice old drunk called Mrs Anstey. However hard-up Aunt Win was, she always seemed to have a good fire blazing away, its smoke adding to the smog that hung over London in the winter. It was quite smoky inside, too, as she was a devotee of Capstan Full Strength, and puffed away most of the time, whether delivering spirit messages or not. Her top lip was permanently stained with nicotine.

During the war, word had got round that Aunt Win was a medium and, at times, when we were sitting by her fire, there would be a knock at the front door. Mrs Anstey would open it and footsteps would plod up the stairs towards us. It would be a woman – it had to be, there were no men – sometimes young and sometimes not, driven mad with worry about her man. Would Win give her a sitting? Money never changed hands for this but sometimes an inducement might be brought, a skinned rabbit in those food-scarce times or, perhaps, a piece of cheese. Whatever.

Not that Win ever wanted anything; in truth, she did not want to give the reading, as it was a terrible responsibility. I would sit on my chair at the table while the tears flowed from the recipient as Win brought the spirits through and delivered messages.

By the time I was at school the war had ended. I was given an embossed V for Victory teaspoon to mark the occasion, which I slung away, now to my regret, as it would be worth a fortune.

Blackouts had been taken down and light poured from windows, streetlights were lit, the cinema opened and we were allowed a quarter of a pound of sweets a week, on the ration book, of course, but none of that stopped the spirits calling at Aunt Win's.

There were no improvised planchette boards there, she was above that. She and I communicated with the spirits mind to mind; or, rather, she did, I listened. Sometimes, of course, they read my mind. While other lads were out booting balls across streets and pillaging bombed-out houses, of which there were many (and I did my share of that, too), I sat with Aunt Win and the spirits. It was fun, they'd tell me what I'd done at school, who I'd met and, on occasion, even what I had in my pockets. Sometimes Aunt Win had a few colleagues round from the Spiritualist church; she felt a tepid warmth for fellow Spiritualists. They were all elderly, or seemed so to me, and this impressionable child would sit among them as the spirits chatted with us, through them. I'd be wide-eyed at all the things they knew.

It was much later, when I was at work and had graduated to sitting in circles with other mediums, that I heard of the Fox sisters. I was told about them by Madame Yolande, a professional and exceptionally accurate palmist, who had a pitch on a seaside pier (I've forgotten which one) during the season and sat with us in the winter.

Madame Yolande told me that Spiritualism had started in America in the nineteenth century, not in the Hollywood of film magazines, but in a remote country village, when two young girls, Kate and Maggie Fox, had heard inexplicable knockings in the night. Eventually, these knocks had been recognised as spirit raps. It was the Great Breakthrough and we, us sitters, were only doing what we did as a result of the pioneering Fox sisters. I was fascinated by them.

Florrie Gooch was the medium of a circle in Streatham in which I sat for years. Florrie was hoping for the Direct Voice that she had been promised, by Spirit, would come. Alas, it never did. Her great hero was Leslie Flint, probably the most famous Direct Voice medium in the world; our whole circle would troop on the bus to his Paddington home for an advisory séance once a year. It was a grand occasion.

Whereas Aunt Win hated everybody, Florrie's hatred centred on men. She had been married, but that had turned out wrong, which was why she hated all men.

Her séances followed a pattern. We sat in black silence for an hour or so, harmonious thoughts concentrated on Florrie who sat in her 'cabinet', a curtained-off corner of her bedroom. She was quite grotesque looking really, scrawny, with a distended stomach, and years before someone had made the grave error of telling her she had lovely hair. It was now a nasty urine yellow streaked with grey, which she wore unbecomingly long for her age.

Such impressions, however, are retrospective. I did not allow them to enter my head at the time. And, in order to encourage harmonious vibrations, and thus attract the right sort of spirit rather than the wrong, I used to try to envisage Florrie, during the séances, in the midst of a golden cornfield, wearing a halo of scarlet poppies, Bambis playing nearby. Like something from *Fantasia*. We'd sing a song if things got a bit heavy; nothing sacred, just a pretty tune or two.

Now and then a visiting medium would join us; no one famous, just someone known locally. I nearly shot out of my chair one evening when I was sitting with Florrie, envisaging the Bambis and poppies, when Betty, a visitor, suddenly yelped out, extremely loudly, a tuneless rendition of *The Roses Round the Door, Make Me Love Mother More*. The shock nearly gave me a stroke; it was horrible. 'That'll liven things up,' said Betty. It did the reverse, it killed the evening stone dead. If any sensible spirits had been around they'd have shot for cover. As much as their capriciousness, spirits are also noted for their love of fine music. Betty's was not fine music and try as I might I could find little that was spiritual in the lyrics. It certainly wouldn't attract me if I were dead: quite the reverse, I'd have gone somewhere else.

The highlight of the circle came at the end. We would be addressed by one or, on special occasions two, of Florrie's three principal guides. These were an Indian (as in Native American) chief, as popular in the 1950s as they had been in the times of the Foxes, called Red Feather, who shattered the room with his guttural bass, a sort of pretend Oxbridge fractured by an indefinable accent; a frail nun who'd had a terrible tragedy somewhere in her earthly past but never directly referred to it; and the inevitable spirit child, Wong. He was for light relief and we always screamed with laughter when he announced his presence, albeit he wasn't all that funny. But he tried.

At least twice a week, my girlfriend Iris and I, with a few lady Spiritualists, attended either Balham Spiritualist church or Tooting Bec. Poor Iris wasn't really interested but I was, so she had to come, that was the deal. She had to sit in the circle, too. Small wonder she married someone else.

Balham church had a stained-glass window that faced the setting sun. I remember the sun streaming through that lovely window; it seemed so appropriate for the higher teachings we were receiving. For all spirit communications were higher teachings. They lived on an elevated plane so naturally they were more highly evolved than us.

Each week there were visiting mediums who, through their psychic ability, would prove there was no death. Not that anyone doubted it. We were all believers. Most of the mediums were pretty good clairvoyants. There was Florrie Something-or-other, who wore her hair plaited earphone style and who suffered from indigestion. She sometimes burped when relaying messages, and when this happened would put her hand over her tummy and apologise, 'Sausages.'

My favourite was Ivy Scott, a plump lady, still good-looking, firmly against book reading (she couldn't read much herself) who had been on the stage and had a gorgeous soprano voice. She would sing the hymns beautifully, her eyebrows lifting as she took her petal-soft high notes.

Her guide was summoned by *Hushed Was the Evening Hymn*. Unless this was sung he did not come through—sensible spirit, it was delightful. Mrs Scott did it full justice, her sweet voice bringing to life the meltingly beautiful melody to which the inspired words of James Drummond Burns are set. Life had few pleasures to vie with that performance, with the stained-glass window as its backdrop. No wonder her guide delivered such convincing service.

I had a private sitting with her once. Her opening words were, 'Who was Arthur? Shot down in an aircraft?' My uncle Arthur had been a rear-gunner in a plane and had been shot down in the war. I did not know that at the time and only found out when my mother, his sister, told me later, when I told her about Ivy's sitting. So how did she know that? A lucky guess? Very lucky to get the right name, right occupation and right manner of death in one sentence. I don't think so.

There were blatant frauds, of course, such as a South African lady who wandered around the hall accompanied by electronic-sounding squeaks. We were informed this was her guide's direct voice. It sounded more like something operated by a battery to me. Whatever it was it was gobbledegook.

There was another one, a ghastly Scottish chap, who announced on one occasion that he had a message in Hebrew for the recipient. He could not speak Hebrew but would repeat what his communicator was saying. He intoned the single word *shalom*. Equivalent to someone saying they couldn't speak French, but would a Frenchman understand *oui*. There were a few embarrassed faces and a stifled giggle or two. Who did he think he was kidding? To the recipient's credit she sat there straight-faced and dignified and murmured 'Thank you'.

Divine healing was popular, particularly among the healers. They would positively tout for customers. I'm sure many gave relief to their patients but there was a dreadful old scoundrel called Mr Scholes, tiny with a bald head with a cyst on top like a nipple—I wonder he didn't get someone to heal that for him.

He was particularly keen on healing the chests of several of the well-upholstered ladies of the congregation. Much to his annoyance he had to do this in company, in the midst of the circle, while we sitters sat around him to strengthen the power.

On high days and holidays there was the Spiritualist Association of Great Britain, housed at 33 Belgrave Square, the heart of embassy land.

This was a much grander affair altogether. The building was, and is, elegant, a pleasure from outside and a joy to walk into. Someone told me the lease was bought in 1955 for £24,500. You couldn't get a parking space for that now.

In those days, if you arrived a bit early, there was a lovely little café on the premises where tea and home-made cakes were served by a mumsy lady in a sunny room that overlooked the small garden.

Then, as you entered the public demonstration room, a dear old queen, with an amethyst on her pinkie, would be gently stroking out *I'll Walk Beside You* from the organ keys, or a similarly delightful tune. You could sit and meditate before the service, and ignore the occasional bickering of the women if someone had taken their favourite seat. It would all settle down eventually; after all, they were there for the higher teachings.

These were lively, fun and, occasionally, inspiring times. Times when you could leave a demonstration pondering on what you'd heard. The pondering might still happen now, but those halcyon days have gone, of course, and with them some of their magic. Or is it just youth that's gone? Nowadays things seem more Spartan, more practical. There seems to be less daring, less controversy in the air, and that's a shame. For Spiritualism was born of controversy; its pioneers were nothing if not controversial.

Albert Einstein wrote, 'The most beautiful thing to be felt by man is the mysterious side of life;' Raymond Chandler, 'Show me a man or woman who cannot stand mysteries and I will show you a fool;' and Quentin Crisp, 'Is not the whole world a vast house of assignation to which the filing system has been lost?'

Spiritualism may not have deciphered the filing system but it spends time and effort trying.

This book concentrates on those heady days of the beginning of Spiritualism and also offers an insight into twentieth- and twenty-first-century Spiritualism, for it is a movement that is still world-wide and thriving. It centres on the Fox sisters who, of course, *are* Spiritualism, but also the many peripheral figures, including the magnificent and extraordinary Madame Blavatsky, who peopled those early séance rooms and brought their own particular colour and gifts to the scene.

And what exactly was the significance of those happenings on that magical, mystical night in bleak New York State on the 31 March 1848?

1

'Her life a beautiful memory'
'His absence a silent grief'
'Remember! and wait for me.'

Can the dead read their epitaphs? Do they watch us weeping over their graves? Can they guide us?

Ghosts have always been with us; their appearances random and fleeting – sometimes comforting, often alarming. Perhaps they glimpse us in the same way?

The first time in modern history that a ghost seems to have succeeded in making an organised breakthrough was in the March of 1848. This was no spirit scientist, no manifestation of Isaac Newton or Galileo come to enlighten humanity, but an uneducated pedlar called Charles Rosna, who claimed he had had his throat slit for his money, his gushing blood collected in a kitchen basin which was then, with his body, chucked into a cellar.

His motive was revenge and his instruments of communication two adolescent farm girls – Kate and Maggie Fox.

March can be a vicious month upstate New York, and it was particularly so in 1848, when much of the land was undeveloped and a frozen wind whipped across the desolate plains. Yet the worst of the winter was over with, sometimes, even a taste of spring in the air, but as soon as this appeared it was quickly soured by the constant and pelting icy rain. Where the ground wasn't still frozen solid it had deteriorated into a sucking marshland. What houses there were clustered together for warmth.

In the hamlet of Hydesville, where Kate and Maggie lived, the only heat and light came from open fires, candles and oil lamps. At night the wind gathered strength and tore through the loose-fitting doors and window frames, making them rattle like dancing skeletons, and the candles flicker eerily.

Outside the darkness was unbroken apart from the sporadic moonlight, which silverly lit the barren landscape when the clouds were blown away for a few seconds. Then the darkness returned, and the pelting rain, reaching into the sodden infinity.

It was easy to believe that the dead walked those lonely moors and many believed they did.

Gathered round the fire in the evenings, Kate and Maggie would listen to their mother's ghost stories, clutching each other in ecstatic fear. It all seemed very real – too real, sometimes.

Margaret Fox, devoted and good mother that she was, believed in ghosts and had no quibbles about letting her daughters know this. She needed someone sympathetic to talk to and got nowhere on this subject with her wiry, dour husband, John. He didn't want to know. An alcoholic, off the booze at the time, John didn't want to know about much.

A blacksmith, they'd married when they were both sixteen, but after four children he left her for a decade or so while he plied his trade, and whatever else he could, on the Erie Canal.

This was not as callous as it sounds. Although four children did not make for a particularly big family then, they still had to be provided for. The canal offered enormous financial opportunities.

Opened in 1825, its construction was the greatest engineering feat of its day. With a length of 363 miles, it stretched from Albany to Buffalo, and contained 83 locks and 18 aqueducts. It was built mostly by man and horse or mule power, the animals towing the laden barges along its length. It brought thousands of settlers. The land was rich and the mobility offered by the canal – roads were built just to get to it – transformed New York into the most important commercial city in America. It also offered great opportunities for a blacksmith.

America was developing fast. Railways were being built and swamps cleared. Tree felling was taking place and forests larger than Ireland, from where many of the immigrant workers came, were cleared. Ireland itself

was in the midst of one of its several tragedies, a potato blight was causing famine and widespread emigration to America.

The Fox marriage was not a match made in heaven. John had finished
with his life of wine, women and gambling but this was not through any
strong paternal urge to be with his family. Having been on the road as a
blacksmith for a decade or so, he was getting too old for his peripatetic
existence and felt the need for home comforts: a warm bed and regular
cooked meals.

Giving up booze had strengthened his religion, which had clearly
lapsed during his canal work. Both he and Margaret were Methodists
and Methodists are staunchly against the abuse of alcohol. It was with
born-again religious fervour that he resumed his position as nominal
family head, sired Maggie and Kate, and looked forward to the cosiness
of an abstemious home life. He didn't find it: instead of enjoining his
new young family to an existence of blameless Godliness, they were to
plunge him into a maelstrom of blasphemous controversy.

Kate and Maggie were both born in Consecon, Canada, Margaret's
homeland just across the border from New York. Margaret was from
Franco-Dutch stock and John had German roots – the family name had
originally been Voss. Kate, or Catherine, their youngest, was born on
27 March 1837 and Maggie, or Margaretta, 7 October 1833. After the
birth of the children they moved to Rochester, New York, then on to
Hydesville.

Their cottage at Hydesville was only ever meant as a standby. Margaret's
family were comfortably off, which was as well for they had helped support her during John's prolonged absence, when payments from him
had been irregular. John was now building a new house for the family
near the village smithy, where he would work, but in the December of
1847 – when bad weather forced him to stop – he'd taken the cottage
as a stopgap. Kate was nearly 11 by now and Maggie getting on for 15,
virtually a young lady.

The elder four Fox children, adults now, had long since set up their
own homes. Ann Leah, who preferred to be known as Leah, was in her
30s, born 8 April 1813. A natural musician with a good singing voice, she
earned her living by teaching children piano and singing and lived with
her only child, her teenage daughter Lizzie, in the up-and-coming town
of Rochester about twenty-five miles away.

Leah claimed to have been married to a Mr Bowman Fish at the
age of 14 and, indeed, was known as Mrs Fish to the local community.

Whether they were legally married or just lived together is uncertain, and no one in their orbit would have been overly perturbed either way providing they adhered to the outward proprieties. Mr Fish abandoned Leah soon after Lizzie was born, which made life financially hard but did not trouble her too much emotionally. Apart from the money she felt better off without him. Leah was an excellent manager and quite capable of bringing up her child alone, and 14 had been an early age to commit to a life-long union.

Perhaps Lizzie's birth was the reason for her husband's departure. Or perhaps the fact that Lizzie was their only child indicated other problems, for they were together a few years, certainly long enough to have had other children. Leah was fond of children, maternal by nature, and the sort to have as many as possible. She welcomed visits from her nieces and nephews and clearly enjoyed their company. The only child she seemed to have had reservations about was her own daughter, Lizzie. Perhaps she blamed Lizzie for the breakdown in her relationship? She brought back too many unwelcome memories.

Margaret, John, Kate and Maggie had stayed with Leah and Lizzie for a while when first moving to New York. She had enjoyed their company and missed them when they left. As life was to prove, Leah was fiercely ambitious, and there were times when the calm respectability of her music-teaching life, fell well short of fulfillment. She felt her resources were not being tapped. Surely life had more to offer? The Foxes had another two daughters, both married. Elizabeth lived in Canada and Maria nearby, married to her cousin. Marriage to relatives was not uncommon. They were not to play an important role in either Kate or Maggie's lives.

The only son, David, in his late 20s, was a big, bluff and popular man, married with three children. He lived close to Hydesville, one of the reasons the Foxes had moved there. He had put them up before they had moved into the cottage. He was a successful peppermint farmer with a large homestead. In the season the pungent smell of his plants permeated the atmosphere and their pink flowers could be seen for miles. It was a peaceful place, and in times of crisis family members converged there. With the good-hearted, down-to-earth David in charge, it seemed a secure haven.

John found it difficult to take over the reins of his new family. He'd been away too long to assert authority. Margaret had run things on her own for over a decade and did not intend to alter her ways now. Although a God-fearing Methodist she had a distinct respect for, and belief in, the supernatural. Her grandmother, so she would tell, had been blessed with foresight, being able to decipher omens, and was uncomfortably accurate in predicting deaths. This clearly ran in the family as grandmother had had a sister who had successfully predicted her own death date. This was common talk in the house.

It wasn't until 29 March 1848 that the family was disrupted by noises at night. The days were still short then, and the whole family retired soon after dark. These noises were not the normal nocturnal scuffles of wild animals, nor the sighs of a house cooling down, but distinct knocks as though someone were trying deliberately to attract attention.[1] The cottage was two stories high, a single large room above four rooms below, comprising of a sitting room, two bedrooms and a kitchen. A pantry in the kitchen opened onto steps leading down to a cellar. Margaret and John occupied one bedroom and the girls the other. The noises were coming from the girls' room.

These sounds were not terrible in themselves and not particularly loud, but it was their manifestation in the dead of night that made them so frightening. They were loud enough to wake John and Margaret who lit a candle and went to the girls' room to investigate. The noises continued while they were there, seeming to centre on the girls' bed. There seemed to be two types of knocks: distinct clicks and a heavier, thudding sound. The latter seemed to make the floor vibrate.

John looked through the other rooms but there was nothing unusual there. The sounds were certainly coming from the vicinity of the girls. All four looked at each other in silence. The girls were so frightened they refused to sleep alone so their bed was moved into their parents' room. But the sounds continued there. John prayed and Margaret wrung her hands but the noises did not stop. Eventually, with great difficulty, the family drifted into troubled sleep.

As dawn lit the house and the countryside, things didn't seem so terrible. Margaret half-heartedly suggested it might have been neighbours playing a trick on them or, perhaps, even the nearby cobbler working late. Even as she spoke she knew this was nonsense. Why would their practical, hard-working neighbours do such a stupid thing as make jokey noises in the dead of night? And the cobbler? He'd never kept such hours before. But it was something to cling to.

That evening before sunset, as they settled round the blazing fire, the talk returned to the raps, which they'd been thinking about all day anyway. Margaret, with her superstitious nature, was certainly not going to let it drop. The children were nervous but excited. Would the sounds come again?

They could hardly miss them.

Loud knocks, even more insistent than those of the previous night, started as soon as they went to bed. The girls were still in their parents' room. This time they seemed to come from all round, on the furniture, floor and even the door. Then footsteps were heard, heading to the pantry and, seemingly, continuing down the stairs to the cellar. Margaret wrote in her statement a few days later, 'I then concluded that the house must be haunted by some unhappy restless spirit.' She thought it was her dead, psychic grandmother. John agreed with his wife's statement and added, 'I do not know of any way to account for those noises, as being caused by any natural means.'

The raps came to a head the next night, Friday 31 March 1848, the date when the new religion of Spiritualism was officially born. It seemed the Gods had something fanciful in mind for the weather had worsened during the day and a downfall of sleet was being pelted by an angry wind against the cottage. It was no weather to be out in. But David called and was upset by the nigh hysterical state of his mother. She told him of the two frightening nights the family had endured. Knowing her fanciful disposition he didn't take it too seriously but comforted her, saying there was probably a natural reason for it all. Odd things happened in the country at night.

This could not continue. Margaret decided that whatever happened that night, even if the raps caused the roof to fall in, they would not rise from their beds. She was determined they would all get some sleep. She was, after all, a mother.

Her resolution was dashed as soon as night fell. With the exception of John, who was sitting up on guard, they all went to bed early, before nightfall in fact, to try to make up for all the sleep they had lost. The raps started at once. Whatever was causing them seemed annoyed at being ignored and was determined to be noticed. They were more insistent, more regular, and unrelenting.

Margaret moaned while the girls huddled together in bed. John checked the window frames to make sure no draught could be causing the noises, there were loose planks outside – he knew no wind could produce such a rhythmic pattern, but with a terrified wife and two young daughters, he was desperate. He had to do something.

The children seemed less afraid now, it was almost as if they had formed some rapport with the sounds; as though the noises had got through to them. To Margaret's horror, Kate had got up and was standing by her bed, listening.

Now, in addition to the knocks there was also the sound of muffled laughter but this had no supernatural source. Torn between fear and exhaustion the youngsters had a fit of hysterical giggles. This was to be a pattern throughout Kate's life. Often, when phenomena was at its height she would nervously giggle.

'Mr Splitfoot, do as I do!'

Margaret jumped out of her skin. The voice seemed to come from the depth of a tomb — but it was no spirit speaking, it was Kate. A single candle lit the bedroom and the words cut through the shadows.

'Mr Splitfoot' was a colloquial name for the devil. On a night such as this, with the wind howling and the spirits knocking, the last thing Margaret wanted was for the devil to be called up. She watched aghast as Kate clapped three times. Was her daughter possessed? She was even more aghast when three raps echoed the rhythm of the claps. In the silence that followed all that could be heard was the howling wind. Then Maggie spoke.

'Now, do just as I do,' she said slowly, in a similarly deep voice to the one Kate had used. 'Count one, two, three, four.' She clapped her hands four times. Four raps followed, again in the same rhythm. The girls suddenly seemed to realise what was happening and grew frightened. There was silence for a while. All sorts of fears crashed through Margaret's mind. Was a Satanic spirit in the room with her two virgin daughters? It was too ghastly to contemplate.

'Oh, mother, I know what it is,' Kate said weakly. 'Tomorrow is April Fool day, and it's somebody trying to fool us.'

Margaret seized on that as a life belt. That's what it was, of course, an April Fool's prank. But who was playing it? She dismissed the idea even as it entered her head. It was impossible for anyone to have entered the house unknown and make these noises. She now took command and devised a test to determine if it was a neighbour or not. Although she could not bring herself to address the spirit as Mr Splitfoot, for she was convinced it was a spirit, she nervously spoke to it.

'Can you rap out the different ages of my children,' she asked. None of the neighbours, to her knowledge, knew their exact ages. Mr Splitfoot seemed to.

He rapped out correctly the ages of her six children and then, after a pause, gave three more raps. Margaret had actually had seven children but one, a girl, had died at the age of three, long before the births of Kate and Maggie. Margaret was sure this was information none of the neighbours knew. She wasn't even sure that Kate and Maggie knew.

'Is this a human being that answers my questions so correctly?' she asked nervously.

Silence.

'Is it a spirit? If it is, make two raps.' Two distinct raps.

'Is it an injured spirit?'

Two loud raps. In her statement she says that these raps made the house tremble. Gathering courage, she asked:

'Were you hurt in this house?' Two raps.

'Is this person living that injured you?' Again two loud raps.

Margaret carried on with the questions and the spirit divulged the grisly information that he had been a man of 31, and had been murdered in the house and his body dumped in the cellar. Margaret thought of the footsteps she had heard the previous night going down to the cellar. It was harrowing.

'Will you continue to rap if I call my neighbours that they may hear it too?' She was in dire need of support. The girls seemed stunned into silence and John could do nothing. He was standing uselessly by, not quite believing what was happening.

Two raps.

There was no way Margaret was going out into the night herself. She sent John, who was quite glad to get out. It was still only about 7.30 but inky black and icy cold. The elements refreshed him. They seemed wholesome after what had gone on. He went to fetch Mrs Redfield, their nearest neighbour. This was a good choice, she was a down-to-earth, practical sort and fond of the girls. Margaret described her as 'candid'. John was by no means convinced it was spirits rapping, but he could think of nothing else. And he did believe in the forces of evil.

Mrs Redfield had actually met Kate coming home from the village school after the first night of disturbances. The excited girl had babbled to her about the knocks, although Mr Splitfoot had yet to make his debut. Mrs Redfield had taken it with a pinch of salt. She'd never been impressed by John and knew how he'd abandoned his wife for years. She was even less impressed with him now as, in grunted monosyllables, he related the ridiculous story. She did not believe for one minute that spirits were knocking at the Fox cottage. John told her Kate had said something about an April Fool's joke and she thought so, too. She thought it was the girls. But she went readily enough with John. What else was there to do in that remote hamlet? A break in routine was welcome, particularly if it was fun, as this promised to be.

As soon as Mrs Redfield entered the Fox home all thoughts of fun evaporated. The atmosphere was icy and the girls were in bed, clutching each other. She was even more disconcerted when Margaret asked Mr Splitfoot some personal questions about her, all of which he answered correctly, including her age. Thoughts of the girls playing a prank were gone. She left more quickly than she had arrived but returned with her husband to witness these strange events. Margaret asked questions about him, too, and Mr Splitfoot answered these correctly.

Mr Redfield then ran off to alert more neighbours and came back with several other couples, including the Dueslers, Jewells and Hydes (Hydesville was named after their ancestors), all of whom later bore witness to the truth of these occurrences. Margaret, forgetting her former terror, now set herself up as Mistress of Ceremonies. She asked Mr Splitfoot if it was any of the neighbours who had hurt him.

Silence. Mr Duesler, a forceful man, took over and blurted out the question she'd already asked.

'Were you murdered?'

Two resounding raps.

Mr Duesler discovered Mr Splitfoot was the spirit of a pedlar called Rosna, who had been murdered by having his throat slit for his money – a fortune of $500 – five years ago in the bedroom now occupied by the girls. He named his murderer as John Bell, a former resident of the house and confirmed his body had been buried in the cellar, together with some of his effects.

He was able to give these pieces of information through a system that the group had devised. The alphabet was called out and he would rap at the letter he wanted. This speeded things up considerably. Mr Deusler is sometimes credited for devising this system of communication but, according to Margaret, it was she, which would seem uncharacteristically practical. Margaret was not quick-thinking, particularly under pressure. Leah, who, to her chagrin, was not there at the time, claims in her memoir *The Missing Link in Modern Spiritualism*[2] published many years later when the sisters were world famous, that the technique was devised in the spirit world by no less a figure than the statesman and author Benjamin Franklin who had imparted it to her. Other accounts give David – at a later session – as devisor. Whenever it was devised, or by whom, it quickly took on and was to remain a staple of rapping mediums for years to come and is still used in some circles.

Meanwhile, the cottage was filling up. Word had spread and fishermen, who had been in the creek nearby, had come in to see what was going on, as had other neighbours. The girls were still huddled in bed. Margaret felt this was no situation for her children to be in. She was also indignant that Mr Duesler seemed to have upstaged her. She and Mrs Redfield took the girls away. Kate and Maggie spent the night at Mrs Redfield's while Margaret went to another neighbour.

John, Mr Redfield, Mr Deusler and other folk who had wandered in seemed set to spend the night in the cottage. Word spread of the miraculous power of the girls, doubtless exaggerated. This was not to John's liking but he could do nothing about it. Some said the raps continued after the girls had left but others denied it. No one knows.

What is known, however, is that the whole of the Western world was buzzing with the news of Samuel Morse's wonderful new code. Morse had created much excitement four years earlier, in 1844, when he had sent an electrically powered message some thirty-seven miles from Washington DC to Baltimore using his new invention, The Telegraph. Electronic dots and dashes represented the letters. Even an isolated hamlet like Hydesville was aware of the Morse Code and how raps could convey messages. Its arrival coincided neatly with the beginnings of rapped spirit messages.

Ever since Benjamin Franklin flew his kite during a thunderstorm and invented the lightning conductor, followed in 1821 by Michael Faraday's experiments with magnets and invention of the electric motor, the very notion of electricity was synonymous with mysticism to many non-scientific minds. As was The Ether, that non-material medium reputed to fill all space and transmit electromagnetic waves. Both The Ether and electricity were to occupy the minds of mystics in the years to come.

Did the raps owe something to the work of Benjamin Franklin or, indeed, the invention of the Morse Code? If so, the spirit world must be in a parallel evolutionary state to our own.

In the morning Margaret collected the girls, intending to return to the cottage. It was not a pleasant sight. The crowd had grown even bigger and spilled outside. People were jeering for the pedlar to make himself known, and for the knocks to sound. If they had sounded they'd have been inaudible amid the din. The confusion of the next days was unbearable. Margaret says that, at times, up to 300 people were present. Eventually the family moved in with David intending to stay there until the furore subsided.

That Saturday night, 1 April, some of the men organised themselves into a party to dig up the cellar and look for Rosna's body, to see if there was any truth in what had been rapped out. Unfortunately, the heavy rain that season made this impossible and after a few feet the cellar floor flooded. Digging was resumed some time later when the weather had improved. No corpse was found, but there was a tin box which might, or might not, have been Rosna's, and a few shreds of bone and hair. No one was sure if they were human or animal. The sort of things anyone might find anywhere if they were digging a deep hole.

Miriam Bucker Pond, who was to marry David's grandson, wrote a biography of the Fox sisters[3] and tells us that David kept the animal remains, human or otherwise, which he would show to interested parties, but they were accidentally destroyed around 1900. The tin box was later presented to the Spiritualist community of Lily Dale in upstate New York.

Before moving in with David, the Foxes spent another few days at their cottage. This was at his insistence, bluff man that he was; he could not help but be intrigued by the sensation his quiet mother and baby sisters had created. He was to become fascinated by it, a believer in the girls and a tower of strength to them all his life.

He had spent that Saturday helping the men dig up the cellar then, ushering most of the crowd away – and they took notice of him for he was a respected man in a position to offer employment – the group spent the night there. There were no raps and they did not resume until the following Tuesday, 4 April.

David learnt from his mother that not only could Rosna hear the girls, as demonstrated by his replicating the number of sounds they made, but clearly he could also see them. Kate had silently held up two fingers and asked him to knock that number. He had done so. This experiment had been repeated several times with a differing number of fingers.

David discovered other things about Rosna. He had said his killer's name was Bell. One of the neighbours, a Mrs Pulver, knew the name well. John Bell and his family had occupied the cottage in 1844, prior to a family called Weekman, who had been tenants before the Foxes. This meant that the Bells would have been living there five years ago, which fitted in with when the pedlar claimed he had been murdered.

Mrs Pulver was a weaver who used to work from the Bell cottage where she kept her loom. She told David how she had gone to work one morning and found an agitated Mrs Bell who told her she had been kept awake all night by the sound of footsteps wandering from room to room. Mrs Bell thought that, at a pinch, it might have been rats but was far from convinced. She was used to rats; they were an annoying but regular part of life. All houses had them. These sounds had been different.

Mrs Pulver now wondered if, perhaps, Mrs Bell's agitation had been a sign of a guilty conscience, a fear of something bad in which she'd been involved? It had not struck Mrs Pulver as particularly sinister at the time, but now she was thinking. Mrs Pulver's daughter, Lucretia, had worked for the Bells and lived with them for several months. She, too, now she thought about it, had heard odd sounds at night, including ghostly footsteps going down to the cellar. She had not thought to mention these things before. To back up her allegations she claimed that a Miss Aurelia Losey, who had been staying with her at the cottage, had also heard raps and footsteps. They had locked the windows and doors in fear.

She remembered that a pedlar, aged about 30, had visited Hydesville about five years ago. He had called on the Bells with his merchandise and been invited to stay the night, as happened with itinerant pedlars. After his arrival, Lucretia had then been sent away for a few days. When she returned he had gone and had not been seen since. This, in itself, was not unusual. Wandering pedlars did call at the hamlet from time to time, and it was possible such a pedlar might have as much as $500 on him if he had been travelling for some time. Had he boasted of his wealth or even shown it to John Bell who then concocted a plan to steal it?

Lucretia also remembered that when she'd returned to the Bells she'd been sent to the cellar to fetch something and had tripped on newly turned earth there. Mr Bell had been working on the cellar floor. Mrs Bell had shown her some trinkets which, she said, she had bought from the pedlar. Other trinkets surfaced in the household from time to time.

Lucretia recalled that the pedlar had worn light-coloured pants and a black coat. People remembered that, the previous year, a Mrs Lape, who lived nearby, had claimed to have seen the ghost of a man in the Bell cottage who was wearing clothes of that description.

Michael Weekman, who had occupied the house immediately before the Foxes, was contacted and he and his wife Hannah stated that they, too, had heard noises one night. In their case it was a loud banging on the front door. It had happened three times in succession and each time he had opened the door to find no one there. Another time he had heard his name called several times by a man of whom there was no trace. His wife told him he'd been dreaming.

Hannah Weekman remembered that their 8-year-old daughter had woken them by her screams one night claiming something cold and clammy had touched her face.

No one knew the whereabouts of John Bell but nevertheless the rumour spread that he was a murderer. Those who had known him did not believe it and swore he had been a friendly, helpful man. Eventually the outcry was so great that forty people signed a petition claiming he was of good character and, in their opinion, incapable of murder – which did not prove a thing.

The general consensus, however, is that he was cruelly slandered by Rosna, whoever, or whatever, Rosna might have been. If he was a spirit, was he settling some vendetta from across the veil or simply lying out of malice? Or had Bell indeed murdered him? Was it all poppycock? By now the entire area was aware of the odd happenings and wild rumours. The first of what was to be many reporters contacted the family. In time both Kate and Maggie were to become expert at manipulation of the press, or spin, to use today's term, but on this particular visit the reporter, a Mr E.E. Lewis, was strangely more concerned with the views of the adults than the children.

On 11 April he collected signed depositions from John and Margaret and their neighbours. These were hastily and distractedly dictated in the company of everyone else and memories were jogged, prompted or invented. Lewis published his research in a pamphlet entitled *A Report of the Mysterious Noises Heard in the House of Mr. John D Fox*. Much of the above information is taken from it and it was to become the starting point for all future investigations of the Foxes.

2

Psychic forces were also stirring in far off Russia. Seventeen years earlier, in 1831, in Ekaterinoslav, Ukraine, a girl, who was christened Helena von Hahn, was born into an aristocratic family.

She was to become a famed mystic who, it was claimed, was in direct touch with highly evolved, sometime discarnate beings she termed Mahatmas, or Masters, who, when incarnate, inhabited an ashram in remote Tibet. Their aim was to restore to the world ancient spiritual teachings, to combat the growing materialism of the time, and they had chosen Helena as their mouthpiece.

In order to do this her formidable intellect was boosted by psychic powers. Her books, among them *Isis Unveiled* and *The Secret Doctrine*, are monumental in size, profundity and occult lore. Yet, like the Fox sisters, she was to become engulfed in a scandal so vast it is still reverberating.

Myths surround her childhood, some instigated by colleagues and others by her sister Vera Zhelikovsky, who wrote about her in the Russian magazine *Rebus* (various translations of this exist in Theosophical literature). Some she founded herself in her numerous writings or were revealed by her many and varied biographers.[1] Some were lies, others *based* on truth and others entirely true. It is a maze to decipher which is which. No one will ever know.

One of the myths is that the priest's robes caught fire during her Russian Orthodox christening, as a protest (by whom?) at having Christianity thrust upon her. Another is that, like Margaret Fox's grandmother, she was able to predict deaths. She was a somnambulist and often sleepwalked through the underground passages of her grandmother, the Princess Dolgorukov's palace at night which, like many old palaces, was reputed to be haunted. Helena spoke in her sleep and some of the servants swore they heard whispered replies. A strange child. It is said that she learnt much from a centenarian apiarist who was a magician. His bees would swarm over him as she sat beside him, unafraid, and absorbing his secrets.

She had incorporeal playmates, unseen by anyone else; one of these was an Asian guardian who, she claimed, although she did not know it at the time, was one of her Mahatmas. Twice he saved her life. In keeping with many ladies of her class, she was an expert horsewoman, but she once had a bad fall. The Mahatma materialised and caught her, lowering her to safety. On the other occasion, she was tomboyishly climbing on furniture and fell again. Again her Mahatma saved her; his presence indicated by a handprint, high above the furniture, which had not been there before.

These anecdotes, in keeping with numerous others, came about when she was famous. However shadowy Helena's past, one thing is certain, that when the time was ripe, and she devotedly started her Mahatma's occult work, the whole world sat up and took notice. Her first steps into public prominence were through Spiritualism.

This is the point where Leah makes her impact or, perhaps more accurately, where Leah starts the story, for without her, the novelty of the sisters might well have fizzled out. Her influence on the girls was enormous. She gave them careers. But for Leah the Spiritualist movement might never have happened and Kate and Maggie would have remained anonymous country girls.

By today's youth-obsessed, stick-insect standard of beauty, perhaps Leah might not be considered a great catch. She was in her mid-30s, regally plump and with a hefty backside. In the 1840s, however, a man valued a nourished woman in her prime, and she was pretty, quick-witted and fiercely independent. Add to this her expressive, dimpled hands, her accomplishment as a pianist and a singing voice that could charm the angels and she was, by the values of the day, an attractive woman. Men tended to like her. She was determined to be recognised as the founder of Spiritualism (alas she failed there) and in *The Missing Link in Modern Spiritualism* she informs us of her many achievements while keeping those of Kate and Maggie to a minimum: 'I regret to be compelled to speak so much of myself', etc.

She tells us that Bowman Fish had abandoned her to marry a rich widow. Apparently no divorce papers were served on either side, which would further indicate he and Leah had never married. For, if Fish had married Leah then his marriage to the widow would have been bigamous. In the unhappy event of the rich widow's death, he would not have wanted some first wife tangling up a possible inheritance. Particularly a first wife as strong-willed as Leah.

With the exception of the patriarch John, there was a strong family bond between the Foxes and Leah kept in regular touch with her mother and sisters, her daughter, Lizzie, often staying with them at Hydesville. It was almost a month after the start of the rappings before Leah came to hear about them. In later life this was a sore point with her as she would have liked to have been in on things from the beginning. At the time, she was deadly bored with life and yearned for something exciting although there seemed little prospect of this. She was frustrated in every way: sexually, artistically and financially. The rappings altered that.

One morning in May, as she was teaching, her pupil's mother disrupted the lesson by bursting unceremoniously into the room with a man, a printer. She was waving proofs of Lewis's pamphlet upon which the printer was working. He knew Leah's maiden name was Fox and wanted to know if she was related to the Hydesville Foxes who were the centre of the marvellous rappings. Leah was given the proofs to read and asked if it was true. She stated that if her father, mother, and brother had said it was true then it must be so. The lesson was cancelled and she rushed to two friends, a Mrs Adelaide Granger and a Mrs Belle Grover, who agreed to accompany her, and Lizzie, to Hydesville to see what was going on. This was the something exciting for which she had been yearning.

They took the packet boat that very night via the Erie Canal to Newark. There, they hired a carriage to take them through the waterlogged landscape to the Hydesville cottage.

The Foxes weren't there, but a few people were hanging around outside, who told them the family had moved to David's. They drove to the peppermint farm, past where work was resuming on the new Fox home. Margaret and the girls were there but John was staying with his daughter Maria. Margaret was reading the Bible, her lips moving as she read. The local preacher had accused them of devilry and some of the rougher locals were resorting to mob rule. What could they lose: they had God on their side? There had been some threatening episodes when people had surrounded the house. Leah tells us that at one point a block of wood was thrown through an open window. There was writing on it, warning that a family member would soon die adding, of dubious comfort: 'She will be happy with the angels.' Leah was convinced no human agency had precipitated this and that it was a spirit message.

There was no further evidence of Rosna's physical remains. David had organised a pump to drain the cellar in the hope that digging could resume, but it couldn't cope with the flood water. Now the raps sounded at David's and he had the girls hard at it whenever he had the chance. This was mostly at night as they all slept in one big room together, in four different beds. Try as they might, neither David nor Leah could get raps by themselves, the girls had to be present. Margaret didn't even try.

A cool head was required and Leah was the woman to provide it. She stayed two weeks at the farm, assessing the situation, during which time she took the girls aside, individually and together, and solemnly questioned them. She made a decision: she would take Kate back with her to Rochester. By separating the girls it would be possible to ascertain which of them was causing the raps or, indeed, whether it was both of them. Maggie was left with her mother and David.

According to Leah the raps started up even on the packet boat back to Rochester, and they were only saved from public notice by the business of the boat having to pass through several locks. Although the raps were not loud, Leah clearly heard them.

They were continuing, too, at David's which answered the question as to which girl was responsible: both of them. It seemed, also, that more than one spirit was involved. At Leah's home other sounds accompanied the raps. The very evening of their arrival, while Lizzie and Kate were in the garden, Leah heard a crash as though a bucket of water had been thrown at the house. She jerked her head out of the window but all she saw were the children innocently playing, apparently, unaware of the disturbance.

That first night Lizzie woke her mother in the small hours with a hideous scream. An icy hand had grabbed her face, rather in the manner that had terrified Hannah Weekman's child in the Hydesville cottage. She shared a bed with Kate who swore she, too, had felt it. Leah read aloud from the Bible then put it under her pillow to protect them. It didn't.

As soon as the lamp was extinguished the Bible was flung across the room by an unseen force. Leah reached for matches but felt them being snatched from her hand by icy fingers. Other disturbances kept them awake till dawn.

It was a fine, sunny morning and Leah's pretty little house in Mechanics Square was surrounded by roses in bloom. As had happened with Margaret, the healing power of the sunlight seemed to dilute their problems. Had it really been as bad as it seemed? Friends called round that evening and, with Leah at the piano, the company sang until dusk. Although the friends were unaware of it, Leah could tell the raps were back, gently beating time to the music. Like snakes, swaying to the pipe of the charmer.

They went upstairs to bed about ten o'clock and slept uninterruptedly till midnight when an extraordinary drama awoke them. They could hear furniture being moved about downstairs followed by footsteps mounting the stairs and marching into a curtained-off recess in the bedroom. Leah tells us that it was as though an unseen vaudeville performance was being mounted in that recess. During this, incredibly, it sounded as though someone did a clog dance, followed by applause. Then there was the sound of an audience leaving. Had the show been put on for them?

The activity always seemed to be centered on Kate. Sometimes Lizzie seemed frightened of this, begging Kate to stop it. She got no support from her mother who would not tolerate her whining. Leah was utterly taken up with the phenomena. The spirits grew spiteful towards Lizzie. They pulled her hair, slapped her face and pinched her. She sometimes had bruises in the morning. Whatever these spirits were they were not very bright and not very nice. What was the purpose of it all?

These new phenomena were far removed from simple raps and although Kate was nervous at times she seems, with Leah's support, to have taken things in her stride. But Lizzie hated it and just wanted to get back to normal. Not so Leah, who silently explored the nucleus of a plan that had come to her when she had first encountered the raps at David's.

Leah was never frightened of the spirits. She writes of her alarm when the matches were snatched from her and the Bible flung across the room, but she tells us these things to impart a sense of wonder at the magnitude of the phenomena rather than to record her fear. She was never the victim of their attacks, which was just as well as they became even more boisterous. Rosna seems to have been shoved aside in favour of a whole host of spirit louts. Nights were full of banging and ghostly steps trod the stairs. The neighbours were no supporters of the spirits and objected to the racket they made. If this was a breakthrough from another world they wanted no part of it.

Due to their complaints, Leah had to move and took a lease on a bigger house on Prospect Street. She had been hard pressed to make ends meet before Kate moved in, but now she had a plan and a bigger house was part of it. It was an investment. The new house was on three floors, the top storey being one big room rather like the Hydesville cottage. This was to be the sisters' bedroom and, like the Mechanics Square house, part was curtained off as a storage area. Three big beds were moved there for Margaret and Maggie were to join them.

As soon as Margaret and Maggie arrived the bizarre nocturnal cabarets recommenced. People could be heard trooping up the stairs to the storage space where giggling was always heard. Whatever was causing the upheavals could clearly see them for, at one point, the end of one of the beds was lifted up and down. A shaken Margaret thought this worse than Hydesville which, indeed, it was, and decided they needed a man about the house. Leah, doubtless bearing in mind the hostility they'd experienced at David's, agreed. They decided upon Calvin Brown.

Calvin, an army cadet, was the orphaned son of a Quaker widow who had been a friend of Margaret's. She had brought him up as her own until he had enrolled in the military academy. He was virtually one of the family.

Calvin listened in horror as Margaret tumbled out the story, was convinced the spirits were evil and advised the ladies to shun them. How spirits that lifted beds could be shunned he didn't say. He was older than Kate and Maggie and, like many a younger man, attracted to Leah. He willingly agreed to spend the nights with them, sleeping in one of the downstairs rooms.

That first night he must have been astounded by the arrival of the spirits, and equally so by Leah's attitude towards them. At two o' clock, while Clavin slept downstairs, footsteps went into the curtained area that Leah had dubbed, in theatrical parlance, the Green Room. The usual giggling was heard and then the sound of someone dancing around Leah's bed. Leah says this amused her. Amused her? A ghost dancing around her bed? This would induce a heart attack in most. She tells us she addressed the dancer as 'Flat-Foot' due to its plodding footsteps, and asked it to dance the Highland Fling while she sang. This was hardly shunning the spirits. After the dance the beds started to bang up and down so they laid their mattresses on the floor to lessen the possibility of accidents. Margaret called for Calvin, who could hardly have missed hearing the racket and came running upstairs.

Things settled down and he returned to his bed. What happened next is contained in both Leah's memoir and Pond's *Time is Kind*.

The spirits took against Calvin, pelting him with objects from his room including a pair of carpet slippers with which he was soundly slapped. Like something from a farce, he grabbed his military cane and, in the darkness, bravely tried to fend them off, hitting nothing, of course. They traded him blow for blow. Things came to a climax when he was struck in the face by a brass candlestick which, fortunately, did no more than badly cut his lip. It could have killed him. He gave up the fight but not before his bed was dismantled and flung about the room.

He lay silently on his mattress, possibly suffering from concussion. The spirits returned to the girls, bombarding them with balls of rag that Leah had stored in the Green Room. Dawn did not come a moment too soon when, with stalwart nerves, Leah continued giving her music lessons. Her lovely voice seemed to calm the atmosphere.

The ladies decided to go for a walk and, as the house backed onto Mount Hope Cemetery, they strolled among the graves, reading the inscriptions – an odd choice of occupation considering the upheavals of the night. But there was no proof these malign forces were spirits of the dead. Rosna had been the only entity who claimed to have been human. Were these forces something else? If so, what? They had made no claims at all.

That night Calvin moved his mattress to the main bedroom to be with the women and they sat by the light of a lamp before sleeping. Suddenly there was a thundering of raps on the roof outside. They each felt a sharp blow to the face. Kate pointed to the foot of the mattress and screamed. She collapsed, not dead but unconscious, and stayed that way for some time. Eventually she groaned and moved, pointing to something no one could see. She did not speak but answered questions by squeezing the hands that held hers.

When she came round she explained she had witnessed the murder of Rosna, seen him in his death agonies; it had been enacted in front of her. He had relived his last moments for her to see. Remembering her Methodist roots, she recited some Biblical verses.

When Kate and Maggie became the most famous mediums in the world, these fits of unconsciousness were to continue with Kate, not regularly but from time to time, when she was stressed. Could they be the symptoms of epilepsy? Epilepsy has many forms and intense research has been undertaken recently on temporal lobe epilepsy. The condition can produce visual, auditory and olfactory hallucinations.

There is a school of thought suggesting that, possibly, some of the great seers of history were temporal lobe epileptics; such visionaries as Saint Joan of Arc or Saint Anne Catherine Emmerich, whose teachings are said to have inspired Mel Gibson to make *The Passion of the Christ*. Saints Joan and Anne had much in common. Both were from peasant stock and both had inspirational messages to impart. Both heard voices and Saint Anne also saw scenes of a mystical nature. She developed the signs of the stigmata and lived solely on the Blessed Eucharist and water for the last years of her life. Kate was to see visions and hear voices, symptoms that fit the pattern of temporal lobe epilepsy.

But she did more than that. Kate was to produce phenomena others could see and hear. This does not fit into the category of temporal lobe epilepsy (although it may into hypnotism) and neither Saint Joan nor Saint Anne, who may or may not have been temporal lobe epileptics, is credited with psychically moving objects. It is possible, of course, that Kate could have been a temporal lobe epileptic as well as a physical medium.

The spirits never took to Calvin. They detested him. Just before dinner one evening, when he had made some disrespectful reference to them, the chair he was about to sit on was jerked away making him fall painfully to the floor and drench himself with the jug of water he was holding. This, too, amused Leah.

Calvin could not stay with them indefinitely. He was attached to a military unit and had to obey orders. He did not want to leave, he hated the spirits, but was concerned for the girls and, in particular, Leah with whom he was by now in love. Leah had to confide in someone about the spirits and she did, quite a few times, and she was not given to understatement. Word spread and the neighbourhood was soon aware that the Foxes were still in touch with the spirits, only more so than ever. Among her confidants were Mrs Granger, who had accompanied her to Hydesville, and Mrs Vick, her next-door neighbour (the house was semi-detached) who became a believer.

More importantly she confided in Dr Isaac Post and his wife Amy, old friends of the family. Post was proprietor of Post, Coleman and Willis, a big store in Rochester. Amy was his second wife, his first wife's sister, whom she had devotedly nursed until her premature death. Post came from an established Society of Friends family (Quakers – so called because the founder George Fox, no relation to Kate and Maggie, bade a judge before whom he was summoned to quake at the word of the Lord) and, although he was to leave the movement, never lost his outspoken objections to capital punishment and war. He and Amy knew the heartache of losing children. From his first marriage he'd lost a baby son and, from his marriage to Amy, a baby daughter.

The Posts were committed to social reform, particularly to womens' rights and the abolition of slavery. His house was the secret headquarters of the Underground Railway, an organisation devoted to assisting runaway slaves on their way to the freedom of Canada. Sometimes he housed between twenty and thirty runaways a night. He was a brave, honourable man and no fool.

The Posts thought, at first, that Leah's imagination had run away with her when she told of the visitations but, after inviting Kate to their home, and experiencing the raps first hand, they changed their minds. Dr Post is another who is accorded the distinction of having devised the alphabet system as used by the raps.

He became convinced of the truth of Spiritualism and developed into an accomplished automatic writing medium, publishing a book on the subject.[2] He and Amy were among the earliest supporters of the Foxes and remained so throughout their many trials to come.

The Posts arranged weekly rapping sessions at their house, one of the first of the soon-to-escalate Spiritualist circles. The spirits had by no means ended their bullying. Now, they had taken to throwing things in a big and nasty way. Among the less dangerous objects were vegetables extracted from the cellar, propelled up to the Foxes bedroom and flung at them. Turnips were included. A hit to the head from a turnip is a serious matter.

They took to coffin building. Sounds of sawing and hammering would be heard through the night and a makeshift coffin found in the morning. Articles from the nearby cemetery were thrown through their open windows and any one of the missiles could have seriously injured them. When Margaret fretted about what was happening her mop cap was torn off and thrown across the room. This happened several times and she was reduced to tears. Leah suggested they should pray. Kate said she felt more like swearing. One evening, as the Posts and other friends were gathered at Leah's, the piano started playing itself. Not a tune, just a single note constantly struck. Leah said it sounded like a death knell and put the lid on the instrument, locking it, but still the note continued.

At one that morning Margaret's son-in-law Stephen, Maria's husband, rode up with sombre news that David's baby daughter, Ella, was desperately ill. He'd come to bring Margaret back to David's and she and Maggie left with him shortly after, reaching David's house just before Ella died. After the mournful funeral Margaret and Maggie returned to Leah's.

The tragedy jolted David's enthusiasm for the spirits. If they knew so much why hadn't they prepared him? Or better still, saved his daughter? Leah recalled the sinister writing on the block of wood that had been thrown through his window when she had been there. She was not comforted by the message 'She will be happy with the angels'.

John had nearly finished building the new house and his master plan was for his wife and two daughters to move in with him and thus become a nice, God-fearing family and forget all the spirit nonsense. This would never happen now Leah had the bit of fame between her teeth and, with the backing of the formidable Isaac Post, she would never let go. A nightmare the spirits might be, but a nightmare of acclaim was better than a nightmare of anonymity.

Kate and Maggie were now local celebrities. This could be frightening when they encountered hostility, as they frequently did but, even at their early ages, they realised they were now somebodies. And, as they later admitted, events had overtaken them by then and were out of their hands.

Margaret clucked along like a mother hen, very much a part of things, fussing over her chicks and having the vapours but determined to stick it out; but Lizzie did not fit in. She hated the rapping and everything that went with it. But when she protested she irritated not just the spirits but Leah. If Lizzie called on Kate or Maggie to stop, then Leah would side with her sisters. Her daughter could be in for a rough ride.

There was trouble with the neighbours again. Mrs Vick had died and was replaced by a 'little man', as Leah described him, who detested the constant disruption. He didn't believe in spirits, he believed it was Leah and the girls being inconsiderate. It was useless for Leah to point to the bumps on her head and claim they came from precipitated turnips, he advised her that if the disruption did not stop he would involve the relevant authorities.

An unwise course, judging by how the spirits reacted to criticism. From then on he and his poor wife were plagued by banging on their roof which, according to Leah, could be heard nearly a mile away. There were also raps of annoyance all over their house. He complained to the estate agent and Leah was, to her indignation, given notice to quit. From then, until she left, his life was hell.

The sisters never renounced their Christian faith and Leah was a great one for reminding neighbours how devout they were. In the opinion of many there was, indeed, need for prayer. The mayhem continued but when Calvin returned to them, from manoeuvres, he found there was now a more organised method of communication. Regular, coherent messages were being rapped out at the Post circles.

The sisters had been told that they were chosen instruments in a breakthrough from the Other Side. Life was continuous, albeit in another dimension. Much of the upheaval they had endured had been attempts to attract their attention (the spirits had certainly been successful in that) when the spirits wished to rap out a message using the alphabet system. In future, when spirits wanted the alphabet called to deliver a message, they would rap five times. This would make things clearer.

One of the more spiritual messages read:

Dear Friends, you must proclaim these truths to the world. This is the dawning of a new era and you must try not to conceal it any longer. When you do your duty, God will protect you and good spirits watch over you.[3]

In deference to the celebrated Samuel Morse, Leah dubbed the raps 'God's Telegraph'. It might be asked where was God's protection when turnips were being thrown, mop caps torn from heads or picket fences being ripped up from the cemetery and hurled through the air? Surely there could have been more sophisticated ways to attract attention? Several have tried to answer this.

One was Madame Helena Blavatsky. Madame had yet to make her mark upon the world, but when she did she wrote of Kate in her *Isis Unveiled*.[4] Her explanation for the cruelly juvenile behaviour was that it had nothing to do with either God or the spirits. It was 'elementals' who had played those ghastly tricks, they could not help it, it was their essential nature to do so.

Elementals, she explained, are discarnate entities that never have and never will take human form, 'tricksy' little beings as she called them, almost affectionately; the imps and goblins of the Other Side – neither human nor spirit.

They delight in playing pranks on humans. Pretending to be the souls of the dead to hoodwink the bereaved was a favourite sport. Since they had never incarnated they had never died so had no respect for the impact of death. Finer emotions were not part of their make-up. They had no conception of good or evil. Madame Blavatsky learned to control these elementals, and had several at her beck and call. Conjuring them into physical form, such as butterflies, was one of her specialities. In his memoir *Old Diary Leaves*[5] Colonel Olcott, her colleague, writes of her setting tasks for them. On one such occasion, she had bidden her maid buy some lengths of cloth which needed to be hemmed into towels.

A sorceress with words and divination, the art of sewing had eluded Madame Blavatsky, she was no seamstress, and did not relish the task. The Colonel, jocularly, bid her get an elemental to do it, and to his surprise she agreed. 'She told me to lock up the towels, the needles and thread, in a bookcase,' he writes. 'After perhaps a quarter of an hour or twenty minutes, I heard a little squeaky sound, like a mouse's pipe, beneath the table, whereupon HPB [Madame Blavatsky] told me that "that nuisance" had finished the towels.' The Colonel unlocked the bookcase and found the towels were hemmed, albeit clumsily so.

The Colonel, a man of unimpeachable honesty, assures us Madame Blavatsky did not approach the bookcase during the interval and that he stayed with her, never leaving the room the whole time. Great as was Madame Blavatsky's command of elementals, even she was their dupe at times, notably on an occasion when her associates found her sewn to the mattress by her nightgown. She had bidden the elementals do some sewing the night before and their pranks had got out of hand.

In her opinion the Fox sisters were not in touch with the dead at all in those first days but communing with elementals. Furthermore, these elementals had, possibly accidentally, gate-crashed the spirit scientists' experiments, hence the chaotic behaviour. The spirits had made the breakthrough but could not keep out the elementals, anymore than a farmer can keep out foxes. Was Rosna an elemental?

Robert Dale Owen had no truck with elementals, being convinced the disturbances were entirely spirit based. He believed it was sheer frustration that caused them to behave so boisterously: 'How are they to make their presence known?' he asks. 'How are they to attract our attention? In what manner does a traveller arriving under the cloud of night, before a fast closed mansion, seek to reach the indwellers? Is it not by KNOCKING OR RINGING?' (his caps)[6]

Others referred to the New Testament and the words attributed to Jesus: 'Ask, and it shall be given you; seek, and ye shall find; knock, and it shall be opened unto you.' The distinguished medium Emma Hardinge Britten surmised that the hysterical state of the Foxes during some of the more violent manifestations only fed the violence: '... the magnetic relations necessary to produce phenomena were very subtle, liable to disturbance, and singularly susceptible to the influence of mental emotions ...'[7].

Leah honoured her eviction notice and with the help of a coterie of admiring, and believing, friends found a house in nearby Troup Street into which she, the girls and Margaret all moved in September 1849. Reporters had kept abreast of the bizarre happenings and written of them in their papers, soon letters began arriving from others who had also discovered that the spirits could rap messages through them. The girls were deluged with requests for sittings. This was what the spirits had been working for, to spread their message, so Isaac Post competently headed a committee to deal with the bookings. As it was impossible for unchaperoned ladies to sit with strangers, one of the committee always sat with them, as did Leah who welcomed enquirers, relaxing them beforehand with polite conversation.

No fees were charged although occasional gifts were accepted. Leah was still teaching but pupils had dwindled into a trickle. With her current reputation, she was not quite the teacher middle-class mothers envisioned for their daughters. Leah would sometimes end a circle by going to the piano and accompanying herself in a song. Her voice wafting through the night inevitably soothed ruffled nerves and made a lovely end to an eventful evening. People could believe the dead really walked in enchanted glades.

Sometimes music came from the spirits. In the dark of the séance room Leah would hush the sitters and, she tells us, instrumental, vocal and even orchestral music could be heard. She sometimes took down music from dictation. The alphabet would be called for and whatever note, A B or C etc. was required would be transcribed to the piano. Leah was instructed to set spirit-dictated music to Felicia Herman's poem *Haunted Ground*, changing the word 'Haunted' to 'Hallowed'. This achieved cult status among Leah's disciples, becoming known as *The Spirit's Song*. She received a distinguished visitor in the form of Swedish writer Frederica Bremer. Miss Bremer was in America writing *Homes of America*. Leah, used to visitors now, told a few friends that she had called but thought no more of it. Her good friend John E. Robinson bought the book, expecting to read nice things about the Foxes but got a nasty shock. Miss Bremer had been less than impressed. The more the Foxes saw of journalists, the more accustomed they would become to their ways.

Leah's psychic powers were developing rapidly although her fame was never to be as durable as that of the girls. Leah saw and felt spirits, one of whom now made itself known by taking her hand at tea times. She believed this was her dead sister, the little soul who had perished at 3 years old.

Lizzie was causing Leah serious grief. This came to the crunch when the Rev. Lemuel Clark came for a sitting. Several churchmen of various denominations had had sittings. Tea had been served and guests, including Clark, were seated around the table. As soon as the raps started Lizzie burst out laughing; Leah was furious. She forbade her presence at future sittings. She was furious with Lizzie much of the time. Her daughter was becoming increasingly rude. There had been several outbursts when circles had started. 'Rap, rap, be sure to rap!'[8] she had mocked once at the start of a circle. 'Why do you keep this up? I'm sick of it,' she burst out another time. Leah packed her off to a friend. Lizzie was glad to go. She hated the spirits and blamed them for making her life miserable.

Clark's sitting was the first in which, we are told, furniture moved upon request as opposed to of its own volition. Clark had heard tales of objects moving of their own accord and put it to the test. The sitters moved away from the heavily draped ten-seater dining table which he sternly bade move towards him. To his amazement it did, slowly but definitely. It stopped and moved to his command. None of the sitters had contact with it, not even so much as a toe-cap.

One of the sitters that day, who became an important part of the girls' lives, was a family friend, the young journalist Eliab Capron. Sceptical at first, he'd come to investigate the girls. In his book *Modern Spiritualism*[9] he tells how he tested the spirits by holding a handful of small shells and asking how many were in his hand. The spirits got it right.

He sat many times and, doubts overcome, became a champion of the girls. A decent man, he was concerned about the detrimental effects a life of Spiritualist circles and spotlit public attention might have on them – something that does not seem to have bothered Margaret.

Maggie was already temperamental, sometimes brooding and sulky when she felt she did not want to work. Kate was getting spoiled, it would have been surprising if she hadn't been with all the attention lavished upon her. She was a 12-year-old child and, like a child, could be aggressive, downright rude, and almost as naughty as Lizzie when the mood took her. Eliab persuaded Margaret to let Kate come and live with him and his family at his home in Auburn. She could go to school there, away from the public gaze. His mother could keep a maternal eye on her and he thought the atmosphere would be more wholesome. He was sincere enough in this, but there was an ulterior motive in that he wanted to study Kate at close hand.

Margaret, too, was on the move again. John's house was completed and she agreed to move back in with him. So Leah's household was reduced to Maggie, Calvin when he was there, and their faithful retainer Alfie. What a pity no one thought to ask Alfie his story, he would have had quite a tale to tell. Benjamin Franklin started rapping at the Post circles. He would be overseeing proceedings there from now on.

Now that the Rev. Clark had started the ball rolling, or rather the table, it became quite a feature during séances, always with the sitters and mediums well out of contact with it. To ensure everything was above board, the heavy drapes were lifted beforehand so that sitters could check that no collaborator was crawling underneath, in any case it would have taken more than one to shift such a heavy piece of furniture.

Thoughts of collaboration could be further banished in that the girls now traveled to sitters' houses rather than restricting circles to just the Post home or Troup Street. They were shown into rooms where there were clearly no collaborators and tables moved there, too. It was extraordinary. Visitors to the Foxes verified that sometimes the laden table would suddenly shift during meal times, when no séance was in progress. Violent as these movements could be, items were seldom spilled or broken, as though whomever was moving it was taking care not to cause damage.

There was little that was religious about those early circles, even though a member of the clergy might attend them. Sometimes a nervous sitter or, indeed, Leah herself, might offer a prayer but that was all. Prayers made no difference to what happened. But the spirits made it known that light could weaken them. They preferred working in the dark.

A shock awaited the household at Troup Street, although it may have been a relief for the faithful Alfie. The raps spelled out that they would be leaving. Emma Hardinge Britten, who knew the girls well and was to work with them firsthand, wrote that the withdrawal was because the girls 'were constantly disobedient to the spirits' requests'.[10]

This took the form of Leah's refusal to hold a public meeting to demonstrate communication. Private séances were not enough. The spirits had requested this many times but Leah was too frightened to allow it. To go public in such a way would make them targets for hostility and there was always the dread that the raps might let them down, or might get things wrong. A final farewell circle was called for. After some raps of gratitude, and affection, 'We will now bid you all farewell' was spelled out and received in stunned silence. This reigned for nearly two weeks. The raps had gone.

For a few days the girls pretended they were relieved but this tailed off. They realised what they had lost. They didn't want the peaceful lives that had been returned to them. Leah realised she'd made a dreadful error of judgement and tried frantically to summon back the raps.

It was Eliab Capron who unexpectedly brought them back. Kate was still with his family in nearby Auburn, and he and his Quaker friend George Willets, a relative of the Posts, called on Leah one evening, to bring news of her. To Leah and Maggie's amazement they learnt that the raps had not deserted Kate and she was attracting many enquirers. It was through her that Willets, a businessman, had become a Spiritualist himself. The spirits had made it clear early on that they would not be inveigled into advising on business ventures, this was not their purpose, but in his case they had relaxed their principles sufficiently to advise the purchase of a piece of land, which he had done to advantageous results. Kate was not only rapping but some sitters swore they could also feel spirit hands touching them in the dark.

Leah crestfallenly told of their abandonment. Eliab, full of his success with Kate, buoyantly announced: 'Perhaps they will rap for us if not for you?' Then, Mrs Britten assures us, 'To the unspeakable joy and delight of all present they were greeted by a perfect shower of the much-lamented sounds.'[11]

The spirits were back and glad to be so, but at that very first reunion they repeated their demand for a public platform. Even Eliab demurred at this, at first, but was assured, by raps, it would be a triumph.

Leah was now ready to comply. She'd had a severe shock and didn't want it to happen again. A public demonstration would be arranged and at the biggest available venue in Rochester. Eliab and Willets were enrolled as part of the venture. No longer would the Fox sisters confine themselves to séances in private houses, they would announce their message publicly and proudly as required – coast to coast if necessary.

As a prelude to the grand event, circles were held for influential people. Mrs Post – Amy – was told to invite sixteen prominent citizens, their names rapped out plus the wording of the invitation. One of the sixteen was the editor of the local paper. Several of the sixteen, not all, did attend. The spirits would answer no questions but merely demonstrated their presence by rapping in various parts of the room, including the ceiling and floor. This was certainly mystifying in itself.

An intensive period of training followed on both sides of the veil. It was decided Kate was too young to be involved in a public demonstration and she would be better off remaining at Eliab's home, but both Maggie and Leah had to practise in front of each other to learn how to address an audience in an authoritative and dignified manner. Isaac Post doubtless helped them in this, as he had had years of addressing public meetings. The spirits, too, had to be tutored from their side; they were unused to mass communication. If they wanted to be taken seriously then they must behave seriously. A major fear was that the raps might be inaudible. What could be heard in a dining or sitting room might get lost in a large hall. The raps seemed to have lost power since their heady days of roof banging when, as many testified, they would make thunder sheets of doors and demolish beds. These more disciplined sounds were feebler, rather like those of the initial Hydesville days.

With practice they did increase in volume, loud enough to be heard in the various parts of a large hall. For they would not restrict themselves to the stage, and might strike any part of the room. Leah's teaching experience stood her in good stead. She understood the need for vocal projection and became mistress of it, possessing natural stage presence. Under her direction the reluctant, nervous and sometimes resentful Maggie practised stage demeanour and how to deliver messages with decorum while under duress.

While this preparation was in progress other mediums were vying to be noticed. One ambitious novice nearly killed a woman whose husband had gone missing. Raps, nothing to do with the Foxes, announced that the wife had drowned the missing man in the canal. The authorities took this seriously and the canal was dragged to no avail. In those days of brisk justice, the wife was actually ordered into the canal to indicate the spot where she'd allegedly done the deed. She was nearly drowned. Some months later the missing man returned home. He had done a bunk across the border to Canada to avoid a debt.

14 November 1849 was the date arranged for the debut and the venue was to be the imposing 1,200-seater Corinthian Hall. A publicity campaign was organised which was not difficult as newspaper editors well remembered the pretty girls and their bizarre claims. In fact, they'd seldom been out of the limelight since Hydesville. Reporters guaranteed they would be there.

It was decided that a whole evening of rapping would be too much. The performance would be divided into two halves, the first to be a lecture on the history of the raps by Eliab, then Maggie would demonstrate. Leah was not sufficiently psychically developed to demonstrate at that stage but would support Maggie by her presence on stage.

Everyone was incredibly brave. What if the raps did not turn up or were inaudible? What if the audience turned on the girls, believing them to be tools of the devil? By now certain outraged Christians had come to precisely that conclusion and threatened to disrupt things. Sermons were being preached against them. As Conan Doyle put it, concerning clerics, 'The majority thundered from their pulpits against them, and the mob eagerly joined in the cowardly sport of heretic baiting.'[12] This, of course, made the reporters even keener to be there.

This tirade had far more effect on Maggie than Leah. Leah easily rode the tandem of Spiritualism and Christianity, but not Maggie. Unlike Leah, Maggie had been subjected to her father's reborn Methodism which had left its mark and all her life she was to be troubled by doubts that she was, by rapping, mocking the Christ that, somewhere deep in her heart, she still loved.

A theatrical performance of any description was not to be taken lightly. Theatre could be a rowdy experience, often nerve-racking for the seasoned performer and frightening for the inexperienced.

A few months previously a riot had broken out at New York's Astor Place Opera House where William Macready had given a performance of *Macbeth*. The disturbance had been organised by his rival, Edwin Forrest. The two actors had been embroiled in a deadly feud for years. Forrest had paid a cabal to pelt Macready with debris on opening night as soon as he appeared on stage. Much of this fell on the audience but some reached its target. The stoical Macready, however, refused to stop his performance.

Word spread and by the second night the Opera House was jammed with a violent crowd out for trouble. The streets from Broadway to Third Avenue were packed with people who had tried to get in. Inside the theatre, paving stones and seats were hurled onto the stage. Things were worse outside where actual murder was taking place. The police were powerless and the police station ransacked. A nervous mayor, who had been in office barely a week, called in the National Guard which fired on the crowd. Several were injured and dozens killed in the resulting stampede. The whole of America including, certainly, Maggie and Leah, was aware of the notorious Astor Place Riot.

Putting aside the physical danger, Leah and Maggie were risking their respectability by merely stepping on a stage. Well-bred ladies did not do that sort of thing. Ladies that did were of dubious reputation.

Public entertainment was divided into categories. Opera for the upper classes, where the last of the brilliant castrati and prima donnas did appear (although some of the prima donnas had a somewhat slippery grasp of respectability, as did the castrati for that matter) but this was Culture and Culture came under Society's patronage – the audience usually chatted through most of it anyway, making it acceptable. One of the leading sopranos of the day was the celebrated Caterina Barilli, mother of the soon-to-be even more celebrated Adelina Patti. It would be in the following year, 1850, that the 7-year-old Patti would make her astounding New York debut. The middle classes had minstrel shows and melodrama.

Entertainment for the working classes was confined to variety shows in saloons, mostly attended by men. It was to be another couple of decades before entrepreneurs were to develop vaudeville (parts of which descended into burlesque), where women came into their own, although few were viewed as respectable. An exception to this was the 'Vaudeville Saloon' which had opened in Boston as early as 1840, but this was a unique, pioneer establishment.

For Leah to launch Maggie and herself as public performers was risking scandal. This was the way, however, Spirit had chosen: a breakthrough by itself.

Their performance was to start at 7.30pm and seats were 25 cents each or three for 50 cents. It was agreed that together with Maggie, Leah and Eliab, other supporters would also sit on the platform, among them the staunch Amy Post, the Rev. Jervis (not all clerics were hostile) and Lynam Granger, husband of Mrs Granger who had travelled to Hydesville with Leah. About 500 people turned up making the place just under half full. Maggie sat on stage, fresh and comely. Nothing could be less ghoulish than this innocent young lady. Leah sat in mature, statuesque splendour besides her. Both wore elegant new dresses.

Reports of theatre riots must have flashed through Maggie's brain as she sat on the platform, waiting to prove there was no death. *Macbeth* was small beer compared to what she was about to attempt.

Things got off to an inauspicious start. Eliab, who had previously written up the girls in his paper, gave a brief history of the raps and what had happened since. Not brief enough. He was not a gifted speaker. The audience had come to hear spirits; no one was interested in history. He lost confidence, faltering alarmingly. He bored the audience stiff.

There was a welcome diversion when John Fleming, editor of a Second Advent paper, angrily shouted that he wanted to address the audience instead. The audience wanted to hear him, anything to get rid of Eliab, so he was allowed to take the platform. Fleming announced he believed the raps genuine and he knew where they came from – hell! The communicator was Satan. The girls should be charged with blasphemy. It was in this unruly atmosphere that Maggie shakily stood up to deliver her maiden demonstration.

She was not an overwhelming success but neither was she the failure she dreaded she might be. The militant Christians did their best to unnerve her with cat-calls but she kept going. The raps arrived punctually and Mrs Britten tells us that, although they were muffled at times, they were easily loud enough to be heard. Their answers to the shouted out questions, which came at random with no system of organisation, were not always accepted as accurate but who cared? Raps had sounded all over the hall and they were inexplicable. Quibbles were drowned out by more questions.

It was an illuminating evening for all. Maggie, too, made a discovery. She realised that, in keeping with Leah, she had a natural stage presence. No doubt her youthful attractiveness helped this but once she had mastered her jarring nerves she found she was at ease in front of an audience.

Leah, too, ensured she was very much a part of the occasion, by rising majestically and clarifying what the raps meant when recipients were unsure. The sisters left an audience divided in its opinions, some were mesmerised, others puzzled and, it must be said, many amused. But some believed. Had the dead been there? A few were sobbing believing their lost loved ones really had come back. Others wondered, was it trickery?

A small committee of prominent male citizens was convened that night to examine the girls and deliver the verdict the following evening. To that end, next morning, Leah and Maggie were taken to the Sons of Temperance Hall where an investigation was carried out. A physical search was conducted to see whether a clicking device was hidden in their clothes. Their ankles and wrists were held to see whether they were clicking their joints. Raps sounded all through this, on the floor, walls, cupboards and the outside of the front door. The girls were motion-less throughout although the floor around them jarred. The committee could discover no physical agency by which the raps were achieved.

A more intimate search was proposed, to which the girls agreed, pro-viding, for decency's sake, this was undertaken by ladies. This yielded the same result. The committee's report was given that night before the performance at Corinthian Hall. Due to the enormous interest, this had been booked for a second performance. Mrs Britten tells us: 'This report was delivered to an eager and excited audience and seemed to fall like a thunder-bolt on many of those assembled, who had obviously come in the expectation of receiving one of a very different and far less favour-able character.'[13] The sisters left behind another audience divided in its opinions.

Not everyone was convinced by the committee's findings and a second committee was formed. This included the Hon. Frederick Whittlesey, former Vice Chancellor of the State of New York. Unfortunately he was disqualified on the grounds of partiality as he was not only a Spiritualist but also a close friend of Leah's. This time they were tested by a doctor who held a stethoscope to their chests, as someone had suggested they might be ventriloquists. He found no evidence of this. Leah, however, found the doctor's ministrations rather too personal and told him so. Reluctantly, the second committee came up with the same conclusion as the first.

Corinthian Hall was booked for a third time and the committee's report delivered to the audience. This time the performance did not go down too well. As Conan Doyle put it: 'So long as the public looked upon the movement as a sort of joke it was prepared to be tolerantly amused, but when these reports put the matter in a more serious light, a wave of blackguardism swept over the town.'[14] Indeed it did.

The jammed house was determined to have fun. Interruptions were continuous, sometimes making the raps inaudible. Both Leah and Maggie were terrified. Maggie's new-found confidence left her. Yet a third committee was set up. Some hostile audience members sarcasti-cally proposed themselves. When one man boasted that he was so tough the girls would not dare cross him, he was chosen on the spot. Another vowed that if he could not discover how the raps were made he would throw himself over Genessee Falls (he could not discover how the raps were made but did not throw himself over the Falls). Another nominee suggested the raps were made by the shaking of ball bearings sewn into the hems of dresses, which was instantly disproved.

The third committee included some church ladies who instigated a thorough and intimate body search, including every article of the girls' clothing, being particularly diligent with their underwear. So painful were their vigorous, spiteful fingers that both Leah and Maggie cried out in pain, which brought Amy Post hurtling through the door in protest. The raps, too, protested loudly all over the room which somewhat disconcerted the church ladies. Leah and Maggie were placed on pillows and stood on glass tumblers – glass reported to be a non-conductor of electricity. Still the raps sounded.

The third committee had to agree with its predecessors. This would be announced at the next performance for a fourth evening had, incredibly, been booked. Money may well have been an inducement for this as the box office was bursting.

Rumour spread that if the third committee found in favour of the girls then the girls would be lynched, and their supporters with them. Demand for tickets increased. Too frightened to go home after the third tests, Leah and Maggie stayed at the Posts'. They both wanted to cancel the fourth performance. The staunch Amy declared that if they did so then she would face the hostile crowd alone if necessary. She could not rap but she could tell people what she thought of them.

This brought Leah to her senses. She was no coward. She told Amy she would go, too, and sit with her, even 'if I go to my death'. But Leah could not rap. Maggie was the rapper and she still refused to go and it was not until Leah and Amy were preparing to leave that Maggie gave in, announcing hollowly, 'I expect we will be killed.' She was very nearly right and but for Willets and Isaac having taken the precaution of alerting the police beforehand they may have been.

The third committee delivered its positive verdict and the audience became a howling mob. Fireworks were thrown and demands made for the girls to be stripped, tarred and feathered – a pot of tar had optimistically been prepared beforehand. It looked like the evening was going to turn into Rochester's answer to the Astor Place Riots.

A heavily built man leap on stage. Leah, in terror, ordered him down, but it was the Chief of Police who assured her he had fifty men among the audience who would ensure no harm came to them. These now revealed themselves and threatened the ringleaders with arrest. It was later discovered that some of the troublemakers were reporters, hoping to heighten their story.

With the Police Chief beside him, the burly Willets who had supported the girls throughout all three performances, informed the audience that if anyone harmed them it would literally be over his dead body. He was a Quaker, committed to non-violence, but he also had a short fuse and believed in the girls. More than once he had torn his jacket off and threatened to take on anyone who insulted them.

But the performance had to be cancelled after all, and the shaken girls given a police escort back to the Posts'. As Mrs Britten wryly put it: 'Thus ended an investigation into the sublime and occult mysteries of the communion between the natural and spiritual worlds.'[15]

The girls, however, had made their mark, one way or another, and henceforth were popularly known as 'The Rochester Rappers'. They stayed with the Posts for a while, refusing sittings, although there were plenty of requests; not everyone had been out to tar and feather them. There had been some among that obstreperous audience who believed, and others who had not dared go to Corinthian Hall fearing a blood-bath, but still believed in the girls.

John Fox in his new, if rather empty, house thanked God he was on the true path. He believed he had been cursed with his daughters and a wife who seemed to have taken leave of her senses by aiding and abetting them. He blamed this on his dissolute earlier life. It was God's punishment. God was to punish him further when Margaret forsook him again, making the house even emptier, to bring Kate back from Auburn to stay with the others at the Posts. Although Kate had made a name for herself whilst with Eliab's family, she was terrified when she heard of the rowdiness. She was still a schoolgirl, with plaits in her hair.

Ruffled nerves were eventually calmed and sittings resumed at Troup Street. Judge A.P. Hascall, a sympathetic member of one of the investigating committees, was one of their first clients who arrived with a group of enquirers. This included two other judges, Summerfield and Chamberlain, plus the Hon. J. Hedden and a Scotsman, Duncan McNaughton. A message was rapped out for McNaughton to recite the Lord's Prayer. When the communicant was asked to identity itself the following message was rapped out, as reproduced in *The Missing Link*. 'My dear son, ha'e ye forgotten your puir auld mither? Repeat the Lord's Prayer.'

Now, this is ridiculous. It's one thing for a spirit to speak in dialect – at that time spirit voices were not heard in the Fox circles – quite another to rap in it. Leah was colouring the story. McNaughton clearly thought it ridiculous himself and refused to accept the message. The raps stopped and there was much laughter at his expense. (Lots of those early séances were fun, contrasting with the piety that pervades so many of today's séances. The spirits quite like a party, I recall unusually accurate messages being given at a function where high spirits and wine were much in evidence.) As otherwise there would have been no continuation of the séance, McNaughton began to mumble the prayer. The raps then demanded everyone join in, and did so themselves by rapping all over the room. As well as having a mother in spirit, McNaughton had also lost a young daughter, and was convinced that she, too, communicated with him that evening. He had arrived a sceptic and left a believer.

This particular séance was the first where a fee was accepted as opposed to a gift. As the party was leaving Judge Hascall discreetly handed Leah some cash. She says she was insulted, and probably was, but realised it was meant sincerely. She accepted, and Spirit made it known that from then on fees must be charged for circles. There was little alternative if they were to carry on. Money had been made from the Corinthian Hall appearances but before that Leah had been drawing on her fast-dwindling savings and David's generosity. Her music pupils had evaporated.

Isaac Post still handled the sittings and these were booked well in advance. Furniture often moved and ornaments were lifted in a controlled manner, not thrown across the room as had earlier been the case. The spirits were strengthening their techniques all the time, now faces were kissed, hands could be felt caressing and spirit lights danced.

3

That year, 1849, is memorable in psychic annals. Not only did it see the first public demonstration of Spiritualism, which launched a tidal wave of passionate interest, it also witnessed the marriage of Helena von Hahn, who became the celebrated Madame Blavatsky.

That event took place in the Caucasus, near Tiflis, when she was 17 and her husband, General Blavatsky, was some thirty years older. Despite the photographs of Madame in middle age, when she was ill and obese, tipping the scales at eighteen stones, she was actually attractive when young, rather in the style of the young Leah with whom she had more than a little in common.

The age difference was not remarkable for those times, but what *was* remarkable was the wife's behaviour, and that would have been remarkable in any time. She refused any form of sexual relationship with the General, any relationship whatsoever for that matter and, within three months, had left him and fled Russia, quite alone with no servants or staff and without a word of explanation to anyone. It was ten years before her family saw her again.

What could she explain? She was, she tells us in her many writings, being trained in occult lore by her Mahatmas to be their spokesperson. She took pains to point out she was not the perfect vehicle for this task, just the best available at the time. She was to tell her biographer, A.P. Sinnett, that she had studied with the Mahatmas in their Tibetan ashram penetrating inhospitable international borders to do so. Elsewhere, she tells us herself: 'I have lived in different periods in Little Tibet and Great

Madame Blavatsky.

Tibet, and these combined periods form more than seven years.'¹ Her study period, including the seven years in Tibet, lasted nearly thirty years and was undertaken in far corners of the earth among remarkable, often bizarre, people and sects. She witnessed levitation, materialisation, pre-cipitation and astral travel.

Before the full realisation of her Mahatmas work, which was to be the formation of the Theosophical Society, she was, together with her occult associate, Colonel Olcott, to become an integral part of the blossoming doctrine of Spiritualism. There, she would demonstrate her own excep-tional powers, champion mediums and expose fakes. She was unlike any other medium in that *she* would command the spirits, not they her.

Back in America, mediums were springing up all over the place. The state of New York was a hotbed of religious fervour and had been so for some time. Conan Doyle suggests this was the reason Spirit chose New York for its attempted breakthrough. There was the Quakers' Holy Sanctuary of the New World. The Quakers developed tremors when in the throes of divine passion and spoke in tongues incomprehensible to many except the chosen few. The Mormons were also there. In 1823, a quarter of a century before anyone had heard of the Foxes, a devout farm lad, Joseph Smith, had seen a shining angel with a face he described as like lightning – brilliant. The angel, whose name was Moroni, told him the whereabouts of The Book of Mormon that would explain many mysteries.

Nearer in time to the Foxes, in 1844, Captain William Miller announced that Jesus would return to earth on 22 October that year. With this Second Advent the world would end and sinners pay for their sins. Many sold their homes and gathered to be saved. The divine non-arrival was referred to as The Great Disappointment. Dates were re-calculated and it was realised Jesus had not intended to reincarnate on earth but to begin a new ministry in heaven: the foundation of the Seventh Day Adventists.

Just prior to this, mesmerist Andrew Jackson Davis, the poorly edu-cated son of an alcoholic cobbler, claimed that he had – perhaps in his physical form, perhaps in his astral, accounts vary – made the forty-mile journey from his home in Poughkeepsie to the Catskill Mountains for a meeting with the deceased philosopher and visionary Emanuel Swedenborg. After this he could, and frequently did, quote from works he had never read in languages he had never learned. His masterwork

The Principles of Nature was published in 1847. He claimed Spirit dictated it and he was merely the amanuensis. Others were to make similar
claims, including Emma Hardinge Britten who informs us that her trea-
tise *Art Magic* was actually the work of the Chevalier Louis, a Master of
more than forty years occult experience who had died in France some
time previously.

Colonel Olcott had his doubts about this, and they were not lessened when he saw a psychically projected portrait of the Chevalier: 'All
those years of profound study,' he observed, 'ought to have made his face
embody the acquired masculine majesty one finds in the countenance of
a true Yogi or Mahatma; whereas in this portrait of a pretty young man
with mutton chop whiskers, the face has the vapid weakness of a "sick
sensitive", of a fashionable lady-killer, or, as many say who have seen it,
that of a wax figure such as the Parisian barber sets in his shop window
to display his wigs and whiskers upon.'[2]

Mrs Britten limited the publication of *Art Magic* to 500 copies and
these were only to be sold to those whom she approved. The printing
plates were then to be destroyed. As no publisher could accept such a
financially suicidal venture she published it herself. *The Principles of Nature*
can still be obtained from specialised outlets. Davis also kept a diary and
an entry for 31 March 1848 reads: 'The good work has begun ... a living
demonstration is born.' This was the very day Rosna had started rapping.

Raps were now sometimes accompanied by electric shocks in circles.
Electricity was the rage, it was considered by some, together with The
Ether, to possess occult value. The shocks were first brought to public
attention by Rachel Draper, a 'magnetic' medium. 'Magnetic' meaning
she rapped while entranced. Trance mediums were later to develop into
controlled mediums, through whom spirits spoke using the medium's
vocal apparatus. During a circle which included Mrs Draper's husband
Nathaniel, George Willets and the Rev. Jervis as well as Margaret, Kate
and Maggie, Mrs Draper contacted Benjamin Franklin who rapped he
was experimenting with electricity, rather unkindly demonstrating this
by 'electricizing' Mrs Draper with a substantial shock. She jumped so
violently that the other sitters thought she had broken her trance. But,
no, still entranced, she rapped what had happened and how it had done
her the world of good, cleared her head and made her see clearer.

When it was asked why Franklin had chosen raps, rather than some
other method to communicate, Franklin responded, enigmatically, that
he was trying out the batteries. He tried them out again by giving Mrs

Draper another shock that did, this time, awake her from her trance. But this was meant to be. He had decided upon another experiment. The party was to divide into two sections; one section, which included Maggie, would remain where they were with Mrs Draper while the other would go to another room where Kate would be the medium.

Raps were produced simultaneously in both rooms, although each could be heard in the other. This caused much excitement and sitters rushed from room to room to listen. After the session the sitters compared messages and found an identical message had been rapped in each room. The content was hardly startling, it announced that there would be great changes in the nineteenth century and many mysteries revealed. Writing in 1926, Conan Doyle had to reluctantly concede this had not taken place to the degree for which he could have hoped. But the sitters were thrilled by the successful duplication and so was Franklin who ordered Willets to send a report of the happenings to the *Rochester Daily Magnet* for publication.

Leah often heard spirit music and took down its notation. Now, spirits were about to appear who could play musical instruments. Sarah Tamlin had come to Eliab Capron's attention while Kate was staying with his family in Auburn. Mrs Tamlin was a rapper but created an even greater stir by setting a guitar in the midst of her dark circle on which recognisable tunes were played without visible contact. The medium herself could play no instruments and had had no musical training. Another of her triumphs was the reproduction of the sounds of a hunting horn and harp, when neither instrument was visible in her séance room.

The tradition of untrained or little-trained musical mediums has carried right through the history of Spiritualism to today. One of the most famous at the end of the nineteenth century was Jesse Shepard, whose musical séances attracted the patronage of the influential and wealthy of America. A supremely gifted pianist he claimed to be controlled by the spirits of deceased composers and pianists. He was also an accomplished singer and one of his specialities was to sing in 'two voices', during which he duetted with a spirit voice.

More recently, the English Rosemary Brown (1916–2001) made an impact on the music world. She had had piano lessons when she was young but showed no outstanding promise. In her 1974 autobiography *Immortals at my Elbow* she tells us that Franz Liszt, who had died some forty years earlier, contacted her in the 1920s when she had been just 7.

It must have been her latent psychism that attracted him for, by her account, she was no embryonic world-class musician. Notwithstanding, he brought other composers, of such diverse talents as Bach, Brahms and Chopin. Chopin, if his earthly memory was intact, could not have had happy memories of England as his last concert in London in 1848 had been a disaster. He was in ill health and his audience so apathetic that the press did not bother to acknowledge his presence. As *The Oxford Companion to Music* puts it, 'it hangs like a pall of gloom over the close of his career.'

Later, Rachmaninoff, Debussy and others inspired Rosemary to take down, note for note, works they had composed since their deaths. She created enormous interest during the 1960–70s not just among Spiritualists but also among prominent musicians. Publishers Novello and Co. have written, '... many musicians of note – among them Richard Rodney Bennett, Professor Ian Parrot and John Lill, have shown great interest ...'

When asked to contribute to this book John Lill, who among other triumphs was winner of the 1970 International Tchaikovsky Competition in Moscow, commented: 'I knew Rosemary Brown well and she was genuine, sincere and spiritually very receptive. Being musically uneducated, her music had to be simplified but to me, there is no doubting the one thing hardest to copy – the composer's style and that style was obvious in her writing. She had many critics and detractors but I'm sure she is having the last laugh!' World famous pianist Peter Katin, an expert on Chopin and Liszt, recorded an LP of her (the spirits') compositions, which was released under the title *The Rosemary Brown Piano Album*. He recalls how this happened and his feelings for Rosemary:

I had never heard of Rosemary Brown when my agent asked me if I would be interested in recording some of her music. I was sceptical when I was told that the music had been dictated by the spirits of past composers, and I wasn't convinced when I received a batch of manuscripts from Beethoven, Schubert, Chopin, Liszt, Debussy and Brahms. Anyway, the plan was that I should record one side of an LP containing the most difficult pieces, and Rosemary would record simpler pieces on the other side.

When I met her, I found her to be a simple 'housewifely' person with absolutely no affectation about her. She told me that Liszt wanted me to make the recording, and the way she put it seemed entirely convincing, probably because she was clearly convinced of it herself. I made it clear from the outset that I was sitting on the fence as far as any authenticity was concerned, and she always accepted this.

One extraordinary thing was that she seemed unable to write music unless it was 'dictated' by one of the composers; in a Liszt piece she said that four bars had to be radically changed, but when I asked her to write it down she said that she couldn't unless she sensed the dictation. When she did, she wrote the four bars very rapidly because, she said, she was afraid that the communication might disappear without warning. Looking at the rest of the score, she was unable to say where these four bars should go. I played the piece to include the four-bar alteration where I felt it might go, but had to try it three times before she suddenly said, 'That's exactly right!' Later, she re-wrote the whole piece without hesitation. I insisted that she must be able to write music but she was adamant that she couldn't without 'outside help', and one professor who met her and tried her on simple tests said that in fact she was totally unable to write down a simple scale when it was played to her.

In connection with this, I was intrigued by her ordinary writing. It had no particular character. Yet before she wrote those four bars, she decided to write down the instructions. I was very surprised at what I saw, because it wasn't her writing. I thought about it a lot and wondered whose writing it could be, then remembered that not long before, I had been given Liszt's visiting card – on the back he had written a message to the person he had visited. And that was the writing.

When we met at Wembley Town Hall for the recording, she was very excited by it, but nothing actually escaped her notice; there was what I knew was an error in the Schubert Moment Musical – probably a missing accidental – and she picked it up straight away. Now, she couldn't point to the place in the score because she couldn't read it, but when we went to the piano I can recall quite a transformation when she sat at the piano. She stared at the score and I tried to point at the mistake, but she said, 'That's no good, I can't read it – oh, here it comes.' And she played the whole section with the error corrected. In fact, I then wrote it in because she clearly had no idea what to do about it.

She was pursued everywhere not only by journalists but notably by psychiatrists. Of these, she said, 'They say it's my mind. All I can say is that I must have a very funny mind!' I frequently had the job of fending them off myself, but although I wasn't too happy about interviewers in Tokyo asking about her rather than about me (!) I did try to set the record as straight as possible, although rationalising was far from easy.

This strange phenomenon went right outside music. There were stories about her being able to paint exactly like van Gogh, domestic tales about her bathwater overflowing, but I can recount a few times when we spoke on the phone and she knew exactly if there was something I wanted to ask her – and sometimes when there wasn't. A notable case was when I moved back to the UK from Canada in 1985 and settled on a house. I phoned Rosemary simply because I wanted to contact as many people as possible to let them know where I'd be. The house had been surveyed, but she told me to watch out for something 'near the back of the house' which she said could exacerbate (she also said she didn't know what the word meant). I decided to take it seriously, and the result was dry rot! Rosemary never saw that house.

Katin points out that Rosemary only received compositions from composers of whom she'd heard and that on replaying the CD recently, 'I have to admit the music I recorded was a pretty weak imitation of the real thing. The Schubert is probably the most convincing (and was Rosemary's favourite) and the Beethoven isn't bad either! And the Debussy the least so.'

Spirit healing was becoming recognised. Those who possessed this power would lay hands on the sick and cures would be effected. In time certain spirit healers became world famous, particularly those of Latin American countries. Among British healers, Harry Edwards achieved enormous fame in the 1960s.

For as many converts as were springing up there was a commensurate number of sceptics. Even John Fox was accused of fraud. *The Auburn Daily Advertiser* reported that the Hydesville raps had been contrived by John using a device of springs and wires. Considering John hated Spiritualism, and the girls were constantly rapping in different houses, not to mention different rooms, this was hard to swallow. The rumour refused to die, however.

Even so, the Spiritualists were holding their own. Leah decided to put Kate and Maggie on a tour of nearby venues, culminating in that citadel of ambition, New York City. She employed a manager, a Mr D.F. Coman, to organise this. Margaret and Calvin would be travelling with them, Calvin juggling his military duties to permit this. The outlay would be considerable, at a hefty $150 per week. But since they were now charging for sittings – $1 per person for an hour and $5 for two sitters or more – this would not only defray the expenses but yield a profit. It speaks volumes for Leah's nerve and organising ability that she conceived this.

Their first stop would be a demonstration in Albany, at the Van Vechten Hall, followed by private bookings divided into three long sessions throughout the days and evenings; whatever else the girls might be accused of, sloth could not be included. Before they left, however, Leah was determined to restore their damaged Rochester reputation by staging another demonstration. The Corinthian Hall debacle still festered and nothing but a successful follow-up would obliterate it. Corinthian Hall was not available, which she deemed a good omen, so another room was taken, and filled to capacity with an appreciative audience. The public perception of Spiritualism had changed. It was no longer the province of cranks, too many powerful citizens had taken an interest. Even Maggie seemed pleased, or perhaps she was just relieved.

Eliab was replaced as Speaker by Universalist preacher, the Rev. R.P. Ambler, a friend of Coman. Eliab had given the girls extensive press coverage, promoting the forthcoming tour and, with co-writer Henry D. Barron, had just published his own compendious pamphlet on spirit research, *Singular Revelations*.

Van Vechten Hall got them off to a good start. No questions were permitted, it was purely a display of power. People queued to book sittings. Leah was elated and tells us the 'elite' of Albany consulted them. The grandees, too, thrilled Margaret, and Kate and Maggie, the stars of the show, were entranced by their fame and popularity. They produced the phenomena easily and efficiently. Due to her age, Kate was often the centre of attention, even cooed over, and that would have been satisfying for any young girl.

The raps, always the staple, were augmented by furniture moving and spirit hands which sitters could feel caressing them. Potent stuff, no wonder they were fully booked. It was no more than a hiccup when a committee investigated them for blasphemy. Leah charmed the party, which included lawyers and a judge, and the girls curtsied when presented by Margaret. No arrests were made and some of the committee booked sittings. They were staying at the best suite in the Delavan House Hotel and gave a sitting to Mr Delavan, the owner. His mother came through and called him, via raps, his boyhood nickname. He was so thrilled he pressed $20 into Leah's hand.

On 24 May 1850 they left in triumph for Troy where they stayed at a suite at the Troy House Hotel. Again they were a success even though some of the Trojan woman instigated a campaign against them arguing that had the mediums been men they would have had far fewer male customers. Undoubtedly true, the majority of their clients were men. The accusation spread. One middle-aged lady with a much younger, and handsome, husband was particularly vituperative. Again a committee of Christian women examined them for evidence of fraud. The raps sounded throughout the examination.

Eventually they left for New York City with a male brass band playing outside their hotel and applause from the crowd.

Disembarking from the New York night boat they took up residence at Barnum's Hotel. This was not owned by showman P.T. Barnum, later to achieve even greater fame as half owner of Barnum and Bailey's Circus, but a kinsman of his. It did, however, lead to a rumour that P.T. Barnum had masterminded Kate's career, which he never did although he was, quite soon, to take an interest in her. It's a pity Barnum never represented Kate as she might have benefited from such an experienced hand at the helm.

The Foxes loved New York, the bustle, the excitement, the enormous buildings and its sheer grandeur and energy. The city reciprocated their delight. It adored 'The Rochester Rappers'; as did Horace Greeley, editor and owner of the influential New York *Tribune*. Greeley, then 39, was a remarkable man and several biographies have been written on him. A New England farmer's son, he left school at 14 and arrived in New York with just $10 in his pocket. He secured a job in the print industry and went on to found the *New Yorker* and edit the *Log Cabin*, both successful, before launching the *Tribune* in 1841. He is credited with creating the phrase 'Go West young man' and its not so well known rider '... and grow with the country'. He was unrelenting in his campaign against slavery.

He was well acquainted with the careers of the Foxes, having carried stories on them, usually contributed by Eliab, in the *Tribune*. He'd run a dignified piece, extolling their integrity, on the day of their arrival in New York. There could have been no finer introduction to New York society. Greeley had actually been instrumental in making them famous, and they were now so well known that popular singer Mary Taylor featured a song on them in her hit Broadway show.

Intrigued by what he'd published, Greeley made an appointment to meet the girls. He was, in fact, deeply unhappy, grieving over the recent death of his young son, Pickie. Calvin, smart in army uniform, saluted him at the entrance to the Fox suite and duly presented the girls who entered, hand in hand, chaperoned by the soberly dressed and bonneted Margaret, and a rather more flamboyant Leah.

There was charm on both sides and, to break the ice, the businessman Greeley gently chastised Leah for working the girls so hard, their three daily sessions were from 10am–12pm, 3pm–5pm and 8pm–10pm, and advised them to up their fees to $5 a head, mainly to keep out the riff-raff. This was sound advice; the girls had already encountered less-than-respectful drunken bucks and were to continue to be harassed by intoxicated buffoons throughout their careers. Leah, however, becomingly blushed at the introduction of so coarse a topic as money and responded quietly that the spirits wanted it otherwise. Their message was for all.

Then the two sweet girls, with their glamorous elder sister in attendance clarifying any vague points, gave him a sitting. He was at once put in touch with his beloved Pickie. Greeley was deeply moved and they promised further contact. Pickie, who had died of cholera as an infant, was just one of the four Greeley children who had succumbed to early deaths: only one of their five offspring was still alive. Greeley had wanted an explanation for the cruelties of life. Pickie, through the Fox girls, provided it.

Thirteen-year-old Kate particularly fascinated him. She could be sulky when things were not going as she thought they should but, even at her tender age, she could also be a flirt. Greeley felt his heart open to her.

The *Tribune*, never hostile, now became a promoter of the girls. Clients crowded the waiting rooms, hoping for a chance of a sitting. Because the *Tribune* so favoured them, some of the competition became, according to Mrs Britten, 'rabid in their denunciations'. But this made no difference to their popularity.

The suite was not big enough to accommodate their by-now vast circles of up to thirty or more sitters at a time, so they moved to one of the big public rooms. Leah increased the number of sittings and often arranged an extra session before breakfast. In addition to 'The Rochester Rappers' they were now known as 'The Lions of New York'. They were also the toast of New York and attended many exotic dinners. Hostesses vied with each other to include them, they were quite a catch. Sometimes they returned to their suite, in the small hours, a little tipsy from the unfamiliar champagne they had drunk. Leah became a shopoholic. Despite not raising their fees the money was pouring in and she poured it out just as quickly. There were new clothes for them, and presents for friends and relatives. They accepted lavish gifts, one delighted sitter sending an antique dinner service valued at over $1,000. Margaret would sometimes mildly protest at the extravagant style they had now adopted but was overruled as she was in most things.

It was not all a bed of roses. Rival mediums could be jealous and there was still resentment from certain members of the church. Once, Leah was presented with a bouquet sprayed with poison which could have blinded her and, occasionally, unruly sitters penetrated the circles. Bodyguards had to be employed but were rarely needed.

Tests continued, as they always would, and the séance rooms and suite were regularly searched. Ladies' committees still prodded their anatomies intimately and revengefully.

At times, at night, when they fell exhaustedly into their beds, Maggie and Kate were frightened. A few knocks in the night had become a national epidemic. But there was nothing they could do about it now. It had all become too big. Such was their success that they extended their stay to three months. A press-cutting of the time (undated and unnamed) reads: 'We saw the table at which we sat, and the door opposite, vibrate with the knocks, and yet we saw none that we could suspect of collusion. The world is curious. These knockings are curious. And these young ladies are worth seeing and the mysterious raps worth hearing.' Eliab wrote: 'Curiosity had so far obtained the mastery of bigoted opposition as to lead many of the most eminent men of the city to give the subject a fair investigation.'[3]

Among those eminent men was James Fenimore Cooper, author of, among much else, *The Last of the Mohicans*, first published in 1826 and still going strong. Cooper, with other literary figures, had a sitting with all three sisters, plus Margaret. Food was served throughout and cigars and pipes smoked, jokes were cracked against the background racket of a busy hotel clearly audible.

Cooper asked many questions and gave no indication as to whether the answers were right or wrong. This was frustrating and, eventually, in a spirit of joviality, the others sitters began rapping their canes on the floor in a parody of impatience for him to either deny or verify the answers. He conceded all were correct. He was particularly impressed when accurately told that he had had a sister who had died fifty years ago after being thrown from a horse. Cooper died a year later and, Leah tells us, before dying he scribbled a few words to the girls, thanking them for preparing him for death.

Meanwhile, a Professor Loomis, in the *Scientific American*, published his theory that the Hydesville raps were no more than vibrations from nearby mills.

The girls now had a coterie of regular sitters, including Greeley, and gave them nicknames, like the Hippopotamus, Slick Wig or The Count. Although there was opposition from various Christian factions, Leah points out that her spirit contacts were invariably Christian. And, whilst eschewing the teachings of hell and damnation, she recommends the pamphlet *Christ the Corner Stone of Spiritualism*.

For their last two weeks in New York the Foxes stayed with Greeley at his home on 19th Street. This was no holiday. They paid for their board with séances – Greeley was keen on tests; he did not need proof himself, he already believed, but he wanted to foil detractors. Among Greeley's many guests was travel writer and novelist Bayard Taylor who, in that year of 1850, had just published to acclaim, both in Britain and America, his novel *El Dorado*. A man of whims, many of them paying off handsomely, he questioned the girls deeply, quite wearing them out. They willingly discussed the raps with all Greeley's friends insisting that they had no idea from where the sounds came. Sometimes their questioners would be unexpectedly titillated when raps sounded near them, stressing what the girls were saying. They listened to all possibilities that were expounded and neither agreed nor disagreed. They simply did not know.

The Foxes were glad when the two weeks were up and they could return to the relaxed atmosphere of David's farm, give out their presents, tell their tales and show what they had bought. Greeley had not wanted them to go although Mrs Greeley did not share his sentiments. She was not, and never became, a fan, always viewing them with suspicion. She was, however, a newspaperman's wife, accepting his interests, so put up with it. Greeley offered to board Kate and Maggie indefinitely at his farm, just outside the city, and arranged for them to be educated in order that they might communicate with an educated world, if not on equal terms then, at least, with a degree of confidence.

Neither was keen. New York had given them a taste for the high life; the prospect of trading that for school was unappealing. It might be thought Margaret would have seized this unique opportunity of an education for her daughters but, if she had wanted to do so, Leah overruled her. There was no way she was going to let them out of her control. Truth to tell, Margaret, too, enjoyed the excitement of their fame, grateful to be part of it. Greeley, however, was not to be fobbed off and put up a strong argument for education. Leah was conscious of the debt she owed the powerful editor and did not want to cross him so a compromise was reached. Maggie had already shown a talent for public work and was older; she would remain with Leah as the public face of Spiritualism.

Kate, although a favourite at séances, was really too young for continuous public work. Leah knew Greeley had a weak spot for her so it was agreed that the reluctant Kate would put herself in his hands and live with him and his unsympathetic wife at the farm while being educated. She would attend school under an assumed name, to protect her anonymity, and continue to give séances for Greeley out of school hours. While the family was at David's, Leah agreed to a séance for a group of his friends who had heard about his psychic sisters and wanted to see what it was about for themselves. David's wife, Elizabeth, who had never had a sitting wanted to join them but was nervous about a séance being held in the house while her children were there. It was decided to hold it at John's, which was the last thing he wanted but the weight of family opinion was against him.

David's faith in the spirits had taken a knock after the death of his baby but was now recovering. He was still intrigued and proud of his sisters' fame. Leah had agreed to the séance, but as this was not a professional booking, and instead a goodwill gesture, she decided her presence was not essential. Kate and Maggie could hold the fort. She agreed to babysit so Elizabeth could join the circle at John's.

Left alone Leah went to her room, put on her nightdress and undid her hair for the night. But she could not sleep and kept thinking about the circle just down the hill. She felt neglected and a little peeved that they had agreed to go ahead without her. She could see John's lighted windows from her room and clearly things were still going on. It was now 2am and the idea possessed her to go and have a look. The children were settled fast asleep.

Slipping a farm hand's coat over her nightie she walked into the blustery night towards John's house. A pang of resentment swept through her again. How dare they enjoy a séance without her? She who had done so much for Spirit. There would be no séances at all had she not got things organised. Mischievously, she threw a stone at the window. No one noticed so she threw a handful of grit. The sitters started in alarm, was this spirit intervention? She heaved the largest stone she could find and broke the window. There were cries and everyone rushed out onto the grass.

She hid behind a bush in fear; it would not do for David's guests to see her – especially in her nightie, worker's coat and unkempt hair. All sorts of conclusions might be drawn. Margaret said that a poacher must have accidentally broken the window but a man denied this and claimed it must have been spirits because he'd seen lights around the window before the smash. The sitters eventually went back in and Leah scampered home, thoroughly ashamed. When David and the family returned she was still awake and they told her what had happened. She said nothing.

It might be expected that she kept quiet about the incident for the rest of her life but this was not the case, had it been so then we would not have known of it. Years later, when her reputation was assured in Spiritualist circles, she confessed to it to the family. It became a part of the Fox legend for Mariam Buckner Pond included an account of it in *Time Is Kind*.

Which leaves us where? Clearly Leah was capable of fraud but just as clearly was capable of voluntarily owning up to it. If her entire life had been based on fraud, and she decided to confess, she would have to have admitted to much more than that single incident. She never did.

Excitement came to an end for Kate when she was packed off to the Greeley farm. Kate, bright, sly and with a zest for life, was not a natural scholar. She neither enjoyed school nor the lonely routine at the farm. Mrs Greeley could be downright hostile at times and the doting, but demanding, Horace was forever inviting scientists to test her. When there were no tests she was expected to contact the energetic little Pickie, sometimes under Mrs Greeley's steely eye. There were times when she was exhausted and longed for a little nip of the champagne that had been so abundant during their public appearances. She was already a city girl.

Leah and Maggie were booked for another round of circles in Buffalo. They were a good team: Leah would greet the sitters and relax them, ensuring they were in a harmonious frame of mind, pointing out how essential this was to the production of phenomena. She would have a few words with Maggie before ushering them in and then would remain at the table during the circle to boost power and prompt the spirits, sitters or Maggie if there was an uncomfortable lull. Among the many mediums practising in New York was a Mrs Benedict. Inspired by Kate's visit to Auburn she had copied much of her technique. Mrs Benedict was chief medium of 'The Auburn Circle', about whom Mrs Britten kindly writes that there 'were to be found several extremely ignorant but strongly bigoted persons'.

Although a rapper, Mrs Benedict was also controlled by spirits who spoke through her, among them St John the Divine, St Paul the Apostle and the prophet Daniel. Teachings arrived from the very apostles who had walked with Christ. The circle was renamed 'The Apostolic Circle'.

Still in kindly vein, Mrs Britten tells us: 'Two or three of "the prophets" would be jabbering in unknown tongues at once, whilst others would be shouting the war-hoop of the Red Indian.' With the help of Baptist minister James D. Scott, Mrs Benedict had the jabberings transcribed into English and published. 'To the disbelievers in the divine origin of these papers they certainly created no little feeling of indignation at the audacity which could append the names of prophets and apostles to their absurd puerilities,' notes Mrs Britten, 'whilst even the most credulous of the well-educated Spiritualists had cause to mourn over the deterioration in grammar and orthology which befalls the exalted dead by a long residence in the spirit world.'[4]

Whereas holding no brief for The Apostolic Circle, Conan Doyle offered an explanation for the crudities that sometimes emanated from the Other Side. He suggested that when spirits start to communicate they adopt the vocabulary, mannerisms and, in materialisation or trans-figuration cases, even the looks of their mediums. They can only use the resources with which the medium is already equipped.

Spiritualist magazines and papers were now enjoying a thriving circulation, among the most popular *The Spiritual Clarion*. Levitation made its debut; one of the earliest recorded incidents taking place in the New York Circle, where both Kate and Maggie had sat. Wealthy New York business-man Charles Partridge patronised this circle and among his many respected sitters was Judge Edmonds, who was already acquainted with the girls. The medium was Henry Gordon who, it is said in various publications of the time, rose in his chair and travelled sixty feet through the air.

Before Leah and Maggie started their Buffalo appearances, Maggie had a fit of resentment against her elder sister's vice-like grip on her life, and wanted to step out into the world alone. She decided to handle her own appearances. This was a mistake as she was inexperienced in practical matters. As soon as she had started as a medium, Leah had run her life – which, of course, was the problem.

She accepted a solo booking in Troy, New York, from a circle headed by a family called Bouton, who proved to be loyal supporters. But there were also enemies in Troy and a hostile cabal soon made its presence felt, threatening Maggie's very life. She fulfilled her engagement, however, and was leaving for home, accompanied by Mr Bouton in his coach. They stopped to board a ferry when five hefty thugs tried to force the driver onto Troy Bridge, a notoriously ill-lit and lawless area where many crimes had been committed under cover of darkness.

The driver managed to turn the coach back to Bouton's house where they barricaded themselves in, Maggie hiding in an upstairs room. She was detected and rocks flung at the window. Attempts were made to kick down the door. The mob whom, as one paper put it, was protesting against the 'unholy work of waking the dead' menaced them for a couple of days, working in shifts to ensure Maggie and the family were thoroughly terrorised. She tried to escape out of the back door but was shot at and ran back in terror.

Word was got to Leah who immediately took the train to Troy. Messages must have been intercepted for she was jostled by roughs and forced to change her seat several times. A carriage driven by Bouton's friends, armed with pistols, was waiting for her at Troy but a howling mob followed them to the Boutons'. Another mob was outside the house and but for the guns, and Bouton's friends who came out to help her, Leah would never have got in. As it was, shots followed them. Maggie threw herself at Leah, paralysed with fear and incapable of speech.

Eventually Bouton's men, helped by the commanding presence of Leah, managed to get them out, driving them to nearby Albany and the sanity of the Delavan House Hotel.

Maggie never recovered from the experience. Not the most confident of people, from then on she harboured a suspicion of the public at large. She never trusted them and never really liked them.

Protection was often needed for Spiritualists. Public séances could be raided, and mediums evicted from their houses and insulted in the streets. Some, like Maggie, physically attacked. Frightening as this was, it fostered a spirit of martyrdom. It became a fine and noble thing to be a Spiritualist: a special ambassador, chosen by the Other Side to impart a unique message. The lonely and despised, when contacted by Spirit, even if only by a rapped message, believed they were chosen to do an important job. Loved ones in spirit would be with them all the way. They were no longer alone.

Many successful people also believed; they spread the message and were shot down for it. One such was John Worth Edmonds, who had risen to the position of Judge of the United States Supreme Court, a jewel in Leah's 'elite' tiara. He had conducted exhaustive tests on the

Foxes involving, at different times, no less than eight scientists, all coming to the same, by now, customary conclusion that the raps were not produced by human agency. A trained observer, used to judicial procedure, he had kept notes and published his evidence in the *New York Courier* on 1 August 1853: 'At length the evidence came, and in such force that no sane man could withhold his faith.' Forming a partnership with medium, George T. Baxter, he contacted Francis Bacon, Lord Keeper of the Seal to Elizabeth I, and Emanuel Swedenborg. Non-believers were unimpressed when Swedenborg spelled his name Sweedonborg; One of those many little 'psychic blips'.

The Judge followed his star and together with Baxter published the two-volume *Spiritualism*.[5] Such, however, was the outrage among the judiciary that he was obliged to resign. He never escaped his 'gullible' label. Over a decade later, when Robert Browning published his satirical poem *Mr Sludge the Medium*, he is lampooned as Judge Humgruffin.

Mr Sludge is Browning's parody of medium Daniel Dunglas Home, whom the poet detested. Home, effete, perfumed and with perfect manners beloved of ladies, epitomised everything Browning abhorred. Browning was a man's man and had no time for Spiritualism. *Mr Sludge* was published in 1864 but written earlier. Browning had not published it for fear of upsetting his ailing wife, Elizabeth Barrett Browning, who died in 1861 and believed in Home. He was not the only literary genius to take against the medium. Charles Dickens, whose *A Christmas Carol* features several ghosts and who wrote other supernatural stories such as *The Chimes* and *The Haunted Man*, bluntly declared, 'Mr Home I take the liberty of regarding as an imposter'[6]. Dickens had not sat with Home in a circle, and declined to do so on the grounds that 'the conditions were preposterously wanting in the commonest securities against deceit or mistake'.

Back in 1850, as that amazing year for the Foxes hurtled to its chaotic end, Leah and Maggie spent Christmas honouring their engagements in Buffalo. Spiritualism was thriving in Buffalo and Maggie and Leah were comfortably ensconced in a suite at the Phelps House. Then the knee-joint theory raised its head.

On 17 February 1851 the *Buffalo Commercial Advertiser* carried a statement signed by three doctors attached to the University of Buffalo, to the effect that the raps were produced by the girls manipulating their knee joints. A medical explanation was included. The accuracy of this report was questioned by the *Buffalo Medical Journal* producing a conflict of opinion among the medical profession.

The *Advertiser* continued: 'A highly respectable lady of this city possesses the ability of developing sounds similar, both in character and degree, to those professedly elicited, by the Rochester impostors.' The alleged impostors had been tested for bone dislocation several times already but a 'highly respectable lady' who could do the same thing as them was a novelty.

Leah sent a reply to the *Advertiser*, co-signed by Maggie, objecting to being labelled impostors and expressing their willingness to undergo tests. She added that no one was more anxious than she and Maggie to discover the origin of the raps. The challenge was accepted and tests were duly held in the presence of experts and miscellaneous witnesses, some literally solicited from the street. The girls were stood on cushions, legs extended and ankles held, then made to shift positions.

It was extremely uncomfortable, both physically and mentally, for the raps did not sound. It seemed the girls had been deserted again, for there was nothing but a horrid silence. Eventually three weak taps came on the back of a sofa. This was not a spirit but one of the witnesses, a man who felt sorry for the two girls and tried to help them out. Leah protested and he was duly chastised. Later, a thump was heard on the door, everyone jumped and a man walked in. He'd heard what was going on and could he join the fun. Maggie burst into tears and permission was refused.

Later, Leah attributed this absence of raps to an inharmonious atmosphere. The spirits were always susceptible to bad vibrations. But the atmosphere wasn't that bad, and everyone was patient, both the tested and the testers who were, after all, only doing what Leah had requested. There was an inexplicable silence for nearly two weeks, Leah insisting the tests continue until raps sounded. There was no way she was leaving defeated, for it was during this Buffalo trip that Leah's own skill as a rapper seems to have flowered.

Eventually, the raps returned with a fusillade under the table, which developed into a crescendo. The spectators were told to thoroughly search the room and did so, finding no collaborators. The spirits then made up for lost time, shaking the table so violently that candles fell from sticks. It was rapped out that three bells, of different sizes, be placed under the table. Everyone was then instructed to sit round, hands visible with the girls' feet placed on the feet of their examiners. It was warned there would be a new phenomenon.

The bells rang vigorously under the table, then struck the undersurface with such force that indentations were later discovered. One of the heavier bells was placed on one of the examiner's feet and pressure applied. Everyone was told to move their chairs from the table. They did so except for one sitter, a Captain Walker – a boat skipper who had been roped into the proceedings, who could not shift his chair. Others went to assist but it was as though it was nailed to the floor. It was not released for several minutes. The bells continued to ring but were silent if anyone lifted the heavy cloth to look under the table. As soon as the cloth was replaced they rang again.

Eliab, who was not in Buffalo with the girls, later questioned some who had been there. He was told that it had been rapped that there were times when the spirits were compelled to assume shapes human eyes should not see. An unpleasant rasping was heard. This was the death throes of the father of one of the independent witnesses. He was pointed out and confessed his father had, indeed, died in such distressing respiratory circumstances.

The purpose of all this erratic behaviour was to prove that the phenomena were physically independent of the mediums, and certainly not caused by the flexing of their knees.

Several witnesses were so impressed that they wrote to various papers at length, telling of these marvels. These were unbiased bystanders and medical men formerly out to disprove any supernatural influence. These extraordinary, sometimes alarming, events heralded a new era for the Fox sisters, and were the first of even greater wonders. Spirit was out to impress.

During these extended sessions it was almost forgotten that a 'respectable lady' who could also produce raps had started it all. She was now produced and did, indeed, elicit a few clicks by making violent and, as it turned out, painful, leg movements. To do this she needed to lean against something and bang her leg against a hard surface. It transpired she had some inborn malformation of the knee that permitted this but she so exerted herself during the tests that she was laid up, unable to walk, for a week afterwards. Mrs Patchen, as was her name, did turn out to be thoroughly respectable and was an old schoolfriend of Leah's, although neither of them realised it at the time. When her husband had learnt that the Foxes were to visit Buffalo, he had mentioned it to one of the doctors who involved her in the tests. She apologised for the trouble she had caused and Leah, not one to bear a grudge, forgave her. Maggie did not.

Bookings had had to stop during the tests, but the results were now announced, producing an even greater demand.

This, though, was not the end of accusations of fraud. In April the Rev. Chauncey Burr produced a statement signed by a Mrs Ruth Culver. Culver alleged that Kate had confessed to her that she and Maggie had produced raps by clicking their ankle joints. They had been abetted in this by Leah's daughter, Lizzie. Ruth Culver further alleged that the girls' ankles had been made flexible by soaking their feet beforehand. Other raps had been made by a Dutch serving girl, hidden in another room. Mrs Culver gave the actual date when Kate had made her confession. Her statement carried weight in that she was David's sister-in-law and, before the families had quarrelled, had been close to the girls.

When the Culver accusation was investigated it was found, however, that on the day of Kate's alleged 'confession', she had been seventy miles distant, staying with Eliab and his family who backed her alibi. Kate denied she had ever confessed to Mrs Culver and the Foxes had never employed a Dutch servant. There was bad blood between the families and the accusation made in a spirit of spite. Nevertheless, the story of the Dutch accomplice grew into a legend that was never to leave them.

The editor of the *Buffalo Commercial Advertiser*, which had carried the 'respectable lady' accusation, and thus instituted the tests that lost the Foxes two weeks of bookings, happened to have the misfortune of checking in to the Phelps House while Leah and Maggie were staying there. In front of the entire dining room Leah loudly demanded he publish a letter from her extolling the validity of the phenomena. If he did not do so then legal action would follow. He said he would gladly publish any letter of hers. When it arrived he found it stretched to several pages but a letter from the famous medium would in no way hamper his circulation.

Buffalo had been eventful and, thanks to Leah and Maggie retaining their nerve, ultimately successful. It was with a feeling of satisfaction that they returned to Rochester.

It was dark by the time they arrived and Leah's housekeeper, Clara, had gone home. With all the spirit communication she felt frightened being alone there at night. But Isaac and Amy Post met them and had made them a hot meal. Next day Leah made arrangements to move to a grander house on Sophia Street which she could now afford. Margaret arrived shortly after to take Maggie to New York where she would stay with Kate at the Greeleys while Leah attended to business in Ohio. The Rev. Chauncey Burr had further slandered them and Leah, who was developing a taste for litigation, was not standing for it.

Burr had become a powerful enemy. He had developed a hatred for the Foxes and was now, together with his brother Heman, touring Ohio giving a series of illustrated lectures repeating his claim that the Foxes were frauds. The illustrated part came when Heman produced raps to a stunned audience. He did this with the aid of an adapted boot that enabled him to rap with his big toe. They sounded remarkably similar to the light raps produced by Kate and Maggie, and now Leah. The hall had to maintain absolute silence while Heman rapped which made for a dramatic atmosphere.

They were currently performing at the Melodian Hall, Cleveland, and Leah was determined to see the show. Travelling with the supportive Calvin, her sister Maria and Maria's toddler Charlie, she checked into a suite at the Dunham House Hotel. She had been reliably informed beforehand that the food there was excellent, which was always a deciding factor with Leah. The Burrs were also staying there and Leah made a point of questioning the staff. She learnt to her satisfaction that Heman's socks were saturated in blood after each show as a result of his rapping, and his foot had to be wrapped in a poultice. Obviously he could not keep this up indefinitely.

It was extraordinary how famous the Foxes had become. Not only were the Burrs trading on their names to fill a hall, at the nearby Universalist Church, lawyer Joel Tiffany was doing the same thing. But Tiffany was an ally, a supporter of the girls. His lecture claimed the raps were genuine manifestations. The Cleveland *Plain Dealer* for 5 May 1851 informed its readers: 'There are to be rapping times in Cleveland this week ... we shall patronize both sides and report progress.'

Burr was winning. The Melodian Hall was full and audiences intrigued by Heman's raps. Something would have to be done, which was why Leah had come to Cleveland. A slander suit did the trick. Tiffany, whose suggestion it was, would handle the case. One of Burr's allegations, made from stage, was that Horace Greeley had become disillusioned with the girls and, as a result, given up Spiritualism. This was not true. In the future his faith did waver but at that time he was still infatuated with Kate and working her to a standstill. And Greeley had the weight and money of his paper behind him.

It had been decided to sue at a lavish lunch, attended by Leah and Tiffany, given by Leah's many supporters in Cleveland at a fashionable water spa, set among sylvan groves. Another guest was John Gray, editor of the *Plain Dealer*, with whom she became friends, granting him colourful interviews and exchanging hospitality with him and his family. That night an incognito Leah, Maria and Gray attended Burr's performance.

Shortly after, Maggie and Kate turned up at the Dunham House Hotel. Leah was flabbergasted; she thought they were at Greeley's in New York. She was even more flabbergasted, not to say horrified, to discover they were in the charge of a Mrs Kedzie, a Rochester lady, who intended in future to represent the financial interests of Kate and Maggie, usurping Leah to do so. She had had the effrontery to arrange séances for them already in Cincinnati. They had broken their journey in Cleveland specifically to break the news to Leah.

Leah managed to maintain her composure while immediately tele-graphing Margaret to come to Cleveland and explain matters. Margaret was no more pleased with the situation than Leah but had been powerless to stop it. Greeley had been away and Mrs Kedzie had arrived with her proposal. Maggie had decided that she and Kate would take it up. In her ineffectual way Margaret had let the whole thing drift out of control.

Leah rectified the situation. The girls were not so daring in front of her and pondered on the wisdom of their decision. Maggie gave in, counselled by Calvin and Maria, and decided to break the agreement and stay with Leah. It was conceded, although not amicably, that Kate could continue to Cincinnati with Mrs Kedzie, accompanied by Maria and Charlie. A truce of sorts was declared and there was a belated, if strained, 14th birthday party for Kate. It looked like Mrs Kedzie had won the day. Kate, an adept medium, delighted a Cincinnati that was bursting to meet her. Her séances were many and successful.

Columbus should have been the next venue but Charlie became seri-ously ill. Until then, he had enjoyed his life on the road pampered by all and allowed to tuck into the rich food. Those were days of high infant mortality and Maria had already lost three boys. No one wanted a fourth added to the list. All séances were cancelled. Mrs Kedzie had no option other than return to Rochester and Kate rejoined her sisters. Thankfully the boy recovered and was returned to Rochester with Maria.

Meanwhile, the Burrs had to be attended to. The suit had been lodged but they were still demonstrating to full houses all over Ohio and con-tinued to do so right until the matter came to court. They were certainly not quitters and the news of the case only enhanced their appeal. Now that Maggie and Kate were with Leah, she had reinforcements. With the help of her manager, she managed to book a string of venues. As soon as the Burr gigs finished, hers started: lively times for the Ohio audiences. For all the strength of her personality Leah was not a strong public speaker, but Calvin was with her, and as soon as the rapping started the audiences were intrigued. The Fox raps were more convincing than the Burrs. And who was going to boo two pretty young girls? Who could resist them?

It hadn't started out that way but Ohio proved another successful tour. Private readings were given and gifts of cash, jewellery and other expensive presents showered upon them. After this, Kate returned rather shamefacedly to the Greeleys.

The slander case came up and Leah arrived for her day at court escorted by fans and family, holding little Charlie above her head to a standing ovation. She was pleased to note, and admirers pointed it out, that outside the court there was still a pottage of eggs and refuse that had been slung at Burr who had appeared there the previous day. The case was resolved in her favour. The Burrs cancelled their act.

There was a brief visit home after which Leah and Maggie fulfilled a Cincinatti booking. Kate had made such an impact that there was a demand for a return engagement. Maggie was an excellent and well-received substitute, filling the hall, even though the city was in the grip of a cholera epidemic.

Back home Calvin was taken ill with tuberculosis. Faithful Calvin, who had been brought up by Margaret as one of the family, and who had been a bastion of strength to his beloved Leah was dying. His doctors announced there was no hope: it was a matter of weeks.

On his deathbed he proposed marriage to Leah. She points out that this was no romantic gesture, rather a matter of practicality. Calvin thought widowhood might confer a degree of respectability on her. It was, of course, by no means certain that Leah was respectable. She probably had neither married nor divorced Fish (no divorce papers had been served), although she claimed to have done both. Had she and Fish married and not divorced then her marriage to Calvin, far from bestowing respectability, would have made her a bigamist.

Whatever the truth, Mrs Fish became Mrs Brown on 10 September 1851. The nuptials must have agreed with Calvin for, happily, he rallied and lived in comparatively good health for another eighteen months.

4

One of the VIP engagements Kate undertook for Greeley was a séance with the legendary Swedish soprano Jenny Lind, when the singer was appearing in New York as part of her record-breaking 1850–52 American tour under the management of her equally legendary impresario Phineas T. Barnum.

Barnum first made an impact on New York by exhibiting a female slave whom he claimed to be 161 years old and whom, he further claimed, had nursed the baby George Washington. In 1841 he introduced a freak show which included a mermaid. Since then he'd never looked back. His clients, who seemed to remain fond of him throughout their lives, included Siamese Twins Chang and Eng Bunker and Tom Thumb, the midget. In 1881 he was to co-found, with fellow impresario James A. Bailey, the world famous Barnum & Bailey's Circus.

Conscious of the influence of this powerful man, Greeley had wasted no time in contacting Barnum and introducing him to Kate. Barnum toyed with the idea of representing her but was fully occupied with Jenny and lost interest. He was, however, aware of the publicity Kate could confer on his client, even one as celebrated as Jenny Lind, and willingly agreed to bring her to one of Kate's séances.

Tales abounded of Jenny's status, how she had received over thirty curtain calls for a performance of *Norma* and how, in Vienna, the Empress had made the unprecedented gesture of throwing her bouquet at Jenny's feet. As Greeley related these anecdotes, Kate listened spellbound, keen to meet the Swedish Nightingale. Such was the demand for tickets for

Jenny's concerts that they were auctioned rather than sold, one eager purchaser paying an astronomical $625 for a single seat. When this was told to the practical Jenny she shrugged and said she thought the man a fool.[1] She had a heavenly voice but her feet were firmly on the ground and, good-natured though she was, there was no one quicker to grasp the terms of a contract.

Her past was steeped in romance. Now 30 years old, and at the peak of her powers, she had suffered from an unrequited love for Chopin. It was said that Hans Christian Andersen had fallen hopelessly and unrequitedly in love with her and his story *The Nightingale* was the result.

The truth is more prosaic. Andersen was homosexual and had fallen for Jenny in the asexual way many a homosexual man falls for a diva; Maria Callas' past was littered with them. Andersen and Jenny had been friends and, according to a new biography on Andersen, Jenny referred to him as her 'brother'. (The term homosexual was not used to describe someone's sexual orientation until coined by Karl-Maria Kertbeny in 1869.) Well-known songs were included in her repertoire, and many became popular because they were sung by her. Publishers clamoured for her to sing their songs. Every soirée worth its salt included a Jenny Lind song.

She was the biggest celebrity ever to visit America; in fact, she was the biggest celebrity America had ever known. Later, under Louis B. Mayer and his fellow movie moguls, America was to become the land of stars but in the 1850s there were none. America was in the grip of Jenny Lind Fever.

It was a triumph on Barnum's part that he managed to get a God-fearing Christian like Jenny to attend a séance in the first place. It was the entertainment value of Spiritualism that had done it for she did not take it seriously. But so many fashionable people had become fascinated, that it became quite the thing to attend a séance. And, like Barnum, she was aware of the publicity value.

Jenny was in jovial mood for the circle, in which Barnum and Greeley also sat. As Kate duly produced her raps, Jenny suspected Greeley of a set-up. He tells us that she admonished him 'in the tone and manner of an indifferently bold archduchess'[2] to keep his hands above the table where she could see them. He sat with his hands on his head like a naughty schoolboy. Kate unprotestingly continued producing the raps; just one more occasion when she was viewed as a figure of fun. She was used to it.

It is not recorded what Jenny's messages were but, although the circle was held in New York, the Cleveland *Plain Dealer*, whose editor was Leah's friend John Gray, carried a report: 'It is said that the sweet song-stress had a very interesting interview with what she believed to be the spirits of departed friends, and when she left, she kissed little Katy, saying "If it were possible for you to make these sounds, I know it is impossible for you to answer the questions I have asked this evening." Jenny had been conversing in her native tongue, and she was so impressed with the startling nature of the intelligence she had received, that she bade Kate good-bye with eyes suffused with tears.'

Impressed she may have been but eyes suffused with tears are unlikely. It is interesting that Jenny asked questions in Swedish – if indeed she did, for the whole sitting was a publicity stunt – and the raps knocked out coherent replies. There are several accounts of Kate conducting rapped dialogues in foreign tongues. She had no knowledge of any language save English. Jenny's message did not convert her to Spiritualism. Shortly after her sitting she was at a reception with her friend Parker Willis, who himself had just returned from a séance with Kate. 'From which world do you come?' she had greeted him gaily. He told her that he had asked the raps whether Jenny had any other talent that she could have developed apart from her voice. 'And the spirits said it was making frocks for poor little children, I suppose,' she replied witheringly.[3]

The fame of the Foxes spread to Europe and it was only a matter of time before Britain started developing its own mediums. Before that, however, the Americans needed to show them how it was done.

The first American medium to visit Britain was New Englander Maria Hayden who went to London in 1852 with her journalist husband. She appeared at several venues and charged a guinea a head for private sittings. Mrs Hayden was a refined and attractive young lady, whose psychic abilities have been described as 'quiet and unobtrusive'. Hardly the requisites, it might be thought, for the instrument of a breakthrough between two worlds. But then the Foxes were always demure on stage, it was the raps that created the attention. She, too, was a rap medium and brought to the rostrum a sober presence that subdued some of the more ribald hecklers, and there were always plenty of those. She impressed one reviewer favourably: 'Many who came to amuse themselves at her expense were shamed into respect or even cordiality by the patience and good temper which she displayed.'[4]

Unfortunately, good reviews were in the minority. The 'ignorant British Press' as Conan Doyle put it, ridiculed Mrs Hayden portraying her as an adventuress. One of Mrs Hayden's disparagers was editor of *The Leader* George Lewes, who lived scandalously with novelist Mary Anne Evans (better known as George Eliot) whose books he did his best to promote. They could not marry as Lewes was already married, although his wife was having a long-standing affair with his business partner Thornton Leigh Hunt.

Lewes sat with Mrs Hayden and it was agreed he could write a question, which the raps would answer. He wrote: 'Is Mrs Hayden an impostor?' There was a sharp 'Yes' in response. Lewes published this, which occasioned an outraged response from, among others, royal physician Dr Ashburner: 'Mrs Hayden is no imposter, and he who has the daring to come to an opposite conclusion must do so at the peril of his character for truth.'[5] These psychic young ladies could certainly stir male blood.

Among those whose blood was stirred was mathematician Professor De Morgan, whose author wife became a Spiritualist and regularly sat in circles. The Professor wrote of his encounter with Mrs Hayden in a preface to his wife's book *From Matter to Spirit*. Mrs Hayden rapped, in a crowded séance, for nearly three hours, making sounds the Professor describes as like knitting needles clicking. Then, as she moved across the room to take refreshment, 'A child suddenly called out, "Will all the spirits who have been here this evening rap together?" The words were no sooner uttered than a hailstorm of knitting-needles was heard, crowded into certainly less than two seconds.'

During another session the Professor questioned the willing raps incessantly. Mrs Hayden was sitting some distance away, apparently in a world of her own, reading the recently published *Uncle Tom's Cabin*. Slavery still existed in America and many Spiritualists were against it. The Professor tells us that most of the raps were heard on the table and elsewhere about the room. As usual, the answers to questions were not always correct. Although puzzled by this, the Professor had no doubt as to the genuineness of the phenomenon.

Mrs Hayden was taken up as an amusing diversion by society. Few really believed in her but in fashionable salons she would wander from table to table, not an equal but something above an entertainer, and perform her raps. Perhaps Mrs Hayden's indifferent British reception made her think the spirits had let her down for, back in America, her appearances as a medium lessened and she became a fraud investigator for the Globe Insurance Company.

Although the new Mrs Brown had recently moved to a grander house she now found Rochester too restrictive. She adored New York and that was where she wanted to live. She proudly took a lease on a handsome brownstone in exclusive West 26th Street and moved in with her husband, mother and sisters. John refused to budge from his house, which suited everybody fine.

The Fox farewell from Rochester was monumental. The station was thronged with friends, well-wishers and admirers. Tears were shed and kisses exchanged. A casual observer might have supposed they were leaving for Tibet. Lizzie was to live with them in New York after a two-year stay in Illinois. Margaret, who felt remorse at the child's separation from her mother, had organised the reunion as a surprise. It was certainly that, however Leah agreed to give her daughter another chance and Lizzie, while never liking the spirits, understood she must not oppose them and, in any event, seemed to have lost some of her bitterness against them. A bonus for her was that she was genuinely fond of Calvin, whom she'd known all her life.

Lizzie had more than the easy-going Calvin to cheer her. She had fallen in love and was already plotting her wedding although that would not be for a couple of years yet. Leah was far too preoccupied with her own success to bother overly about her daughter's marriage; she was probably more than glad that Lizzie was to be happily settled away from her.

Lizzie chatted about her plans to Maggie and Kate, as any young lady planning her wedding might. She was certainly more cheerful than the sullen teenager of two years ago. Her happiness was infectious and, not surprisingly, Maggie fell in love shortly afterwards. This was to have a more drastic affect on Leah than her own daughter's engagement, and she was to do all in her power to kill it stone dead, irretrievably alienating Maggie in the process. For Maggie's beloved abhorred Spiritualism; he thought all mediums fraudulent and the Foxes a pack of charlatans (which in no way dampened his ardour for Maggie).

> If ever any beauty I did see,
> Which I desir'd, and got,
>   'twas but a dream of thee. (*John Donne*)

Maggie met 32-year-old Dr Elisha Kent Kane in the autumn of 1852 in Philadelphia, where she was giving sittings. Leah was still in New York; there was too much work for them to rap together nowadays so Maggie, with Margaret as chaperone, usually rapped alone as Kate was still with the Greeleys. There were so many offers for work that Maggie could have taken her pick, but Philadelphia was a Quaker town and the Spiritualists had many Quaker friends. It was Quakers who had arranged this itinerary.

Kane, now celebrated for having established new Arctic shipping routes, had a remarkable past. Unlike other celebrities, he was not to make a brief appearance in the Fox lives then disappear. He was to remain in Maggie's life forever, long after his premature death. Their doomed romance is Spiritualism's greatest romantic tragedy. It brought her a few periods of ecstasy for which she was to pay with years of bitterness. Her life, after Kane's death, was one of unrelieved anguish. It ultimately brought her downfall.

Kane had studied medicine and while at university contracted the rheumatic fever that was eventually to kill him. Never a well man, this was rarely apparent from his demeanour. Slight, short and not particularly good looking, there was a glamour attached to him that made him stand out. He was dashing and had left a string of broken hearts in his wake. After becoming a doctor he'd joined the navy as a ship's surgeon, journeying to Madeira, Bombay, Rio, Ceylon, Egypt, Greece, France and the Philippines, where he'd descended the live volcano Taal, which erupted again in 1965.

There is no doubting his courage. In 1847, during the American-Mexican war, and a year before the first rappings, he had requested a posting to Mexico City. There, although badly wounded and working in primitive conditions, he managed, through surgery, to save the life of a general's son. He returned to America a hero. In 1850, while Maggie was the toast of New York, he had left on an Arctic expedition to search for the ill-fated Sir John Franklin, who had never returned from his search for the North-West passage. His wife, the iron-willed Lady Franklin, would not rest until every possible chance of finding her husband had been exhausted. Many able-bodied seamen had been sent to their deaths under this privileged lady's futile determination to retrieve her husband, corpse or otherwise.

Kane had had no more luck than the others but he had kept notes and was writing a book of his adventures. He was also determined to mount another search and was raising funds to that purpose. He met Maggie in the Bridal Suite of Webb's Union Hotel where she was staying and giving sittings. He had had a few hours to spare before a meeting one morning and, glancing at the local paper, noticed one of her advertisements. He was curious; who had not heard of Maggie Fox? He did not believe in spirits, he went for a laugh and a chance to meet an attractive woman. Spiritualism broke all sorts of taboos.

Arriving just before ten o'clock, the door was opened by the servant. Margaret was there with 19-year-old Maggie, who was sitting at the window, the sun streaming on her, reading a book of French exercises – the well-connected all spoke French. Elisha apologised for his unannounced intrusion, saying he must have come to the wrong room, as he was seeking a medium and surely these attractive ladies could not come into that category? He was assured he was in the right place.

Margaret sat him at the table where Maggie joined him. He asked questions and the raps responded while Maggie continued to read her book to prove her impartiality and keep her hands in view: the same technique adopted by Mrs Hayden. Messages came from Elisha's dead young brother. He was invited to look under the table while the raps sounded. He politely asked that Margaret remove her hands from the table, which she did, and still the raps continued. He noticed a slight vibration on the surface even though there appeared to be no human contact.

Elisha came to scoff and went out smitten. They fell for each other on that first day although it took Maggie a little time to accept this. She was different from anyone he had met before. In that hotel séance room, something built up between them far more potent than ectoplasm. He was everything she'd ever dreamed of, charming, rich, attractive and aristocratic. Although Elisha became the love of her life, if he had not come along when he did then someone else would have. Inexperienced romantically, she was pining for love. She wanted to give her heart and Elisha came at the right moment. She was accustomed to the indelicate comments of some of her more debauched sitters and had met plenty of elderly, scientific and grief-stricken men, more interested in romancing the dead than the living, and there had been a few decent young bucks for whom she yearned, but she'd never considered romance. Few had attempted to romance her. Maggie was difficult to court and Spiritualism's racy reputation distanced her from many respectable circles.

Smitten as he was, Elisha did not believe for a second that it was spirits knocking. He thought it was Maggie, it made her more intriguing. The Kanes were well known, his brother's death common knowledge. That she purported to bring a message from him meant nothing. It was a short reading and he would have liked to stay to talk but this was impossible. Margaret explained other sitters were already in the waiting room.

He came back the next day with a group of friends for a sitting. This time he managed to exchange a few words with her and chided her, gently, that this was no life for a young lady.[6] Margaret explained that it was not their chosen path but one chosen for them by Spirit. Elisha let that ride, although he was to pick up on it with a vengeance later. He came every day, often bringing friends; sometimes he called two or three times a day. Eventually he summoned up courage to ask, hesitantly, if he might bring his cousin, Helen Patterson, to tea, to meet them. Arrangements were made for them to go on a carriage ride.

More drives followed, where Margaret occasionally let them walk for a few minutes while she waited in the carriage. Sometimes Maggie took Tommy on their drives. Tommy was a white poodle whom Maggie adored, given her by actress Charlotte Saunders Cushman. He had unusual blue eyes. No more unusual than Miss Cushman herself. The Massachusetts-born tragedienne had returned to America in 1849 after a triumphant tour of Europe. The 40-year-old boot-faced thespian, who had filled theatres with her acclaimed portrayal of Lady Macbeth, was also known for her 'breeches' parts, among which was Romeo to her sister's (also an actress) Juliet. Her many admirers included poet Walt Whitman who described her acting as 'among the most intense ever felt'.

At the time she consulted Maggie she was experiencing intense feelings of her own, being in the midst of, what was to be, a decade-long affair with actress Matilda Hays. They dressed identically and their relationship was acknowledged, as Elizabeth Barrett Browning put it, as 'a female marriage'. Females were not reckoned to possess feelings of lust so the union was judged, if judged at all, as non-sexual. In 1852, after Miss Cushman's sittings with Maggie, although not as a result of them, she moved to a lesbian community in Rome where she fell in love with sculptress Emma Stebbins. Miss Hays discovered Charlotte writing a love note to Miss Stebbins and a violent fight ensued followed by a court case resulting in Charlotte handing over a large sum of money.

This was not the end of romance for the insatiable Charlotte who moved on to 18-year-old actress Emma Crow, 'my little lover' as she called her. Unfortunately, her little lover ditched her to marry Charlotte's nephew. Charlotte's full life had a happy ending of sorts in that, although she died of cancer aged 59, Emma Stebbins returned to nurse her to the end.

Considering the vicissitudes of Charlotte's life it is not surprising she sought guidance from a loftier source. Hopefully Maggie provided, through the spirits, useful guidance. The actress was sufficiently grateful to buy Tommy for the animal-loving Maggie. These were the sort of clients who flocked to Maggie's séances, those who, it could be said, led lives in the fast lane. It might be thought that the Foxes, themselves, came into that category.

They were not the type to which the Kanes were accustomed. Elisha knew this, but Maggie was to find it out the hard and painful way. The adventurous side of her nature, by and large, had till then thrived on the unplanned course her life had taken but, by now, she had seen enough of society to want to be a part of it, to feel secure and not have to rap for a living. She wanted the respect of the middle classes as opposed to being a fairground attraction. But Leah constantly warned her that if they stopped rapping they would be destitute and there was no way Leah was going back to piano teaching.

Elisha was the essence of decorum. His cousin Helen seemed to have taken to Maggie and whispered, flatteringly, how fond of her Elisha was. When the snow was thick on the ground the three of them went sleigh riding. There was no need for Margaret with Helen as chaperone. They were noticed – such a famous pair could not escape attention. Soon Maggie ceased to care, she was head over heels in love. It was returned; in his selfish, masculine way Elisha did love Maggie, as much as he was able to love anyone.

He flirted irresistibly, constantly buying her flowers and gifts, always through Margaret as decorum dictated. He playfully asked her if she had ever been in love. She told him to ask the spirits. That sharp Philadelphia autumn of 1852 was one of shivering beauty for Maggie. It was as well she had some happiness. It came crashing down too soon.

Towards Christmas Elisha had to go to New York on business and, with Margaret's permission, called to pay his respects to Leah. He planned this well, taking a party of friends for a group reading and laden with letters of introduction, family greetings and gifts. Leah, who had been informed of his relationship with Maggie, was not pleased to see him. She attacked him, virtually on sight, terrified he would take her gifted sister away from her. He was shocked, unused to this hostile treatment.

George Du Maurier was to publish his novel *Trilby* towards the end of the nineteenth century in which he introduced the evil genius Svengali (well captured in the 1954 film of that name starring Hildegarde Knef and Sir Donald Wolfit) to a delightfully horrified world. Had Du Maurier sought guidance as to Svengali's nature from Elisha, he might have come up with Leah. Having met her he knew why his beloved Maggie was living this life of deception. It was Leah's fault; she was the Svengali who had driven her into a life of disrepute. They hated each other as long as they both lived.

He had better luck with 15-year-old Kate. She adored him, but would have welcomed any distraction from the Greeleys with whom she was still being educated and churning out séances. Elisha provided this; he would take Kate back with him to Philadelphia as an unexpected Christmas surprise for Maggie and Margaret. This was a happy reunion as the girls were always close. They bonded together to protect themselves from the gusty Leah. He showered everyone with Christmas gifts and although this touched Maggie, presents did not bring the excitement they might once have done. Their suite was full of lavish gifts sent by grateful message recipients. They could have opened a shop, there were so many.

On one occasion Maggie glaringly demonstrated the difference in protocol of their worlds by taking him through her bedroom to show him a magnificent cake someone had sent. He was shocked to the core that an unmarried lady could be so indecorous. After Christmas Kate returned to the Greeleys and Maggie continued with her Philadelphia sittings. Early in 1853 they became secretly engaged and he gave her a diamond ring. But Maggie could only wear this in private and had to keep it hidden.

Elisha assured her that, when the time was right, he would introduce her to his family. The oldest story in the world but Maggie swallowed it because she was naive and because she wanted to swallow it. He probably hoped this might be possible, Elisha was an optimist but, in his heart, he knew how his parents would react if he introduced a medium as his bride-to-be. He knew he was on a collision course with his family. There were times when the futility of the situation hit him. Then he could be cruel and, in frustration, tell her she was not worthy of him, could never raise herself to his level. He begged her to give up a life that he viewed as one of deceit without guaranteeing her the compensation to do so. Maggie was not entirely aware of Elisha's family situation, but the fact that she had not met his parents indicated all was not well.

The Kane family had found out about them, which was hardly surprising since much of Philadelphia had seen them together. Kane had to admit the dalliance to his parents who, as he knew they would, begged him to give her up. Then there was the matter of his official betrothal. Elisha was already engaged to a young lady of acceptable social standing. He'd told Maggie this but assured her it had taken place before they had met and he would, in due course, put matters right.

He couldn't leave Maggie, and there were times when he was the most caring of lovers, full of tenderness. But, as Maggie was to find out, Elisha also had violent mood swings. She first experienced one of these when he had returned to New York on fundraising business as he often did – he was a good and colourful speaker – leaving her in Philadelphia. He had taken his brother, John, into his confidence, and persuaded him to deliver a letter to Maggie. Out of the blue, this informed her that they were finished and must part; their lives were too different for the relationship ever to work. He ended with, 'Remember Dr Kane of the Arctic Seas loved Maggie Fox of the Spirit Rappings.'[7] This line was to be much-quoted throughout the years.

Margaret was outraged, which did not help Maggie at all. She was wounded and humiliated, her love betrayed. All remaining Philadelphia bookings were cancelled and Maggie and Margaret left, in distress, for home. Leah was delighted. She insisted Maggie should have nothing more to do with him and was appalled at their secret engagement. He had abused the spirits and the Fox sisters *were* Spiritualism. By his betrayal Elisha had shown himself in his true colours.

This denunciation had the reverse effect to the one Leah intended. Maggie turned on her, blaming her for making her a medium, something she'd never enjoyed. Maybe Elisha was right, she should give it up. After a week of misery for Maggie, Elisha called and apologised for his behaviour which he blamed on pressure of work. Maggie was overwhelmed, he was back and that was all that mattered. Her pride had taken a blow but so what? Alas, they would break up again. This was only the first of several ruptures to be followed by Elisha's apologies and renewed declarations of love.

On the whole Margaret was relieved he was back. The improvement in her daughter was instantaneous. Unaware of the degree of Kane family opposition, she held hopes of a marriage between the families. Leah demanded a meeting with him. *Time Is Kind* gives a verbatim report of their conversation, Leah high handed and Elisha conniving, but as only Elisha and Leah were present, this can only be based on family lore. Whatever was said, it was not amicable. Leah wanted him out of their lives. He wanted Maggie to renounce Spiritualism. He would not give up Maggie but neither would he publicly declare his love. The population of the United States was around twenty-five million and a million of these were Spiritualists, the number swelling all the time. Leah headed the Spiritualist canon. The idea of Maggie retiring was preposterous to Leah.

Maggie and Elisha resumed their courtship, although Maggie tried to keep Elisha and Leah apart. He beseeched her not to allow Leah to poison her mind against him, to have as little to do with her as possible and to renounce Spiritualism. Occasionally she asked when she might meet his family and he stalled saying that the family mansion was being renovated so now was not the time.

Kane's hatred of Spiritualism or, as he considered it, the lies of Spiritualism, tore Maggie apart. She had her own demons concerning the spirits. She knew she had to fabricate certain things at times, too many people demanded too much of her. But many sitters believed all she told them and it left her wondering if, perhaps, the fabrications were true and that she had not made them up? She sometimes had to make a silk purse from a sow's ear; people had paid and wanted value. She was confused and Kane made her more so. Still their love affair grew.

Elisha was a distinct irritant but the worldly Leah never believed for an instant that he would marry Maggie. Apart from Maggie herself, no one who gave it much thought did. Kate was too young and Margaret, although always a parent who cared for her daughter, bent whichever way the wind blew. So Leah flourished, sopping up the cream of society or, at least, that intrigued section of it that came to her door.

The teenage Kate was restless to leave school. She languished at the Greeley farm amid the cattle and crops, sometimes treated as a goddess, at other times an object of ridicule. She envied the glamorous lives of her sisters. Maggie and Leah called a truce in that they did not discuss Elisha. He continued to warn her about the terrible implications to him if she were discovered to be a fraud. All hopes of financing another Arctic expedition would be dashed as he, too, would be tainted.

Lizzie's uncomplicated romance did not help Maggie but instead highlighted the problems she faced. Lizzie was not in love to the all-consuming degree that Maggie was, but the likelihood of the finely balanced Maggie ever sustaining a straightforward courtship was remote.

In the company of the well-bred Elisha, Leah's new-found grandeur began grating on Maggie, as did Margaret's compliance with most of Leah's suggestions. Although always close to Kate, Maggie was growing apart from her family and beginning to despise her mother. She loved her, but scorn tainted it. Closeness was needed among the Fox clan, for competition had sprang up to such a degree that most of America sat up and took notice. Of all the states for this to occur, it was happening in Ohio, where the Foxes had made such an impact. Not in the big cities, but in a remote hamlet, seventy miles from the nearest town, rather as the raps had started at Hydesville.

Newspapers forgot the Foxes and syndicated stories of the amazing spirit communications produced by farmer Jonathan Koons and his sons. Koons called his spirits 'The Invisibles' and had built a Spirit Room for them deep in the heart of a forest, near his farm. Visitors flocked there to hear spirit music. Mrs Tamlin and her musical instruments were still performing in New York as were other musical mediums. A pretty young medium, Miss Brooks, was, at that very time attracting a large following through her ability to produce music from a closed piano simply by touching the lid.

These were amateurs compared to the spirit virtuosi at the Koons. Guitars and other instruments were strummed in the darkness, sometimes there were soloists, other times orchestras. Spirit pictures were also produced. Scenes from the Other Side were impressed onto plain paper – waterfalls, seascapes and fields, all glimpses of the paradise that awaited believers after death. The Invisibles demanded a trumpet, not a musical instrument but something resembling a lightweight megaphone daubed with luminous paint, through which their spirit voices could be amplified to address the sitters. Usually the trumpet levitated while this was happening.

The wealthy Mr Partridge, who had held levitation séances in New York, was one of the many visitors who crowded the Spirit Room. It was there that he first heard the spirit John King. John went on to become a celebrity, appearing in circles all over the world. Towards the end of the nineteenth century Colonel Olcott wrote of his encounters with John King when King was communicating with Madame Blavatsky:

She [Mme B.] gave me some séances of table-tapping and rapping, spelling out messages of sorts, principally from an invisible intelligence calling itself 'John King'. This pseudonym is one that has been familiar to frequenters of mediumistic séances these forty years past, all over the world. It was first heard of in the Spirit Room of Jonathan Koons where it pretended to be a ruler of a tribe or tribes of spirits. Later on, it said it was the earth-haunting soul of Sir Henry Morgan, the famous buccaneer, and as such it introduced itself to me. It showed its face and turban-wrapped head to me at Philadephia during the course of my investigations of the Holmes mediums, in association with the late respected Robert Dale Owen. (*Old Diary Leaves*)

The Holmeses were to be another of the great Spiritualist scandals (covered further on) of which the Colonel wrote in his comprehensive *People From the Other World.*[8]

The Colonel refers to John King, untypically and ungallantly, as 'it' because he was not quite sure whether or not King was an elemental. You never knew with Madame Blavatsky's callers. If Madame Blavatsky knew, and she probably did, she did not tell the Colonel. The locals did not take kindly to John King nor the rest of The Invisibles, and even less kindly to the troops of city folk trespassing on their land. They attacked the Spirit Room and smashed all paraphernalia. The Koons were lucky to escape with their lives. As Sir Arthur Conan Doyle put it: 'Koons and his family were driven from their home by the persecution of the ignorant people among whom they lived.'

Judge Edmonds was still being ridiculed by the press, notably the *National Intelligencer* of Washington. Outraged by this the Hon. Nathaniel Pitcher Tallmadge, former Governor of Wisconsin, wrote a long piece in Edmond's defence in the *National Intelligencer*, ending, 'I knew him to be a man of unimpeachable integrity. I concluded that if he had become a believer in "spiritual manifestations" it was at least a subject worthy of investigation.' He had investigated and become a Spiritualist himself, receiving several communications, through different mediums, from his old colleague John C. Calhoun who had died in 1850.

Another supporter of Edmonds was General Waddy Thompson, former Minister for Mexico whose 1846 book *Recollections of Mexico* is considered authoritative of the time. A man of substance and experience, the General arranged for the Fox sisters to come to Washington for a series of séances with himself, Tallmadge and others. Leah could not fulfil these bookings (and as a result does not mention them in *The Missing Link*, which firmly keeps appearances of Kate and Maggie at arm's length) due to other commitments so, in the February of 1853, Maggie, Kate and Margaret conquered Washington. Kate was thrilled to be going, glad to be away from Greeley and looking forward to seeing the big city.

Maggie was indifferent. She was peeved with Elisha believing he had left town for lecture engagements in Boston without saying goodbye to her. In fact, he had called for that very purpose but Margaret had not let him in, fearing Leah's wrath, and had not mentioned he had called. But through Kate – who was now living at home although still under Greeley's auspices – he had sent Maggie a letter asking her to meet him clandestinely, which if she had done so and they been seen together would have jeopardized both their positions. In the end he had compromised by sending her a beautiful travelling bonnet for the Washington journey. Before her Spiritualist days, she would never have been able to afford such a hat and certainly never have had occasion to wear it.

Calhoun rapped through Maggie in Washington and Tallmadge wrote of these sessions to his Spiritualist friend, the Rhode Island poetess Helen Power Whitman.[9] Miss Whitman was still recovering from the trauma of a hellish earthly engagement to Edgar Allen Poe during which she had vainly tried to wean the famous writer off the bottle. Stronger forces than she had tried that and failed. However, now he was 'in spirit' their relationship had stabilised.

On earth, Calhoun, hailing from South Carolina, had been known as the 'cast iron man', earning this title through the various causes he had espoused including slavery and war between America and Britain. He was the seventh Vice-President of America and, vain as a peacock, the first to have his photo taken. Now, through Maggie, Calhoun informed the group that the purpose of the raps was to draw mankind together in harmony. Like Poe, Calhoun had changed in the spirit world.

Maggie, who seems to have been the dominant medium, was at the peak of her powers and the Tallmadge séances must have been extraordinary. As was now routine at a Fox circle, the heavy table around which they sat moved about the room of its own accord and raised one end several feet off the ground. Tallmadge was then invited to try to upend the table himself but it would not budge. He asked the spirits to release their grip and he was able to lift one end. These séances seem in many ways identical to those that had occurred in Buffalo when Maggie had been with Leah.

Tallmadge, who weighed about 200 lbs, asked the spirits to raise the table while he was sitting on it. They suggested a smaller table and one was brought in from another room. He sat on this, Buddha style, while Maggie, Kate and Margaret placed their palms on it. It rose about six inches off the floor and remained suspended there for a few moments before gently sinking to the ground. The hands of the mediums and Margaret's were visible the whole time, not that they could have lifted him between them, but the Governor says a mild vibration could be felt as though the spirits were utilising some electrical device.

For the next séance, Calhoun ordered a guitar and three bells of different sizes, similar to those requested at Buffalo. An emptied-out, upturned drawer was put under the draped table and the bells placed on it. Both raps and chimes were heard and the bells thumped against the underside of the table, knocking candles from their sticks. Then a hand grabbed one of Tallmadge's feet. The guitar replaced the bells and this was played softly then built to a crescendo before fading again. Tallmadge described the music as 'vibrating echoes of the most indescribable beauty and sweetness'.

At another session a General Hamilton joined them. A closed Bible was placed on the upturned drawer under the table while the sitters resumed their positions. Darkness and closed spaces were always helpful to phenomena. After a while the Bible was inspected and found to be open at the third chapter of John. Raps instructed verse thirty-four be read aloud: 'For he whom God hath sent speaketh the words of God: for God giveth not the Spirit by measure unto him.'

At another session paper and pencil were placed on the drawer. After a while the sitters were told to look under the drawer. The paper was now underneath and, in Calhoun's handwriting, which both the Governor and the General knew well, was written the sentence, 'I'm with you still'. Calhoun's son authenticated the writing as that of his father.

Governor Tallmadge had four daughters and they all, spurred on by their distinguished father, became mediums. Much of his later years were spent writing religious tracts. He remained a friend of the Foxes, particularly Leah with whom he enjoyed many subsequent séances. She brought back to him his wife and dead son William. He wrote to Leah from his home at Fond du Lac: 'I had no peace for years till I began to communicate with him through you.'

They returned to a forlorn New York brownstone. Calvin really was at death's door this time. Everyone was upset but Lizzie particularly so; he had been a real friend to her. The sisters may have preached that Spirit is a world where there is no death, but they were far from happy at the thought of the supportive Calvin going there. Friends gathered around, including the Posts. Isaac, to his joy, had discovered he was a medium himself and possessed the gift of automatic writing. For this a pencil is lightly held in the medium's hand and becomes motivated by Spirit to write; quite different from the writing that had taken place under the Washington table, where no human agency had been involved to hold a pencil.

Kate was to become a prolific automatic writer, particularly the mirror form, where the characters are transcribed back to front and can only be read by holding the paper on which they are written to a mirror. At the height of her career, during her lengthy séances with wealthy banker Charles Livermore, she was able to write automatically, mirror fashion, with both hands simultaneously. What Phineas T. Barnum could have done with that!

Isaac was not that dextrous but competent enough. Benjamin Franklin, Swedenborg, Thomas Jefferson, Voltaire and George Washington all wrote through him. The compassionate old Quaker had published these communications[10] because, 'This very subject, so much ridiculed, is now forming a platform, whereon thousands will be placed, who are now wading through the slough of despondency, willing to catch at a straw to save themselves from sinking to the bottomless pit, which they have been taught to believe in. This is given to bless the whole human family and wipe out the blot of ignorance and superstition, so that man may be free as God made him.'

He added: 'As my object is only to give facts, I leave the book to stand upon its own merits.' Benjamin Franklin contributed the hefty introduction, including the sentence, 'I leave the reader to calmly digest in his quiet moments what is here offered.' Included among the offerings were rapped communications from Leah, who was delighted to be placed among the immortals. The Foxes specialised in bringing back dead children and Isaac himself had lost a son, Edmund, at 5 years of age. With Leah as medium, Edmund had rapped out a poem to console Isaac over the loss of someone else:

Now, Father, she has gone to join the throng Of Heavenly angels, dear;
To unite in song, and the joys prolong, while we are lingering here.

The whole family loved Calvin. Sick and failing, he still exuded a calming influence on the household. He was no match for Leah but she was fond of him and he could, and did, diffuse many a difficult situation. Maggie adored him because he always spoke well of Elisha, as a military man Calvin had an appreciation of the explorer's courage. He had frequently comforted Maggie when Leah was being vituperative. In John's absence Calvin was the only male member of the household, indispensable when an escort was required.

Towards the end of April he started haemorrhaging midst a raging fever. This quietened and the bleeding stopped. For a few days he was peaceful.

Calvin died on 4 May 1853 aged 28 years. In his short life he had been attacked by spirits, seen the birth of a radical new religion and married one of its high priestesses leaving her a comely, if slightly eccentric, widow. More than some achieve at thrice his age.

The funeral sermon was conducted by Universalist pastor Professor Samuel B. Brittan, editor of Spiritual publications and personal friend of the Poughkeepsie Seer Andrew Jackson Davis. The Professor came to Spiritualism after having sustained a coma for twelve days and being unable to eat for twenty-one. He awoke from this condition as inexplicably as he had fallen into it, converted to Spiritualism by a spectral visitor who had visited him during his delirium. From then on Professor Brittan was a man with a mission. Madame Blavatsky would have described his spectral visitor as a Mahatma.

Among the tributes to Calvin was a eulogy by Judge Edmonds during which the room was filled with raps of approbation. The funeral itself was at the house of Amy and Isaac. Due to Leah's widowhood Lizzie, who in truth could not wait to get away from the spirits and begin married life, had to postpone the ceremony. Calvin was buried at Mount Hope Cemetery, a place where Leah had often walked in contemplation when she had been Mrs Fish. It had brought her peace and it was profoundly to be hoped it would do the same for Calvin. The family then stayed with David at the peppermint farm for a few days. This was far from recuperative as David's small son Georgie suddenly died. The wretched man had been cursed with the early, tragic deaths of his children.

Back in New York, Leah took over the main parlour for her mourning while Kate and Maggie occupied the smaller rooms for séances. Kate was back at school, but for important sittings, returned to the brownstone. Margaret now acted as booker. Isaac had relinquished this post to

Calvin and now it was Margaret's turn. Care was taken to ensure only serious callers were accepted but, with two attractive girls on offer, albeit chaperoned, plus a ripe widow, some of the rougher sort crept in.

Under Judge Edmonds' supervision, Leah agreed to more test sittings. A party of six eminent men conducted these who, in addition to the Judge (newly resigned), included two doctors, a major in the US Army and Charles Partridge. Major George Washington Rains, was an electrician, a master of that force then so revered by Spiritualists. He constructed an iron chair in which Leah sat, suspended above a steel platform and beneath a glass canopy while her investigators stood on magnets. While the raps sounded the Major prodded her with his 'electrometer', and the doctors listened through stethoscopes for any possible electric emissions from her body. There were none. The raps were still a mystery.

Various 'experts' constantly tested the sisters. Mysteries abounded. At one circle coins were scattered under the table which, afterwards, were found in neat piles. At another a male sitter wearing gaiters, found one had dematerialised. Tables would now glide over the floor with two or three on board. Sitters flooded in, and thousands of dollars with them. Carriages sometimes blocked the street. The money was quickly and often foolishly spent. As Leah put it, Mammon had no temple in their home or hearts. It went straight to the shops to maintain their lavish lifestyle; clothes were ordered, expensive food eaten and fine wines flowed.

It was sometimes asked, as indeed it is today, why communicants who had enjoyed a reputation for intelligence on earth, came through with such trivial messages. It was a point the Foxes usually could not answer. They did not attempt to do so; they were merely the mediums not the technicians. There were raps about 'experiments' and the like but no more. Elisha was sure he knew the answer and continued to beg Maggie to desist from what he believed to be her life of deception. He told her she must abandon her existence of lies and cultivate the demeanour of a lady at all times, ensuring she was appropriately dressed in public with her shoulders and arms demurely covered, something Maggie could be careless about. He sent her so much bossy advice that he adopted the nickname of Preacher, which she delighted in calling him. They had several nicknames for each other.

The time for his expedition was approaching. He would sail from New York on 31 May 1853 in command of shipping magnate Henry Grinnell's sponsored brig *Advance* with its crew of eighteen. His rheumatic fever had flared up while she had been in Washington making him uncharacteristically depressed. He had written her that he was lonely with no one to care for him, a hint that things would be better once they were married. She wrote back at once and he told her her letter had done him more good than the doctors.

This was literally the case and he proved it by, ill as he was, arriving unannounced in Washington, with his brother, whilst the Foxes were in the midst of their noisy séances. To Margaret's rather delighted consternation, he had taken a suite above theirs in the hotel. She was so flustered she had even permitted an hour alone, unchaperoned, which was, truly, taking things too far. Unpredictability was part of Elisha's armoury but Maggie knew that his journey to the Arctic was totally predictable and would not be put off. Adventure was his life.

In his blithe determination to make Maggie a lady, acceptable to his family (although he knew that she would never be acceptable), Elisha had found a place where her rough-hewn education could be refined while he was away. There was, of course, a hidden agenda, for she was to be secreted in the depths of the Philadelphia countryside. Undoubtedly, she could concentrate on the polishing of her accomplishments there without distraction, but the attractive young exotique would also be far away from the eyes of other men. He did not want her snapped up by someone else in his long absence. Not that there was the slightest chance of that; Maggie was a one-man woman, and that man was Elisha. He would cover all expenses, secretly, as he did not want his family to discover what he was doing.

His aunt, Mrs Lieper, was taken into his confidence. She owned an estate in Crookville which she had leased to a yeoman tenant, a Mr Turner, a straightforward Scots family man. He was to take Maggie in as a boarder where she could be tutored by his daughter, a governess, whom Elisha charmingly described as 'ugly as sin'. She certainly would not be attracting suitors. There, under the sheltering pines of the estate Maggie would further her studies in music, French, handwriting, embroidery and other essential accomplishments for a lady of quality. How Maggie now regretted having turned down Greeley's offer of an education. After a summer thus spent Maggie was to enter Madame Montenard's academy for young ladies at Albany.

Maggie was content to comply. She would have done anything for Elisha and, after all, it was to prepare her for their marriage and her consequent elevated position in society. She would not miss the spirits. She was becoming increasingly impatient with the endless parade of sitters, all demanding something special and who callously drained her energy. Aside from her admirers, Washington had been full of drunken politicians. She would not miss it.

Margaret condoned these arrangements. Maggie would have been her enemy forever had she vetoed them. She never gave up the forlorn hope that Maggie might, perhaps, one day marry Elisha. He, always courtly, took Margaret to meet the Turners with whom Maggie would be living. There was nothing about them in which to object to – to Leah's fury.

Just before his departure Elisha fell ill again, and recuperated at the home of his patron Henry Grinnell. Elisha was a man to constantly astonish and, for all his fear of scandal, he invited Maggie to take tea with him there. His intentions to Maggie constantly vacillated and, perhaps, he was seriously thinking that if she was to be his wife then she must meet his colleagues.

For Maggie, his invitation was a statement of intent. Anxious to prove what a good wife she would be, she was on top form. Mrs Grinnell was intrigued by her carefully monitored accounts of her associations with the Generals in Washington. As a last minute thought, Elisha commissioned Maggie's portrait to be painted by the fashionable Italian artist, Joseph Fagnani, famed for his portraits of European aristocrats and who had recently moved to New York. Fagnani's portrait of *The Nine Muses*, now in the Metropolitan Museum of Art, had caused much interest in that the muses were all famous beauties of the time. Maggie's portrait was for Elisha to take to sea with him. In times of danger he would strap it to his back.

While Maggie had taken tea with the Grinnells, she had astounded the company, doubtless intentionally, by telling them that she was to give a private sitting to Jane Appleton Pierce, wife of President Franklin Pierce. A bomb exploding could not have created greater shock.

Elisha was the most shocked of all. She had promised she would give up Spiritualism while he was away and he had expected the embargo to start immediately. But she would not be diverted from this prestigious engagement; it was to be her perfect swan-song. She assured him that, after she had seen the President's wife, there would be no more.

Pierce had just been elected (1853–57) but his victory was soured by the death, two months earlier, of his 11-year-old son, Benny, in a train accident. This was the third child the Pierces had lost. The first had died in childbirth and the second aged 4. The whole nation had joined the President elect in his and his wife's grief, to such an extent that the customary Presidential inauguration ball had been cancelled.

Olive Tardiff writes of Mrs Pierce[11], 'She never knew a moment's happiness during her husband's four years in the White House. Most of the time she stayed in seclusion while her aunt acted as official hostess. On the few occasions when Jane appeared in public she was described as having a "woe begone face ... sunken eyes, skin like yellowed ivory".'

A minister's daughter and suffering from tuberculosis since childhood, Mrs Pierce spent much time in prayer. When she told Benny that his father was running for President he had replied, to please his mother, 'I hope he won't be elected.'[12] She fainted with horror when told he had been. When his term was finished Mrs Pierce was so ill she had to be carried from the White House. She died aged 57 in 1863 after a life of gloom. The Foxes were specialists in reuniting dead children with their parents and Maggie was able to comfort Mrs Pierce who spent much time after that writing letters to dead Benny. She deserved consolation and Maggie had certainly brought her some.

Elisha was fully occupied with his forthcoming trip but, if he couldn't see Maggie, he sent his man, Morton, with messages and presents, one of which was a handsome new travelling trunk. Morton was close to Elisha and had travelled with him in the past and was to accompany him on this latest venture. Morton told her of the comforting superstition that if a sailor threw a rosebud, which his beloved caught in her mouth, it would ensure his safe return. The romantic Elisha was more than capable of throwing a rosebud.

Elisha was eager to take Maggie to Crookville and see her safely installed with Mrs Turner and her ugly daughter, both of whom Maggie grew fond. He was still far from well but would not hear of his trip being postponed. The 31st of May was actually a postponement of an earlier date. Elisha's father had admiringly summed up his son as a man to 'die in harness'. Elisha was determined to live up to this description. With Margaret as escort, and Tommy in her arms, they took the train to Philadelphia. Tommy was never fond of Elisha and had nipped him a couple of times. The ladies were to overnight at the Girard House Hotel, and Elisha joined them for a final supper before returning that night to New York. It must have been heartbreaking for Maggie, and Margaret had the sensitivity to leave them alone while they said their farewells.

Next day Maggie and Margaret made, in the carriage Elisha had hired, the four-hour drive through the pretty May countryside to Crookville, where Maggie was kindly welcomed by the Turners and bade farewell to her mother. It was not the saddest of farewells for Maggie as her relationship with Margaret had cooled even more. She resented Margaret's intrusive presence during her farewell to her lover. Truly, she could not wait for her to leave, her very presence was irritating. Sometimes Maggie hated people.

Pressed for time as Elisha was, he returned to Crookville for another farewell to Maggie. Now that Margaret had fulfilled her duty by escorting them on the journey, he craved a few minutes intimacy. He had brought her a few small personal items including her canary, which she had forgotten. Alas, in his agitation to get to Crookville he left the bird on Philadelphia station. It was not seen again. Maggie was ecstatic at his unannounced arrival; even the lost canary couldn't dampen that. Back home, he asked his friend Cornelius Grinnell, the magnate's son, to be sure to buy Maggie another canary in his name.

It seemed that half of New York turned out to cheer the popular Elisha on his expedition. Military boats fired guns in salute and the crowd roared its approval. The *Advance* was expected to arrive in Newfoundland two weeks later, where it would restock, and any letters from Elisha to Maggie would be sent to Cornelius who would forward them to her, and likewise forward hers to him as they could not correspond openly.

Somehow news of Maggie's withdrawal from Spiritualism, and New York, had been made public. Few, however, knew exactly where she was. Her heart was aching and the empty countryside did little to ease it.

Leah missed Calvin dreadfully, he had been a good husband and it had been a friendly marriage. He had also, as much as he could, kept his hands on the business side of things. The imprudent Leah had made and spent a fortune and now found herself financially pressed; she had even been reduced to persuading a reluctant Maggie to tap Elisha for a $100 loan on her behalf.

The trouble was that she could not hold séances during her husband's mourning period which drastically shrank her income and, now that Maggie was not sitting, there was considerably less coming in. Sooner than was altogether proper, Lizzie had married her beau hoping, futilely, to shake off the taint of Spiritualism, and this had incurred Leah more expense.

The answer was for 17-year-old Kate to be put into full-time harness. Although taking part in the occasional public séance, notably at

Washington, Kate had been eclipsed by Maggie while under Greeley's control. Now, he conceded, it was time for her to occupy her rightful position in the public eye. Living with Leah had incurred a certain stress among the Foxes so he generously found a house for Margaret and Kate on Tenth Avenue. All parties were happy with this arrangement and Kate was more than happy to step fully into the public eye and become mistress of her own fate.

Things were not going so well with Maggie who was seriously lovesick. The Turners watched in dismay as she grew daily more morose. She sent letters to Elisha, care of Cornelius, telling how she yearned for him, reminding him of times they had spent together and how they had planned to honeymoon in Italy. He wrote when he could and his letters were filled with love and concern. Always he encouraged her to be diligent in her studies, take exercise although she could grow as fat as she liked, and to laugh and have fun, which was a lost cause when stuck in Crookville. Always, he reminded her to keep to her promise to abandon séances and to see as little of Leah as possible and never spend even a single night in her house.

The *Advance* left for the unexplored Arctic wastes and Maggie could expect no further letters till autumn at the earliest. Elisha had asked several friends to make sure Maggie kept as well as possible and one of these was Ellen Walter. She had already met Maggie, through Elisha, and called at Crookville to see her. Far from the chubby beauty of whom Elisha dreamed, Maggie had lost weight and looked unwell. Ellen was so alarmed that she insisted, to the consternation of the Turners, on Maggie returning with her to recuperate at her New York home.

It was the right decision. Ellen put her in the hands of a Dr Edward Bayard, who diagnosed brain-fever which would probably translate today as a nervous breakdown. He prescribed rest – although it might be thought she had had enough of that at Crookville – and suggested a little diversion would be beneficial, anything to stop her fretting for Elisha. Ellen did what she could and she and Maggie became firm friends. She began to rally, much to the relief of the Turners, and after some weeks returned to Crookville but slipped into a depression again and returned to Ellen.

The best therapy came in the form of a letter from Elisha. It was a love-letter as were all his letters from sea. Far away, locked in the inhospitable Arctic with just her portrait to fire his love interest, he let his feelings loose. Things could be sorted out when he returned. She felt and looked better instantly.

Kate, too, gained the patronage of a powerful man. This, however, was no lover; this was businessman Horace H. Day, who employed her on a regular basis. Day was the wealthy founder of a flourishing India rubber works and was convinced of the reality of spirit communication. To spread the word he hired a large building, 553 Broadway, the centre of New York, and transformed it into the headquarters of the Society for the Diffusion of Christian Spiritualism, known among its inmates as the Spiritual Depot. The President was Governor Tallmadge, and among the several Vice-Presidents were four judges, a major, and some doctors.

The Depot, which had its own press for printing Spiritualist publications and a library, employed mediums whom the public could consult free of charge every morning for five days a week. The President, Governor Tallmadge, had insisted Kate be one of these mediums and another was Emma Hardinge, before she became more famous under her married name of Emma Hardinge Britten.

Born in England in 1823 Emma started her public life as an actress, arriving in America in the 1850s to fulfil theatrical engagements, when the Foxes were already well known. She soon became a prominent medium herself. Her reputation was established when a shipping company sued her for slander after one of its ships was lost at sea. She had forecast the death of all aboard. It was too horribly true and the case was dropped. She demonstrated all over America, Canada, England and Australia. When she died, in 1899, her funeral was attended by nearly every Spiritualist of note. By then Spiritualism was internationally established, and it was the likes of Emma who made it so. A born organiser and competent editor and writer, Emma helped the Depot considerably. She founded *Two Worlds* magazine, which is still published today, and wrote several books on the early days of the movement. But for her we would know considerably less than we do.

Day was a generous boss and paid Kate the liberal salary of $25 for five mornings a week, allowing her the afternoons free for private work. But the work was relentless and unforgiving and she was soon disenchanted. As clients were getting their readings free they did not always value what they got. Sometimes it was downright thankless. In her autobiography, Emma[13] recalls seeing Kate at work. She writes that on entering the Depot she would pause on the first floor to hear 'poor, patient Kate Fox, in the midst of a captious, grumbling crowd of investigators, repeating hour after hour the letters of the alphabet, whilst the no less poor, patient spirits rapped out names, ages and dates to suit all comers. A few minutes spent in that quarter, with a few words of pitying sympathy from me, and a furious thunder of rapping greetings from the spirits, and I ascend to the next floor.'

The Depot became the hub of the Spiritualist world, buzzing with gossip as callers came to sit in circles, read the magazines or merely pass the time of day. Alas, by 1857 the Society had to close down. Even a man as wealthy as Day could not sustain things indefinitely; as it was he spent over $25,000 on the venture.

A certain young medium, Mrs Seymour of Waukegan, was attracting attention through her psychic writing. But instead of writing on paper she wrote on her left arm with the index finger of her right hand and then vice versa. The writing was invisible but after a few moments words appeared in luminous red weals which would fade after fifteen minutes or so. Whatever the cause, it was certainly not phosphorous which would have burnt her. Inspirational dancing was now exercising members of several circles where sitters who were sitting quietly would be jerked into involuntary violent motion. These energetic dances could last more than an hour, bringing to mind the frenzies of voodoo practitioners preparatory to their trances.

A certain Miss Bangs, a teenager with no musical training, suddenly developed an ability to play complicated music upon the piano. Others soon followed suit. Eliab Capron was witness to a peculiar demonstration from a Miss Laurie who could command a golden ring, taken from her finger, to dance unsupported in the air, passing over her head and down her back.

Horace Greeley sometimes covered these things in the *Tribune* but the more extreme the phenomena the more reserved he became.

While the tree of Spiritualism was spreading its branches, yielding some charming, many capricious and some positively freakish blossoms, Maggie unenthusiastically, although now on a more even keel, practised her refinements, hoping it would make time pass quicker, but embroidery offered little challenge to her enquiring mind. It seemed pointless but the whole idea was to prepare herself for marriage. Elisha would appreciate her all the more when he returned from his frozen world to find her a finished lady. But at times her life seemed as barren as the Arctic seas Elisha was exploring.

As the rain dripped from the trees, she nostalgically recalled their theatre trips, secluded in boxes, in which they had, almost light-heartedly tried to dodge attention. Their secret hand-holding, kisses and cuddles – their vows of love.

She thought about his hatred of her lifestyle, his disbelief in spirits. She, herself, was never convinced the raps were from dead people. Was she making it up? Was she wicked? The depression, never far away, descended again. She could confide none of this to the Turners who had instructions from Elisha never to discuss the spirits. It was to be a closed book. Her seclusion gave rise to the rumour, still circulating, that she had given birth to Elisha's child. Was Dr Bayard's treatment for brain-fever a cover for this? Had Elisha organised these things before leaving? Would that explain why Margaret was willing to let Maggie be nursed by a stranger, Ellen, a friend of Elisha's, rather than in her own home?

There is no evidence that Maggie ever gave birth to a child – living, stillborn or aborted. Among the Kane-Fox documentation lodged at the American Philosophical Society in Philadelphia is an undated letter, bearing no address, from Maggie to Elisha. In the letter Maggie writes: 'Little Tommy is very well. Pretty little fellow. Do you want to see him? He always loved you very much.'[14]

Little Tommy is the poodle Charlotte Saunders Cushman bought for Maggie. She is being sarcastic as he was a snappy little brute who bit Elisha more than once. In other letters to Elisha she refers to Little Tommy as her constant companion. If it was not known she was referring to her dog, then Tommy could be construed as her son. This, as Earle E. Spamer of the American Philosophical Society puts it, is 'how rumours begin'. Maggie adored Elisha. If she had had a child by him under any circumstances, she would have kept it no matter what the repercussions. Although Maggie certainly never became pregnant she and Elisha both gave rein to their passionate natures. He constantly wrote to her of his warm hands, glowing kisses, her hair tumbling over his cheeks and how he loved her 'dear little deceitful mouth'. Hardly the language with which to address a virgin lady unacquainted with physical passion. This is the language of lovers.

In the autumn of 1854, after an absence of letters, news of Elisha's ship being in trouble reached Maggie. The *Advance* was locked in ice and crew members had died. It was feared Elisha might be among them. In April 1855 two ships, *Arctic* and *Release*, embarked in search of him.

But Elisha was not dead.

Despite his daily proximity to death and chronic ill health, he was assiduously researching meteorological conditions, charting Greenland's western coast and surveying the Humbolt Glacier, notes which would form the substance of his forthcoming book *Arctic Explorations: The Second Grinnell Exhibition in Search of Sir John Franklin, 1853, 54, 55.* Plagued by scurvy and other demons, he'd penetrated further north than anyone to date charting the Smith Sound, later named Kane Basin in his honour.

He'd managed to survive death, as did most of his men, through the help of the Inuits whose hunting ground was nearby. They proved life-savers, and when a renegade party absconded from the *Advance* and floundered on the wastes, it was the Inuit who brought them back to safety. Elisha was later commended for his humane treatment of these mutineers. As it was impossible to free the *Advance* it had to be abandoned. Elisha led his men on a 300-mile trek across the ice, dragging boats filled with supplies behind them, which eventually brought them to the open sea. They then rowed for a further 1,300 miles to Upernavik, Greenland where, 250 miles south of this, in September 1855, the *Arctic* and *Release* met them.

Until the autunm of 1855, when Maggie learnt that Elisha was returning safely to New York, she had spent a year in a hell of miserable uncertainty. She had received no solace from the spirit world, not a grain of comfort came from beyond. Neither Leah nor Kate brought their sister hope. The spirits could be very cruel.

Life was to get even crueler for Maggie. 'The return of Dr. Kane to New York was the occasion of a wonderful excitement,' wrote the *New York Daily Times*. Papers again linked their names, suggesting there might soon be a marriage. These rumours were immediately quashed by the Kane family. All lethargy left Maggie as she raced around, heart thumping, to make sure she looked her best for her man. She decided to meet him at Ellen's, where their reunion could be uninterrupted and told Cornelius Grinnell, who would be seeing Elisha, to give him the message.

He docked on the morning of 11 October and was justifiably given a hero's welcome. As the *Daily Times* says '... the familiar face of the Doctor, bronzed by exposure and adorned with a heavy beard, was looked upon like that of an old friend.' Alas, Maggie, his mistress, could not look upon it. Guns had roared in welcome and the crowds had cheered. Maggie sat in silence and waited with Ellen. He did not call. He had people to see and reports to deliver but there was no word for the woman who loved him with every fibre of her troubled soul. She who had waited, with no other thought than him, for over two years. After a desolate day, she went to her mother's house where Dr Bayard arrived late at night with a message from Cornelius. Elisha would call at Ellen's next morning. She rushed back.

Elisha spent that night with his family. Secure in the trappings of success and feted by all, his perspective shifted. Maggie did not seem as essential as she had been when he had been trapped in the immovable ice for months on end with just her portrait for love interest during the endless hours. His slight to her was deliberate and the hurt terrible. He had decided on the voyage home that he would bring their relationship to a close. What Ellen had not told Maggie was that Cornelius had requested, on behalf of Elisha, the return of his letters. In *Time is Kind* it is stressed that this was at the instigation of Mrs Kane.

He arrived at Ellen's at nine the next morning, resplendent in his naval uniform. Hurt at his refusal to see her she, at first, refused to see him. Whatever both their resolutions they dissolved immediately their eyes met. Passion flared and they fell into each other's arms. The intended words of rejection faltered in his mouth. He told her he loved her. She would forgive him anything and that was put to the test. When he recovered his equilibrium he remembered his intention to finish their relationship. With family help he'd drafted a document for her to sign, stating their relationship had only ever been one of friendship and the question of marriage had never entered into it.

Displaying great dignity, lacking in Elisha, and masking her dreadful pain she coldly complied. He returned a day or so later and handed her the document to destroy. She tore it up.

Maggie moved back with Margaret, and Elisha regularly called. The papers reignited their engagement stories. They were among the most famous couples in New York. Elisha was, in fact, the perfect man for Maggie Fox. She needed to be emotionally bruised. Her brooding temperament was ideally suited for a masochistic relationship. A dependable man would have lasted no time at all. Things in her past haunted her and had to be atoned for. Happiness was not her due. Elisha saw to that.

Gossip of their forthcoming marriage was rife. Horace Greeley, who was paying for the house in which Maggie lived, thundered in the *Tribune*: 'What right has the public to know anything about an "agreement" or non-engagement between these young people?' At the onset of her career, Maggie had been flattered by the limelight but now she began to detest it.

Elisha sent her an engraving of himself for Christmas, which she hung in her room. As the New Year, 1856, approached they began to be seen in public again. He presented her with another ring, a curiosity he had found somewhere in the Arctic. That year *Arctic Explorations* was published which became a best seller and Elisha made plans to visit Lady Franklin in London to personally give her news of his expedition. New York was sweltering that summer so Margaret and Kate made arrangements to visit relatives in Canada. In order to escape the constant public scrutiny, Maggie agreed to go with them.

Leah had now somewhat distanced herself from the three of them and Kate resented Maggie for refusing to give readings, feeling this left her with an unfair burden. Maggie cried with loneliness in Canada. It had been a mistake to leave Elisha. He was far from well himself as his health had taken another tumble and the rheumatic fever had flared up again. Maggie tells us in *The Love-Life of Dr Kane* that she had nightmares that he would die and never return from England.

In the same memoir she alleges they married upon her return to New York, immediately prior to his London departure. This took place in their new home – they had moved to 22nd Street – where Elisha called in a state of excitement. He told her as far as he was concerned she was already his wife, then repeated this in front of Margaret, Kate, Mary the maid and a friend who happened to be visiting. He is quoted in *Time is Kind* as stating: 'Such a declaration, in the presence of witnesses, is sufficient to constitute a legal and binding marriage.' In *The Love-Life of Dr Kane* he adds, 'Maggie is my wife and I am her husband. Wherever we are, she is mine and I am hers.' That narrative, ghost-written under Maggie's direction, continues, 'What had passed made them as indissolubly one as if performed in a church.'

She cites instances of similar bonds, all deemed by her to be legally binding and that he promised to undertake a public marriage ceremony upon his return from London. It became the foundation of her existence.

Elisha's visit to Lady Franklin was not a success. His illness flared up to such an extent that he was forced to convalesce in the country, away from London's congested air. Cornelius Grinnell, who was already in London, went with him. It was serious and doctors were summoned. For a man who had gained his reputation by exploring the Arctic their treatment was ironic. He must leave for the tropics immediately. Warm air was what was needed. Not wishing to alarm Maggie he wrote, his last letter to her as it happened, merely saying he had arrived safely in London.

She knew more than that. It had been reported in the papers that he was en route to Havana for health reasons. She did not suspect the awful truth that he was dying. Before reaching Cuba, he had a stroke which paralysed his right side. Again, Maggie learnt of the seriousness of his condition from the papers. In terror of losing him she booked a passage to Havana.

Before she could leave the papers gave her even grimmer news. He had died on 16 November 1857. *The Daily Times* reported: 'His mind remained clear, and his disease, while making rapid headway, left him moments for calm reflection, and gave him a peaceful end.'[15] His obituary concluded: 'His best and most enduring record is found in the remarkable acts of a crowded life.' No one could disagree with that.

Maggie's mental health, always precarious, slipped out of control. The black abyss enveloped her. Madness was never far away, sometimes present. Elisha had hated the spirits and she began to hate them too – with calamitous results.

She was consumed with hatred, guilt and disappointment. Only one thing brought relief; it had been tried and tested over the ages by numerous others. Her father was an alcoholic. It was in her genes. Slowly, but ever so surely, she trod the path to hell.

5

Leah was the centre of an eager band of disciples who applauded everything she did. So, while Kate solidly beavered, producing ever more impressive phenomena, some of which actually frightened her, and Maggie locked herself away in misery, Leah sat on the throne.

Leah was now mistress of a whole repertoire of phenomena, the apex of which occurred one evening as she held a séance, where Margaret was present, during a thunderstorm. Among the sitters were two doctors, Wilson and Kirby. Both men saw their respective dead mothers in the midst of lightning flashes and heard a man calling to them. This shook Margaret who burst into the hymn *I Am a Pilgrim*, which steadied things.

The Foxes were to learn that atmospheric conditions deleteriously affected the spirits. The information came through Kate, years later, when she was automatically writing for some friends, George and Sarah Taylor: 'As the weather, the atmosphere, is so much against us, we would only harm ourselves by trying to come in form' and 'Our delicate particles feel the changing atmosphere.'[1]

Such marvels, irrespective of weather conditions, were regular occurrences at Leah's. So, when the phosphorus affair raised its head, or rather its hands – for she was suspected of producing spirit lights by rubbing phosphorus on her hands – and suggestions of fraud were murmured, it was indeed as though another meteorological upheaval had taken place, namely a thunderbolt. She was devastated.

Phosphorus glows in the dark and if smeared on fingertips that are moved in the dark, it will give the effect of spirit lights. It will also give a nasty burn and is a dangerous thing to do. Phosphorus was a regular standby of fraudulent mediums, of which an army had sprung up when they realised money was to be made from the gullible. It was painted on objects that were hidden from the sitters, and when lights were extinguished these were retrieved and waved about, glowing in the dark. A favourite item was a cardboard star which, if a confederate in dark clothing was involved, as was frequently the case, could be silently moved about the room producing a wondrous effect. Luminous garments were invaluable as foundations for materialisations.

The potential Leah scandal came after lights had appeared in one of her circles and she suddenly had to leave the séance room due to intense pain in her hands. She hurriedly rinsed these and then went into the garden for some air. It had been raining and she soothed her searing hands in the damp soil. Next day, the earth was glowing with phosphorus crystals. It was decided, in some embarrassment, Leah must provide an explanation. She, being merely the medium, could not answer for the ways of Spirit.

One of her sitters, Daniel Underhill, defended her honour. He was the wealthy President of the New York Fire Insurance Company, a staunch admirer of Leah's, in every sense. The Underhills were prominent Spiritualists and Daniel's mother was famed for moving tables while his sister spoke in tongues. He was convinced there was a spiritual explanation for the presence of the crystals in the soil that had nothing to do with the chicanery that was being whispered about. Strangely, Spirit made no comment on the matter through the other mediums.

Another séance was held, with Kate as well as Leah, and advice sought. The spirits instructed that an impartial sitter, a Mr Henry Sheldon, bring a box of earth with him to the next sitting. He dug this from Brooklyn Heights, sealed it in a box and brought it, intact, to the circle to be opened. Leah dipped her fingers in the unpolluted earth and her hands slowly became luminous. The earth was then examined and found to contain phosphorus crystals that had not been there before. Two conclusions were put forward by Mr Underhill; either Spirit had manufactured the crystals to illustrate its superior knowledge of the laws of nature, or the crystals had been extracted from the brains of the sitters. The latter was not the most comforting of thoughts for a nervous sitter. It was rapped that the ubiquitous Benjamin Franklin had conducted the transformation. In any event, Leah was exonerated but it had shaken her. She was grateful for Mr Underhill's support.

Other mediums were causing astonishment by talking, when under control, in languages they had never learnt. One such was Judge Edmonds' daughter, Laura Edmonds, who spoke in, among others, Latin, Portuguese, Polish, Hungarian and various Indian dialects, her only formal language training having being in English and French. The young Jenny Keyes sang in Italian and Spanish, languages with which she had been previously unacquainted, while others jabbered in such exotic tongues as Chinese, Hebrew, Greek and Malay. Kate, herself was to become adept at automatically writing in French and Italian.

Transfiguration mediums were appearing. These allowed their features to be overshadowed by their controls. Many sitters claimed to recognise loved ones from this technique without the controls having uttered a word. A low light was needed in order for the transfigured face to be seen. Through the glow of an oil lamp, often filtered in red, the medium's face gradually metamorphosed into that of the overshadowing spirit. Some mediums could transfigure several times a night as one spirit took the place of another.[2]

In the case of Direct Voice, the utterance did not emanate from the medium but directly from The Ether, sometimes sounding on the opposite side of the room to where the medium sat, or behind the sitter. Many sitters recognised a voice before a name was given. Direct Voice medium Leslie Flint, whose control was a cockney boy called Mickey, would sometimes speak while Mickey was speaking so the sitter heard both voices simultaneously, one direct, one from the medium. There was no question of Leslie being in a trance and he would often take a lively part in the debate.

In the 1950s and 60s, right up to his death in 1994, the biggest name in Direct Voice was Leslie Flint. People travelled from all over the world to consult him. He lived in a magnificent Addams palace, which had connections with Brunel, off Westbourne Terrace in London's Paddington. It cried out for a celebrity to live there and for a while had been the London home of Hollywood star George Arliss. The style of people who crossed its threshold didn't alter much when Leslie took over, and it was visited by many theatrical and film stars, both clients and guests, both alive and dead. Among the dead were Welsh composer Ivor Novello, but the guest of honour was silent movie star Rudolph Valentino whose premature promotion to Spirit in 1926, at the age of 31, had prompted several suicides. Newspapers published mocked-up pictures of Rudi being greeted in heaven by legendary tenor Caruso. Silent screen siren Pola Negri,

Leslie Flint
with ectoplasm.
(*Courtesy of
the Leslie Flint
Education Trust.*)

preceded by an eleven-foot wreath, had been restrained from throwing
herself on his grave, prostrate with grief.

Leslie was born illegitimately, far from glamour, in 1911 in a Salvation
Army hostel in London's Hackney and as a boy worked in a cinema. He
first saw Valentino on screen and fell in love with him. While still a boy
he saw spirit forms. He went to a Spiritualist church where a medium
told him he had a 'guide' who was 'not really an Arab, he was someone
dressed up as an Arab'.[3] It was, of course, Valentino, dressed in character
as *The Sheik*, the eponymous hero of one of his most successful films.
Leslie later received a letter from a medium in Munich who claimed
that Valentino had come through to him and was trying to contact Leslie.
Valentino had given the medium Leslie's London address. Meanwhile,
Leslie joined a circle in London where another message from Valentino
came through. Contact was established and sustained.

Before Leslie had mastered Direct Voice there were some embar-
rassing incidents when the voices unexpectedly burst through, which
happened once when Leslie was in the cinema. However, with persever-
ance, the technique was mastered on both sides. He took off in a big
way and filled out into a portly, bespectacled epitome of respectability.
Although Valentino had started the ball rolling, Leslie's chief guide was

Mickey – the cheeky London boy who had been run over and killed in Camden Town in 1910. Anyone who has sat in one of Leslie's circles has heard Mickey's humorous down-to-earth cockney.

Like the Foxes, Leslie willingly underwent scientific tests: 'I think I can safely say I am the most tested medium this country has ever produced. I have been boxed up, tied up, gagged, bound and held. Still the voices have come.' He had had his mouth filled with coloured dye and still the voices came. According to him, they issued from a place 'a little above my head and slightly to one side of me' where Spirit had constructed an ectoplasmic larynx.

Sitters were welcome to record messages, and many did. He recorded many himself, usually those from the famous dead, such as Madame Blavatsky. Madame must have overcome her pronunciation problem in Spirit as according to her contemporaries she had spoken English with a thick Russian accent; the recordings played to the author resembled no one so much as the late Dame Edith Evans in her celebrated portrayal of Lady Bracknell – an impression Leslie himself sometimes delivered at parties. But then, it is well known that spirits can only use, though use to the full, the resources already possessed by the medium.

The voices only came in dark circles. Not so much dark as pitch black. At a public demonstration he gave in Reading, towards the end of his career, a wooden hut, like a sauna, was placed on stage. He sat in this, invisible to the jammed audience, next to a bucket of ice – it was a hot day and he suffered in the heat – and a microphone. Not much to see but lots to hear. All manner of amplified voices bombarded the audience and were received enthusiastically.

Among the distinguished sitters in Leslie's home circles were Air Chief Marshal Lord Dowding and astute film critic Alexander Walker, the latter on record vouching that he could find no evidence of trickery. But, as with the Foxes and all psychic work, there was a degree of hit and miss. When the author was a young man, he took part in a group sitting with Leslie and half a dozen Spiritualists. Young sitters can be difficult if they know few people who have died. This was the case with me. Other sitters had chatted with their beloveds, and it was either a case of me being ignored – and we'd paid a guinea a head, a not inconsiderable sum then – or given something.

'Hello, son,' an unknown voice husked out of the blackness. Mickey explained new communicants often croaked out their messages, being unaccustomed to ectoplasmic techniques. Voices were not always recognisable. I felt my face burning and although it was pitch dark could feel every eye on me.

I bleated out, 'Grandfather?', he being the only person I knew who was dead, although it didn't sound a bit like him and why should he come to me? He'd had zero interest in Spiritualism – or me for that matter – and it was entirely mutual. I'd barely noticed he'd gone. However, something had to be said, so a few pleasantries, the like of which we would have never engaged in on earth, were exchanged while the rest of the sitters made encouraging noises. The Ether was pierced for this?

Not all the other sitters were thrilled. Gladys Lorrimore, a rather grand actress, in manner rather than achievement, was contacted by a roughly spoken man who claimed to be her husband. She heatedly denied it. As has been proven, the spirits can be as capable of duplicity as the rest of us. The rest of the sitters were less than pleased with Gladys Lorrimore. It was as though she'd broken some unspoken agreement.

Leslie, who had a private cinema, ran the Rudolph Valentino Appreciation Society and, on Valentino anniversaries, showed his movies such as *The Four Horsemen of the Apocalypse* or *The Sheik*. These evenings were straight out of Sunset Boulevard with old people who had been connected with his films sitting around reminiscing, actors, actresses or writers not heard of for years, as the old black and white movies flickered through the night. After the showing we would adjourn to the sitting room where, under Valentino's invisible portrait as the lights would be turned off, the long dead megastar would salute his colleagues and admirers and welcome newcomers like me.

A generous man, Leslie often helped other mediums and when the biography of Bertha Harris was published, threw open his lavish doors for a celebratory party. Bertha, by this time, was well in her 80s and long past her glory days when she had been Sir Arthur Conan Doyle's personal medium; Sir Arthur lecturing on Spiritualism and she bringing back the dead to prove it – or the times when she had been whisked to France for a private consultation with de Gaulle.

Christmas and birthdays were marked when yesterday's West End stars such as Olive Gilbert and June Bronhill sang Ivor Novello hits, accompanied by Leslie's Steinway. They were wonderful evenings. Spirits respond to music so it was no wonder so many congregated there. Leslie Flint was unique, a dinosaur in today's ever-decreasing world of physical phenomena.

Valentino was no stranger to Spiritualism while on earth. His wife, Natacha Rambova, likened by journalist Ruth Waterbury to 'a yellow orchid shining forth from a vase of black onyx' but credited, less gushingly, by others with ruining her husband's career, was famous for holding séances at her Hollywood apartment. George Sand, Byron and Walt Whitman were frequent visitors.

Valentino admitted, in a 1921 interview, that he was a Spiritualist and had had messages from both his dead parents.[4] The following year, when *The Young Rajah* was released, in which he played a clairvoyant Hindu, costume designer Cora McGeachy demonstrated automatic writing to him and Natacha: 'The more we investigated this remarkable gift,' wrote Natacha[5], 'the more convinced we became of the great truth which lay behind it the truth of communication with the so-called dead.'

Natacha claimed Valentino was a natural psychic and worked through his guide Black Feather. He posed as Black Feather, in loin cloth and feathers, for several photographs, believing his guide transfigured him. He published a volume of spirit-inspired poems, *Day Dreams*, which became a best seller, its title page adorned by a solitary black feather. While entranced, Natacha conceived the idea for *Cobra*, a movie they would independently produce and in which they would both appear. Actress Colleen Moore claimed Natacha wrote the script by automatic writing. If so, whoever was guiding the pencil had an insecure grasp of the movies as it was one of Valentino's rare flops, the *New York Times* dismissing it as 'quite absurd'.

With medium Blanche Wheaton, Natacha held sittings to help earthbound souls and the possessed. She also worked with medium George Wehner who claimed, during storms, to see elementals dancing. Natacha's Uncle Dickie was a member of the *Legion de Service Spirituelle* in France. When Wehner visited there with Natacha, the portrait of Madame Blavatsky which dominated the room unnerved Wehner, who claimed her eyes 'follow one about with a mysterious persistency as if trying to pierce one's very soul'.[6]

During the 1920s Natacha and Wehner held a séance in the Mormon Tabernacle, Salt Lake City, where messages were received from Mormon founder Joseph Smith. Wehner '... saw the whole interior of the Tabernacle shimmering in a glorious blaze of golden light, in the midst of which appeared in the air above the organ, the figure of a young man in blue robes holding a long trumpet of gold. From my clairvoyant description of the radiant being, my friends recognised the spirit of the Angel Moroni.'[7]

After Valentino's death, Natacha met writer Talbot Mundy, aka Makundu Viazi, literally translated as 'White Arse'. Mundy's most famous book is *King of the Khyber Rifles* but he was then writing his reincarnation novel *Om*[8] while staying with ex-medium turned Theosophist, Katherine Tingley, known to her *intimes* as Mother Purple due to fondness for clothes of that colour. Natacha was to become a part of Mrs Tingley's inspired, but ultimately doomed, Point Loma commune.

The prolific Mundy, a significant name in occult circles, also wrote *Nine Unknown Men* based on a 2,000-year-old sect, founded by the Emperor Asoka, whose purpose was to secure occult knowledge from falling into the wrong hands. A principle Madame Blavatsky slightly bent in *The Secret Doctrine* that revealed a distillation, nevertheless potent, of a fragment of this knowledge. Natacha moved to New York, to the newly built Master Building, the model for the building in *Ghostbusters* and with Mundy and Wehner, set up an establishment to foster Spiritualism. (It was through Mundy's efforts that George Wehner's autobiography *A Curious Life* was published in 1930 by Horace Liveright.) Mary Baker Eddy, founder of Christian Science, was a regular communicant. A short-hand typist was employed to record the conditions of the medium when entranced to discover exactly what happened.

Sadly, this was hampered when Wehner, who had a history of nervous disorders, became unbalanced again. This was brought on when he gave messages to Mundy from Mundy's lost brother who described his tragic death in Egypt, only for Mundy to receive a letter from his brother a few days later, who was still very much alive. Yet another example of the hit and miss of Spiritualism.

After his release from the sanatorium, he received spirit music from dead composers, as was to be the case with Rosemary Brown. A concert was planned but abandoned when he became ill again. He attempted suicide by trying to throw himself off a balcony and scriptwriter Dawn Allen, who was to become one of Mundy's several (one at a time) wives had to hold him back. He bowed out of Spiritualism after this. Natacha continued her research but diverted her enormous energy to Egyptology, and became an acknowledged expert in the field.

The Art Deco movie world of Valentino and Rambova was a far cry from the extraordinary ectoplasmic materialisations of the Victorian circles – a channel in which Kate was shortly to excel.

Ectoplasm is the building block of materialisation, a luminous thick vapour exuded from the medium which is moulded by Spirit into the shape required. Medium Elizabeth d'Esperance excelled at materialisation and, in her 1897 autobiography *Shadow Land*, a sitter describes the building up of one of her guides: 'First a filmy, cloudy patch of something white is observed on the floor. It then gradually expands, visibly extending itself as if it were an animated patch of muslin. Presently it begins to rise slowly; by the time it has attained two or more feet it looks as if a child were under it. Its form can be seen as if arranging the folds of a drapery about its figure. Presently the arms rise considerably above the head and open outwards through a mass of cloud like spirit drapery, and Yolande stands before us unveiled, graceful and beautiful having a turban-like head-dress, from beneath which her long black hair hangs over her shoulders and down her back.' Yolande was just one of the many beautiful young spirit ladies popularising materialisation circles.

William Eglinton was another successful materialisation medium, although male materialisation mediums were the minority in this female-dominated field. One of his sitters tells of a séance when the entranced Eglinton paced the room then:

> began gently to draw from his side and pay out at right angles a dingy, white-looking substance, which fell down at his left side. The mass of white material on the floor increased in breadth, commenced to pulsate and move up and down, also swaying from side to side ... the 'form' quickly and quietly grew to its full stature. By a quick movement of his hand Mr Eglinton drew away the white material which covered the head of the 'form', and it fell back over the shoulders and became part of the clothing of the visitor; the 'form' advanced to Mr Everitt [another sitter], shook hands with him, and passed round the circle. (*Annals of Physical Science*, Vol 11)

Mr Eglinton paced the room but, usually, a 'cabinet' is required for materialisation, in which the medium sits and where ectoplasm can be amassed. Cabinets vary from a curtained-off corner, to a full-scale enclosure, rather like a confessional. This enclosure may have an aperture through which a head or partial materialisation can show itself.

Sometimes full facial materialisation is not possible and bits are missing. Colonel Olcott wrote of such an occasion:

> A more dreadful sight I have never beheld ... The lower portions, including the wavy silky beard, were perfectly formed, as also was the brow; but the eyes were not materialised, and the cavities they should have filled

were edged with ragged rims, as though the face had been made of wax and the eyes melted out by the application of a red-hot iron.(*Old Diary Leaves* by Henry S. Olcott pub. Theosophical Publishing House, 1910)

Ghastly indeed.

An infamous case of the imprisonment of a materialism medium took place not in the nineteenth century but the twentieth, in 1944! The medium was Helen Duncan or Hellish Nell as she was known. Tipping the scales at twenty stones, she was a working-class Scot and mother of six with a ready mouth and fist to match. This wretched lady had the distinction of being the last person to be imprisoned under the 1735 Witchcraft Act. She was arrested and tried at the Old Bailey and sentenced to nine months in Holloway. It was over a century since anyone had been tried under such an act. Prime Minister Winston Churchill was outraged by this 'absolute tomfoolery' and wrote in protest to Home Secretary Herbert Morrison.

Nell's crime, which took place during a séance in the Second World War, was to tell a mother that her son had been killed in a sunken British warship, HMS *Barham*. This was information that the War Ministry deemed a threat to national security and had not revealed: how could Nell have been in possession of it? Whatever the source, the court was told she was 'attempting to bring about the appearances of the spirits of deceased persons', with the added misdemeanour of taking money under false pretences as she'd charged an entrance fee. *Daily Mail* columnist Michael Hanlon, writing of Nell in 2005, says: 'There is ... no doubt that her sessions and séances probably gave a great deal of psychological comfort to her many clients. In some ways, spiritualists behaved as counsellors for the bereaved. And it is hard to see how that can justify nine unpleasant months in jail and a reputation in tatters.'

Nell sat in a cabinet while her materialisations made their appearances, clothed in pungent ectoplasm. Nell and her husband, who was also her manager, allowed flash photographs to be taken but the results, crude artefacts, were no proof of life after death, rather the proof of fraud. Which they actually were; Nell did stoop to fraud. But this did not mean all she did was fraudulent.

A portion of Nell's ectoplasm still exists, housed at the University Library, Cambridge. It was snatched from her during 1939 at a séance in Wales. In his biography of Nell[9] Malcolm Gaskill tells how this came about:

Several sitters noticed that the medium was out of her chair when she was supposed to be in trance and a Mr A J Miles was unconvinced by a manifestation of his brother, which lacked an identifying deformity. Deciding enough was enough, Miles and another sitter grappled with the burly Helen who punched Miles in the eye to retain ownership of the cloth, but in vain.

The cloth was the ectoplasm. Having stolen this which, in daylight, did not disintegrate and looked like blood-smeared fabric, Miles added:

> the cloth was damp but I'm not sure whether the stains were fresh. I did not examine it owing to the terrible odour that was issuing from it and from the smell of it quickly suggested where it had been concealed. I suggest that it was concealed within the lower portion of her body.

Nell had been searched before the circle, as was usually the case, but not internally.

Gaskill viewed the cloth at Cambridge: '[It] is a large piece of white satin, or perhaps cotton-silk, measuring eighty by a hundred centimetres, faintly stained at regular intervals. These marks, a typed note by Mrs Goldney [of the Society for Psychical Research, who examined the item] suggests, were caused by the cloth being folded and secreted in the vagina where blood seeped in.'

The substance was also examined by writer Marina Warner[10] who found 'a folded heap of dressmakers' lining material, a cheap man-made fibre now yellowing in colour'. She provides a quote from Gaskill who not only viewed the ectoplasm but handled it: 'I let it catch the air, and watched it billow and shimmer, only to be sternly reminded by one of the University Library staff that they preferred readers not to throw the manuscripts around the room.'

All of which indicates Nell was a cheat. But a cheat in possession of military secrets? Moves were made recently to the Criminal Cases Review to extract a pardon for Nell. So far this has been rejected as not in the public interest, but her supporters' interest has not flagged.

A variation of automatic writing, slate writing, had a vogue. Two slate-boards were needed, of the type used in schools – sometimes sitters brought their own – and a piece of chalk. The medium would put the chalk between the slates, bind them together and place them under the table. Scratching could be heard and when the slates were withdrawn a message would be chalked on the inside of one of the slates.

One of the most successful slate writers was materialisation medium William Eglinton. Aside from English, this extraordinary practitioner could respond to questions put to him in Greek, French and Spanish, the slate answering in the same languages. In the 1880s no less an establishment figure than the future Prime Minister of Britain, the Rt. Hon. W.E. Gladstone, sat with him. Although never declaring himself a Spiritualist, Gladstone was sufficiently impressed by what he saw to join the newly formed Society for Psychical Research, founded 1878. This aroused a certain amount of scepticism to which Gladstone responded, in *Light* Magazine in 1884: '[Scientists] not infrequently attempt to deny that into which they have never inquired, not sufficiently realising the fact that there may possibly be forces in nature of which they know nothing.'

One of Eglinton's clients, a Miss Amy Fisher, testified that she not only received slate-written messages from her deceased brother, signed with his name, which Eglinton did not know, but shadowy forms also roamed the fire-lit room. Eglinton levitated, for which she had certainly not bargained nor, indeed, paid for. Leaving his chair he rose so high that she was obliged to release his hand which she had been holding onto. He flipped into the horizontal and remained suspended for a while, before sinking back into his chair. Music was often heard at his séances but his reputation was somewhat blackened, literally, when instruments daubed with soot, thus rendering them invisible, were discovered in his séance room. Matching blacking was found smeared on his hands, suggesting that he had played them.

Sir Arthur Conan Doyle airily explained this away by stating that when ectoplasm was retracted it took with it whatever substance it had absorbed while out of the body. Soot was on the wicks of the oil lamps and grate of the séance room. He cited the case of another materialisation medium, Mrs Goligher, who had agreed to be experimented upon and allowed carmine dye to be smeared upon ectoplasm that had emanated from her body. After absorption this, too, was discovered smeared upon her person. Conan Doyle was not the only supporter of Mrs Goligher; another was Dr W.J. Crawford, Extra-Mural Lecturer in Mechanical Engineering at Queen's University, Belfast. He was convinced of the reality of ectoplasm and wrote three books trying to prove it. In his opinion, ectoplasm was responsible for levitation. Ectoplasmic rods emanated from the solar plexus and cantilevered mediums off the ground.

Even Sir Arthur could not explain the clockwork toy discovered in Eglinton's séance room; a mechanical frog which, when released, would jump around the room, invisible in the gloom, creating thumps, sounding for all the world like spirit steps. Mrs Sidgwick, wife of Professor Sidgwick, one of the founders of the Society for Psychical Research, investigated Eglinton: 'For myself,' she wrote, 'I have now no hesitation in attributing the performances to clever conjuring.'[11] Mrs Sidgwick had an ally (albeit an unwilling one) in Archdeacon Colley.

The Archdeacon's faith in Spiritualism was tested after an Eglinton materialisation during which a bearded, robed figure emerged from the cabinet. The apparition allowed bits of its beard and robe to be cut off for souvenirs. As with Nell Duncan's ectoplasm, this did not dematerialise when the figure returned to the cabinet.

Next morning, when looking for Eglinton, the Archdeacon entered the medium's empty room and saw his open suitcase lying on his bed containing a false beard and robe identical to those worn by the apparition. The souvenirs fitted the places where material had been cut from the beard and robe.

Eglinton begged his supporters to speak up for him; hundreds did, asserting he had brought them into contact with dead loved ones. He continued to practise.

Also prominent were the Davenports, who were purely a stage phenomenon and never gave sittings. These brothers, Ira, born in 1839 and William, born in 1841, were sons of a Buffalo policeman and gained national recognition during the 1850s and 60s. Charming, moustachioed young men, their potential was quickly spotted and they were taken in hand by what author Ronald Pearsall[12] terms 'a good public relations staff'.

These were Restoration Movement Minister the Reverend Dr Ferguson, Mr D. Palmer, described as an 'operatic manager', and Mr William M. Fay, a conjuror whose wife was a medium. The audience tied the Davenports to chairs, their hands bound, and they were placed in a seven-foot-long closed cabinet, together with musical instruments. These would play, singly and together, sometimes making a cacophony which would not have been out of place in a mad house. The din would fade, the cabinet opened and the brothers be found, secure in their knots, in their chairs.

In June of 1857 the *Boston Courier* offered a prize of $500 to anyone who could produce psychic phenomena under test conditions set by examiners from Harvard University. The challenge became known as

The Cambridge Investigation, Cambridge being where, in Massachusetts, Harvard is situated. The chairman of the examination board was mathematician Benjamin Pierce, and his associates were Professors Agassiz and Horsford and Dr N.B. Gould from Albany Observatory.

Among those who took part were the Davenports, Kate and Leah. For the Davenport session, according to their biographer Dr Thomas Low Nichols,[13] holes were bored in the cabinet and five hundred feet of rope passed through with which the boys were secured. Chairman Pierce sat between them in the cabinet, and held the instruments, which had also been placed there, firmly between his knees.

Reports circulated later that a phantom hand had struck Pierce, untied the Davenports and tied him up in their place. The *Courier*, however, repudiated this as 'shamelessly false'. (Information included on 'Survival After Death' website.) But the instruments did not play. The Davenports were a failure.

Kate and Leah did little better. Raps were heard but so faint as to be dismissed. Other tests were applied which the girls also failed. They could not repeat a word spoken in another room, words written on paper they had not seen, nor could they tilt the lightest piece of furniture. These failures were attributed by the Spiritualists to inharmonious vibrations. The Cambridge Investigation did Spiritualism no favours at all.

Whilst in Massachusetts, Kate and Leah were examined by a group of Unitarian clergymen, in Boston. They were old hands by now, and slipped into the routine of standing on cushions, skirts delicately raised to allow ankles and feet to be held by a party of ladies. According to Leah raps sounded all over the room; what a pity they had not been so energetic for the Harvard professors.

The Unitarians had prepared a feast in their honour and with this success under her belt, Leah fell to with relish. It was a jolly party of clerics who waved goodbye as the Foxes' coach bore them to their hotel where a further party was going on and in which they joined. It would take more than The Cambridge Investigation to dent Leah's confidence.

The same could be said for the Davenports. After ten years of touring America, the brothers went to England where they were acclaimed in the salons of the likes of actor and playwright Dion Boucicault, who invited a flotilla of pressmen along to witness their phenomena and who gave the boys rave reviews. Their stage performances, however, were not so successful. The houses were full but attracted a rough element. Things went too far in Liverpool when audience members, invited to tie up the mediums as part of their act, wrenched the knots so sadistically tight they hampered circulation. Understandably, the Davenports walked off. Equally understandably a riot broke out.

The next night something similar happened and the boys again walked out. The tour had to be abandoned. It has been suggested that a rival performer, a conjuror, had organised the turmoil. They moved on to France where things were, initially, almost as tricky, but settled down after the boys performed for the Emperor Napoleon who was greatly taken by them. Belgium and Russia were also successful and, in Russia, they performed for the Tsar.

Returning to England, the Anthropological Society proposed a test séance but the Davenports, fed up with tests and ill treatment, turned this down. They returned to America where they continued to be a draw until one of the boys died. The Rev. Ferguson, who toured with them, genuinely believed spirits caused the manifestations, but the Davenports, themselves, never claimed this, any more than Maggie Fox did. The public had to make up its own mind.

The conjurer Maskelyne considered them 'great jugglers' noting they 'did more than all other men to familiarise England with the so-called Spiritualism, and before crowded audiences and under varied conditions, they produced really wonderful feats'. Houdini, too, was an admirer but writes in *A Magician Among the Spirits* (Harper & Bros, 1924) that Ira Davenport, who became his friend, freely admitted privately that spirits had nothing to do with their act. It was after seeing the Davenports that Houdini revived his flagging interest in Spiritualism.

The same could not be said for Michael Faraday. In 1864 the Davenports invited the physicist to examine their act. He replied: 'I have been so disappointed by the manifestations to which my notice has at different times been called, that I am not encouraged to give any more attention to them, and therefore I leave these to which you refer in the hands of the professors of legerdemain. If spirit communication not utterly worthless, of any worthy character, should happen to start into activity, I will leave the spirits to find out for themselves how they can move more my attention. I am tired of them.'[14]

A misconception of Houdini is that he hated Spiritualism, which is not true; he hated fraudulent mediums. He visited many mediums in the hope of contacting his adored dead mother, and wrote, 'I would have parted gladly with a large share of my earthly possessions for the solace of one word from my loved departed – just one word that I was sure had been genuinely bestowed by them.' (Cited in *The Secret Life of Houdini* by William Kalush and Larry Sloman, pub. Pocket Books, 2007.) Fraudulent mediums could experience Houdini's fury but he did not hate the subject. It intrigued him and had done so for years.

He struck up a friendship with Conan Doyle who recommended several mediums he considered genuine, among them Miss Ada Besinnet and Mrs Annie Brittain and her child guide Belle. Sir Arthur was an enthusiast of child guides and wrote:

> The author has made the acquaintance of many of these little creatures in different parts of the world. Feda, Belle, Iris, Harmony, and many more, prattle in their high falsetto voices, and the world is the better for their presence and ministrations. (*The History of Spiritualism*)

Belle's falsetto prattling did nothing to convince Houdini. Nor, it would seem, did she convince a magistrate's court where the unhappy Mrs Brittain was sent down on charges which, at this point in time, seem obscure.

Ada Besinnet, of Toledo, was versatile. She could produce Direct Voice, materialisation and apports, the latter rivalling those of Madame d'Esperance's Yolande who once produced twenty-seven roses at a single séance. Miss Besinnet's materialised control was a husky Native American. It was as well to have a muscular guide as there were times, by no means uncommon, when unscrupulous sitters tried to grab a materialisation, as was to happen in the case of Helen Duncan. Madame d'Esperance herself had suffered physical and psychological damage as a result of the voluptuous Yolande being grabbed by an over-enthusiastic admirer.

Regarding Miss Besinnet's materialisations, Sir Arthur observed that if she were in poor health then her figures would look very like her, but the heartier her condition the more dissimilar they became. She must have been in the peak of condition when the muscular Red Indian appeared. The Direct Voice control was a deep bass, who sometimes duetted with a spirit soprano. There were also spirit lights, such as Leah would produce, which Sir Arthur likened to fireflies. He was charmed, at one sitting, when a smattering of these landed on his walrus moustache. But Miss Besinnet, also, cut no ice with Houdini.

The medium with whom Sir Arthur mostly worked was his wife. Lady Doyle was an automatic writer and, in New York, she told Houdini that his beloved mother was about to control her. Lady Doyle drew a crucifix and Mrs Weiss (Houdini's real name was Weiss) wrote in perfect English of her delight at being able to communicate with her son and their great work for Spirit. Mrs Weiss was Jewish, hardly likely to draw a crucifix, and had had a poor command of English, far removed from the elegant phrasing of Lady Doyle. Again, he was unimpressed.

Spiritualism was Sir Arthur's life, his very existence. He never forgave Houdini for what he considered to be his treachery, and Lady Doyle never forgave the slight to her powers. Sir Arthur lost face somewhat when, together with certain members of the Theosophical Society, he was taken in by the Cottingley fairies – two Yorkshire girls photo-graphed drawings of fairies which they had cut from books and, for a while, fooled some of the world, and definitely Sir Arthur, into thinking they were the real thing. He would go into the woods with his camera hoping to photograph some himself as did hundreds of others.

Many books have been published on the great man, including two in 2007, the biography *Conan Doyle: The Man Who Created Sherlock Holmes* by Andrew Lycett and a volume of his letters, *Arthur Conan Doyle: A Life in Letters*, edited by Daniel Stashower, Jon Lellenberg and Charles Foley. The whole Spiritualist world is indebted to Sir Arthur for his support and, perhaps at times too uncritical, promotion of Spiritualism. His *The History of Spiritualism*, together with Emma Hardinge Britten's *Modern American Spiritualism*, provides an invaluable record of the early days of the movement.

6

Leah, the Widow Brown, was living in comfortable circumstances in Ludlow Place, being sedately courted by Daniel Underhill. They complimented each other: Daniel rich and conservative and she racy and glamorous. Lizzie was now married and running her own home far removed from Spiritualism, which was exactly how she wanted it.

Kate, a hard-working professional, lived sometimes with Leah and sometimes with Margaret on East 22nd Street. John had moved in with his wife and Maggie, who was still in a state of despair. She looked alarming with her wild eyes and hair shorn, on the doctor's orders to preserve her flagging strength.

Elisha's funeral had been magnificent, with all the ceremony due his status. This made her feel worse. To be unacknowledged as his widow, or even a part of his life, was harrowing. She had given up séances. It had been Elisha's wish and she could not bring herself to go against it. He had not believed in spirits, convinced she was making everything up. She was convinced God had paid her back for her wickedness by taking away Elisha, the only man she had loved. There was no substitute for him nor did she want one. She wanted to be alone with her misery and the Bible.

Biblical lore occupied much of her thoughts and she felt close to Elisha when she read the Bible. She turned to the Catholic Church. Her father was Methodist and Elisha Presbyterian, but the rites of Catholicism drew her. The Confessional was a great boon. She had no income; Leah and Kate were doing well and with David's help, supported her. But the

coolness between Leah and Maggie had intensified. Elisha and Leah had
not liked each other, he had warned her to stay away from her elder
sister who in turn had tried to split them up.

Maggie wrote to Elisha's brother, asking gingerly if Elisha had left any
memento for her. He had known he faced death on his expedition; had
he made no provision for her? Maggie was not mentioned in his will
but, touched by her circumstances, his brother saw that she was given a
small allowance.

In 1858 two ceremonies took place in the Fox family. In August, at
St Peter's, New York, Maggie, dressed in white, in the presence of Kate,
Margaret, John, and a flower-decked altar, was formally baptised into
the Catholic Church, and in November Leah married Daniel Underhill.
Maggie wanted no congratulations after her ceremony. She immediately
decamped to her solitary room, to commune with Elisha, which was
a celebration in its way. Her baptism was not so much a pledge to the
Church as a pledge to him. A rosary was never far from her nervous,
clutching fingers.

Margaret and Kate repaired to Leah's. The fact that Leah had not
attended the ceremony was significant of the deteriorating relationship
between the sisters. Leah had no objection to Catholicism; she always
linked her Spiritualism to Christianity. John returned to the East 22nd
Street house with Maggie but he saw nothing more of her that day. He
sat downstairs alone and she pined upstairs alone.

Of Leah's three husbands Daniel, eight years younger than her but
already a widower with a daughter, was the most suitable by far in that
he was rich and indulged virtually her every whim. Although enjoying
the attentions of men, and responding to them within the parameters
of respectability – discounting her dalliance with Mr Fish, whom she
may or may not have loved – Leah was never troubled by the pangs
of romantic passion. They were married on 2 November, at Horace
Greeley's house on 19th Street, with the resultant splendour that a
wealthy newspaper editor could provide. Once the ring was on her
finger, Leah announced she would be giving no more public sittings
or demonstrations. That would be unseemly for a lady in her elevated
station in life. Many times John must have wondered what his loins had
unleashed on the world.

Maggie, looking far from jubilant at her conversion, did manage to
attend the ceremony. She made the considerable effort if not actually to
join in the celebrations, at least to be present. Leah welcomed her with

open arms, pleased to heal the rift. Or so she hoped. For all her resentment, in her way, Maggie truly wished the newly-weds well. Leah was, after all, her sister. The Underhills moved to 150 West 37th Street, one of Manhattan's smartest addresses, where Leah presided as a society hostess. She missed the razzmatazz that had been Spiritualism but it had to be. Quasi-respectable old age beckoned.

As Lady of the Manor or, rather, Lady of the Manhattan Town House, Leah began extending invitations to those members of society who would accept hospitality from a former professional medium, albeit one who now had a rich husband, which made a difference. Murmurs of the phosphorus affair bubbled up now and then, but these were brushed aside by *intimes* as not worthy of the air on which they wafted.

Without Leah, the girls began to slip from public view. They were icons, and remain so to this day, but the public began to lose interest. Other more spectacular mediums eclipsed them, who were building even more fantastic edifices on Fox foundations. John, Margaret and Kate, at Greeley's suggestion, moved into his sumptuous house on 19th Street where Kate resumed her sittings, with Margaret as chaperone, booker and cashier. He was seldom there but liked to have Kate at his beck and call, should he feel the need. Mrs Greeley was now unwell and seldom seen, which suited the Foxes fine.

Maggie's emotional state darkened. She could not bear company at all, not even Kate. She found Margaret particularly hard to take, with her unsatisfactory marriage to John. She felt Margaret could never understand the depth of her despair and she was probably right. In her desire to be alone she took a small apartment nearby, which she turned into a dark and pokey shrine to Elisha. She lost herself in the labyrinthine tendrils of the Catholic Church. The more she absorbed, the closer she felt to Elisha, who was now surely in heaven, and the more wicked her past became. She forsook the raps for the rosary and spent hours telling the beads. She wanted nothing outside her monochrome world of mourning, except the forgiveness of Christ, which meant the forgiveness of Elisha.

Meanwhile, Leah, with the liberal aid of Daniel's bank account, gaily turned the Underhill home into a palace of ornate and cluttered splendour. She installed the latest chandeliers, furniture and fittings including an aviary of tropical birds. There was an elegant new piano and her lovely voice could be heard ringing out, vying with the birdsong. Sometimes passers by would stop in delight to listen.

In 1861 in Britain, after the death of her beloved husband Prince Albert from typhoid fever, Queen Victoria's depression vied with Maggie's. She wore the black of mourning for the rest of her life and, like Maggie, lived in virtual seclusion, robbed by death of her soulmate.

It is said that spirits had fascinated her long before Rosna started rapping. That she had sat with clairvoyants was attested by a watch which used to be exhibited at London's College of Psychic Studies bearing the inscription: 'Presented by Her Majesty to Miss Georgina Eagle for her Meritorious and Extraordinary Clairvoyance produced at Osborne House, Isle of Wight, July 15 1846.'[1]

Unfortunately, Miss Eagle never received the watch as she, herself, entered Spirit before it could be delivered, and it was passed to Spiritualist publisher William Stead who, in turn, gave it to American medium, Etta Wriedt. Mrs Wriedt, whose reign started in the early twentieth century, was a Direct Voice medium of formidable power. Like Leslie Flint, she was never entranced when the voices came, and sometimes as many as four different voices spoke at once, and she would sustain a lively conversation with them all. If she did not agree with what they said, this could develop into an argument. Unlike Flint, her voices were amplified by the aid of a bulsa wood trumpet and in one such dispute the trumpet flung itself to the ground, having been in levitation while in use, and sulkily refused to move or utter for the rest of the séance.

Conan Doyle has verified that during a séance in his home with Mrs Wriedt, while they sang the mandatory opening hymns, a spectral soprano, unexpected and uninvited (although none the less welcome) sang in unison with them. This, in his own home where no conspirator could be stowed away.

As Mrs Wriedt's time to take the Final Adventure neared, she felt Queen Victoria's watch should be returned to its homeland and entrusted it to Mackenzie King, Spiritualist Prime Minister of Canada. On his next visit to England, he gave it to the Duchess of Hamilton who, in turn, presented it to the London Spiritualist Alliance which became the College of Psychic Studies. It was exhibited there for years until it mysteriously disappeared, believed stolen.

Her Majesty clutched at any straw to prove Albert was waiting for her behind the veil and, as she was Queen of England there was no shortage of mediums waiting to assure her he was. According to *One Hundred Years of Spiritualism* one of these was Robert James Lees who, judging by his extravagantly signed photograph, possessed the most maniacal eyes.

The terrifying Lees told Her Majesty that her gillie, John Brown, was a medium through whom she could contact Prince Albert. It was Brown's mediumship that linked him to his Queen. Spiritualism cut through the ranks. You were as likely to find a séance in a working-class home as that of a Duchess or, for that matter, the Queen of England. Elegant drawing rooms might form the background for a society medium such as Leah, but much the same procedure could be found in more humble surroundings.

Leah could not cut herself off entirely from her impoverished past; she didn't want to, it held too much that was precious. A shabby kitchen table provided the link. This stood among the grand furniture of her dining room; it was the table around which the Foxes had held their first circles. She'd had it transported from Hydesville and it held pride of position as a shrine. It was an emblem of all Leah had achieved. She told visitors it had a psychic power of its own. Many believed her.

Leah's New Year's Day parties were becoming legend. She, decked in the latest fashions from Paris, a little too daring for Margaret's taste, welcomed her guests beneath rose-tinted chandeliers. Judge Edmonds and his medium daughter Laura often attended as did Governor Tallmadge, Horace Greeley and a senator or two. The spirits had certainly rewarded Leah for her loyalty.

Maggie did not attend as there was nothing to celebrate in her life, just another year of drudgery, but Kate came. Sometimes Kate seemed to resent Leah's good fortune and would annoy her sister by wearing a shabby dress at these grand functions. As Leah's décolleté grew ever more striking so Kate's became more demure; she adopted the look of a field mouse, a look that in an older woman might be described as spinsterish. Leah would have bought her any dress she wanted, and matching accessories, but that was not Kate's point.

By 1861, when civil war broke out, there was no way Leah could sustain her withdrawal from the limelight. She announced she would preside over a series of Thursday evening 'Conversaziones' which meant séances. Handsomely embossed cards were prepared and distributed to suitable sitters.

Among these was Emma Hardinge Britten. At one séance, she opened the proceedings by performing at the piano a medley of stirring war songs, including *John Brown's Body*. Sounds of battle were heard in the séance room, including musket fire and screams. The sitters had been transported to a war field. The circle that night was to help lost souls who had been precipitated to the Other Side by the war.

At the end of the séance, Leah lit the room with her highly celebrated chandelier powered by newfangled gaslights: a triumph of science. The onslaught of science, coupled with the war, had caused many to rethink their religious beliefs.

Science had been internationally celebrated a decade and a half earlier, in 1851, in London's Hyde Park by the Exhibition to Promote Peace and Understanding. Housed in a magnificent glass tower, dubbed by *Punch* the Crystal Palace, eleven miles of stands demonstrated the advances of civilization, including the latest slave restraining equipment.

In 1859 Darwin had published *The Origin of Species* where centuries of belief were questioned. Was life really just a matter of natural selection? Living things not perfectly made upon arrival, as stated in the Bible, but gradually evolving in order to survive? Was God man-made, rather than man God made? It was a snake-pit of insecurity. The infallibility of the Bible was questioned by no less an authority than the Bishop of Natal. In 1862 he published the first of his mammoth seven-volume work *The Pentateuch and Book of Josiah Critically Examined*, querying its historicity. This caused calls for his resignation which, in fact, took place, but it did not stop him publishing the further six volumes, all of which sold well.

In 1867, hot on the heels of Darwin and the Bishop of Natal, came Karl Marx with the first volume of *Das Kapital*, calling for a revision of the world's economic system. People wanted answers. Someone who thought he'd found them was Robert Dale Owen. He believed they lay in an understanding of the Other Side and he joined Leah's circles to learn more. They'd met when he'd accepted an invitation, as a celebrity, to one of her conversaziones. He was enjoying a success with his recently published *Footfalls on the Boundary of Another World*, a compendium of Spiritualism through the ages, and was currently researching its follow-up *The Debatable Land Between this World and the Next*. He intended to include Leah as a part of this and she was so honoured she invited him to stay with her and Daniel, which he did for three months.

A man of principle, he was born in Glasgow in 1801, son of socialist Robert Owen, founder of the Co-operative movement and much else, who had also converted to Spiritualism. He was educated at his father's school in Switzerland, immigrating to America in 1825. In New York he edited *Free Enquirer*, a publication opposing organised religion and among his compendious works is *Moral Physiology*, the first American book to promote birth control with emphasis on coitus interruptus.

A socialist himself, he worked as a labourer before serving in both the Indiana House of Representatives and the United States House of Representatives where he fought for fairer divorce laws for women and the abolition of slavery. In 1853 he was appointed US Minister at Naples from which he retired, at the age of 57, to devote himself to Spiritualism.

Late at night, when the servants were in bed, Leah and Daniel, often joined by Kate and other regular sitters, held circles for Owen where the phenomena were truly spine-tingling. Doors were locked and hands held to increase power. Rapping would start and the chandelier was extinguished. Owen recalled that, during one circle, there were rustlings, as though caused by a lady's dress. The open-leaf table, around which they sat, slowly parted to reveal a whirlpool of lights. The form of a woman stood before him, veiled from head to toe but he could tell from her movements that she was young. She touched him and, through her veil, offered a chaste kiss.

Through the gloom he saw that the other sitters were still in their places, holding hands. He spoke to the phantom and she tried to answer but this was plainly difficult and, apparently, painful. She managed to gasp three short words: 'God ... Bless ... You'. She faded away and cupboards opened and keys could be heard turning in locks. Sometimes these keys, and other objects from the room, were placed in Owen's lap.[2]

Leah was sure the phantom was Emily, her sister who had died in infancy and grown up in Spirit. If spirits mature then why do child guides come through at the ages they were when they died? Is the reverse possible: can old people come back as youngsters? Experiments were conducted to investigate Spirit's ability to increase or lessen the weight of an object. The movement of furniture had demonstrated this many times. A weighing device, called a steelyard, was placed in the room and the table weighed at various times during the séance. This did vary but no explanation was offered as to how it happened.

Leah demonstrated she could produce raps outdoors and there were several jovial outings in carriages and boats where raps were heard on trees, rocks, sand and even sea. But there were neither apparitions nor levitation of objects. The spirits needed dark circles for these.

Owen's belief in Leah shines through *The Debatable Land*; he is full of wonder at her magic. A bright, new life, and death, beckons him. The spirit lady appeared to him several more times and, a decade later, he was to see another young spirit lady in another circle, and fall deeply in love with her. This was the infamous Katie King, spirit daughter of that ubiquitous manifestation John King.

On one momentous occasion the reclusive and glowering Maggie joined him for a séance. She had called on Leah for some reason while Owen was there. He was intrigued and persuaded her to sit with them. No sooner was the room dark than the table shuddered to a thunderous crash. Other alarming crashes followed. Owen feared the table would be smashed and makes it clear no human fist could have made such violent sounds. The circle was hastily brought to a close but the table found unscratched. Leah confided to Owen that similar ferocious manifestations had happened on a couple of occasions when Maggie had joined the circle.

Why was Maggie, who had renounced Spiritualism, still sitting in circles? A newly converted Catholic, she believed her beloved had been taken from her as a punishment for her involvement in Spiritualism. Why did she sit with Leah, for whom she felt considerable animosity? Was it to flaunt the strength of her mediumship, the irresistible lure of fame? Were the crashes manifestations of Maggie's hatred for the whole movement?

In the self-imposed exile of her tiny apartment Maggie grew ever more distant from the world. Kate called every Sunday, and Margaret and John kept an eye on her as best they could; in their old age, her parents had grown closer. It brought her no gratification. There were few other callers.

Surrounded by pictures of Elisha, and the gifts he had given her, she would re-read his letters, gathered together by a ribbon, until the writing on them became smudged by tears as she held them to her mouth and sobbed. She knew them by heart but had to read them, fingering the paper that he had fingered. The diamond of her ring sparkled like another tear. Spiritualism was the reason they had not officially married, and she rued the day she had first heard raps. No spirit came to console her. She, who had brought so many back from the dead to comfort the living, received no spectral comforters. Neither she nor Kate heard from Elisha. Neither expected to.

Panic began to gnaw into Maggie's misery. Apart from the small allowance, her only source of income was mediumship, the very thing Elisha, and she now, abhorred. Her rare sittings with Leah had been to prove she could still perform and, if necessary, more powerfully than Leah. She could see ectoplasmic fingers beckoning with money in them.

Reluctantly at first, she began to give a few sittings; it was her only way to avoid poverty. She knew she was betraying Elisha.

Kate was horrified when, one Sunday, she found her drunk. Maggie now drank regularly and heavily. She knew this would have nauseated Elisha. When she was drunk she didn't care. Unfortunately Kate was not the only witness. There were a few shocking occasions when the famous Spiritualist was evicted from saloons for being drunk and disorderly. Worse, there were times when she gave sittings while drunk. Leah was outraged as friends commiserated. Smelling salts were wafted and heads sorrowfully shaken behind feathered fans. Her hard-fought position in society was being jeopardized by a drunken sister.

The darker Maggie's fate, the lighter Kate's became. She had captured the eye of a young, rich, handsome and influential banker, and even better, he was a widower. Charles F. Livermore, in his early 30s, was in love with his beautiful wife, Estelle, whom he had tended until her premature death. He needed Kate to bring her back.

At 24, Kate had none of the chubby voluptuousness of the ever-expanding Leah, nor the dark attraction of Maggie (when she was well) but she was petite with big grey eyes which she used to effect, and her mousy image was being replaced by a more winsome appeal. Instinctively she knew how to flirt. There had been nothing further than that with Livermore, no impropriety, but Kate had an eye to the main chance – most women of her age, that she knew, were married. Leah had become Mrs Fish at 14.

Livermore was, at first, solely interested in contacting Estelle but the fact his medium was attractive helped broaden his aims. His colleague, Dr John Gray, a Spiritualist, had recommended her as a diversion, thinking circles might alleviate his grief. Their first circle was a small, intimate affair, held in daylight with Dr Gray present to steady Livermore's nerves.

Livermore was sufficiently intrigued to book another session. He soon became a fervent Spiritualist, sitting several times a week in dark séances. It wasn't, however, until after many sittings that he received a rapped message from Estelle in which she promised to show herself to him. Spirit lights danced and he felt her touch on his cheek. Livermore was ecstatic; as she had done with hundreds of others, Kate replaced hopelessness with hope.

Full materialisation had never occurred in Kate's circles. There had been ectoplasmic hands and faces, but neither she nor Maggie had had a full blown materialisation, such as Owen had experienced with Leah. If Estelle were to take physical form this would be a first for Kate.

At Kate's insistence Margaret had waived her chaperone duties so their circles usually consisted of just the two of them, sitting close in the dark and holding hands to increase the power. Estelle's first appearance was hazy. A veiled female figure built up and drifted about the room. The raps told Livermore this was, indeed, Estelle but he could not see her face. By now their séances had increased in frequency to virtually every night, sometimes they were held at Kate's home, at other times at Livermore's, occasionally they were joined by Dr Gray. Estelle's first recognisable appearance developed out of a flood of crackling luminescence; Livermore is at great pains to tell us of the crackling, electronic sounds that accompanied the build up, then beneath a veil he recognised his beloved wife's features.

She approached and bent towards him, her dark hair brushed his cheek. He knew he must not touch the form without permission as that could be injurious to Kate, and indeed Estelle, but she could lightly stroke him. He held Kate's hands throughout, lost in wonder. Estelle silently withdrew and stood opposite for a while. He could see her form reflected in a mirror across the room.[3]

In the dark the séances continued. Livermore held hands with Kate and sometimes he believed he was holding hands with Estelle. They merged into the same being. Sometimes he felt her caressing him in the dark and their caresses became kisses. Her face seemed to take shape before him and the kisses became more intimate although, as he wrote, he felt as though he was kissing her through muslin. She was not able to materialise at every séance, due to atmospheric conditions, not to mention the strain on Kate and Estelle. Sometimes he was simply aware of her presence; sometimes, just her hands were visible or her softly glowing veiled face. There were times when the muslin feel disappeared and he felt her unprotected warm, tender lips on his.

She never spoke but she wrote. He was told to bring pieces of blank card with him. A piece was placed lightly between his fingers, the end pointing upwards, and then Kate took his hands in hers. He felt the card being gently removed and returned. There was a message written in French – he and Estelle often spoke French together. He knew it was the same card that had been returned as he had marked it beforehand, just as he knew Kate did not speak French.

Both Kate and Livermore relished the intimacy as he communicated with the silent but effusive Estelle through her vaporous veil. There seemed to be no lack of tactility in the spirit world and physical desire seemed as vibrant there as here. That there was a limit to what could be expressed seemed to make what was possible more erotic.

One evening at Livermore's home, two forms materialised simultaneously. Estelle was present, flowers decorating her lovely hair, then a burly man also manifested. It was rapped that this was Benjamin Franklin. Both Robert Dale Owen and Dr Gray, although they had not been present agreed, after considerable thought, that it was, indeed, the great man, who had made so many appearances at Fox circles.

Livermore noted that, at times, he caught sight of Kate's face, reflected by the luminosity of the materialisations, and she seemed frightened by what was happening, as though she had no control over it and feared for her safety.

Owen was unconvinced by accusations that a good magician could duplicate the Fox sisters' effects: 'My faith is not at all shaken by reflecting that a Signor Blitz, or a Robert Houdin,[4] having a theatre at command, arranged with ready entrances and exits, with practical trap doors, with dark lanterns in the wings, with the means of producing dissolving views, could probably reproduce all I witnessed. But here were a few ladies, in private life and in moderate circumstances, quietly meeting in two apartments ... The coin of the realm may be counterfeited, but the coiners must have professional skill, and appropriate location, and expensive machinery.'

An enthusiastic review of *The Debatable Land* was published in 1872 in the *Quarterly Journal of Science*. The reviewer concluded that if spirit effects were down to trickery, then why did scientists not properly investigate these tricks instead of 'exhibiting prejudice'.

Franklin became a regular visitor at the Kate and Livermore sessions. Once, at Livermore's house, he called for matches which he struck illuminating his, and Estelle's faces. This was to show they could be seen by earthly light as well as in their luminous spirit forms. In addition to Dr Gray, they were occasionally joined by Estelle's brother, Jacques Groute. Initially a sceptic, he became a believer, convinced his dead sister was communicating.

The sessions were interrupted when Kate became ill which, she claimed, was due to overwork. Leah was in Europe on holiday and Margaret was becoming increasingly infirm, in need of attention. Materialisations were now expected at each sitting, which was draining. She craved Maggie's support. Kate, a modest and sometimes not so modest tippler from an early age, encouraged by the many bottles of fine champagne with which she had been presented, had become a soak with Maggie. They had alcohol-drenched evenings. The ageing Margaret was worried, and convinced Kate's illness had less to do with overwork than with alcohol.

Margaret had grasped the truth of this when her daughter had failed to appear at breakfast a few times. She had been horribly hung over. Margaret's husband was a reformed alcoholic; she knew the symptoms, the debilitating effects of alcohol. She was in despair over Maggie and for another daughter to follow the same bleak route was a body blow for the old lady.

Maggie's neighbours had experienced the symptoms of her illness. When the fit took her she would play and sing dirges, irrespective of the hour. Not possessing Leah's vocal talent, Maggie could be a passable singer and pianist, but her voice, now stained by alcohol, shrilling out in the night, sounded like that of a mad woman. Leah was deeply shocked when, on her return from Europe, she called on Maggie with some gifts, and found Maggie and Kate together drunk. Her horrified reprimand was answered by abuse. She hastened back to her waiting coach and footman, praying to God no one she knew had witnessed the exhibition. It took a long while for her trembling to stop.

Kate was not drunk all the time. She couldn't be. She was a professional woman with a thriving practice. There were times during the day when she yearned for a drink but had to discipline herself in order to earn her living. Part of that living was undergoing tests. Cromwell Fleetwood Varley, who masterminded the Altantic Telegraph Company's electric cable had considered the possibility, as had others, that the raps were electric in origin, testing Kate extensively, and sometimes painfully, to this end. After much research, he discarded the idea and Kate, and devoted his attention to another Victorian fascination – mesmerism.

But it wasn't the last Varley was to hear of the raps. He later claimed they saved his wife's life. He regularly put his wife into trances, when she spoke in 'controlled' voices, often about treatment for her precarious health. Upon her entranced advice he hired a nurse. It is a pity those who spoke through her did not oversee the interviews as the nurse turned out to be a drunk. Varley was awakened one night by three loud raps and hastened to his wife's room to find the nurse in a stupor and Mrs Varley in a state of catalepsy. He was convinced that had the raps not woken him she would have come to harm. But he had not heard

them since his experiments with Kate some time ago. Why should they
suddenly come back? To the end of his life Varley puzzled as to the
origin of those nocturnal raps.

In 1861, the same year that civil war had broken out, Abraham Lincoln
had become the sixteenth President of the United States. He really had
no choice other than to be interested in Spiritualism as his wife, Mary
Todd Lincoln, was besotted by it. A woman of delicate emotional bal-
ance, this was intensified when, in 1850, her second son, her beloved
Eddie, had died in infancy. In 1862 another son, Willie, also died while
still a child. She spent years consulting mediums, desperate to establish
contact with her children.

It is believed by some Spiritualists that the Emancipation Proclamation,
which brought freedom to slaves and over which Lincoln presided, was
expedited by spirit intervention. This is explained by medium Nettie
Colman Maynard in her book *Was Abraham Lincoln a Spiritualist? Or
Curious Revelations from the Life of a Trance Medium.*[5] Nettie first met the
President when she was 19, in the December of 1862, in the Red Parlor
of The White House, and she kept the confidentiality of that meeting for
thirty years before revealing all. By that time Lincoln was long dead and
she a sick woman, confined to her bed.

The invitation to The White House came from Mrs Lincoln via
Washington medium Margaret Laurie, daughter-in-law of the Rev. James
Laurie, founder of the New York Avenue Presbyterian Church close to
the White House, where Lincoln would pray. Mrs Laurie had a daughter,
Belle, also a medium and married to Lincoln's friend James J. Miller.
Belle's Washington séances were immensely popular and no wonder.
Her speciality was playing the grand piano while controlled, during
which the end of the instrument would beat time to the music. The
press had delightedly written of Belle and her 'waltzing piano', as they
dubbed it. It was not just Belle's piano that waltzed, so did other pianos
that she played elsewhere. It was claimed that, sometimes, when she had
stopped playing, she would stand, placing her hand on the instrument,
and the whole thing would levitate to a height of several feet. If this
were not enough, another reason why her séances were eagerly sought
was that many politicians interested in Spiritualism assembled there and
they were a good place to lobby the famous.

Mrs Lincoln invited the three mediums to The White House: Nettie,
Margaret Laurie and her daughter Belle. As was her custom, Belle,

entranced, moved to the grand piano and started to play. The hefty end steadily rose and fell, marking time. The President, who was not expected, stood in the doorway, attracted by the noise; a grand piano is no light instrument to have marking time. Belle snapped out of her trance. Lincoln was introduced to the awestruck guests and a séance was mooted, during which Nettie came under control and spoke to him for over an hour unaware, at the time, of what she was saying or who was saying it.

The Emancipation Proclamation was the topic, and Nettie, speaking in a deep, masculine voice advised the President to expedite its enactment. When she came round she found the President looking above her at a portrait on the wall. This was of Daniel Webster, renowned for his oratory, who had died in 1852. Nettie was sure it was he who had spoken through her.

The President, she says, put his hand on her head and told her: 'My child, you possess a very singular gift.' Whatever the influence of Nettie, or Webster, the Emancipation Proclamation, which freed four million slaves, took effect in 1863.

Another Lincoln séance over which Nettie presided took place in February of 1863, at Margaret Laurie's home in Georgetown. Mrs Lincoln was expected but the President was not. Nettie's child guide, however, told the company that he would be there. He did, indeed, arrive with his wife, wrapped in his long dark cloak, and was surprised to be told he had been expected. He had been leaving The White House as Mrs Lincoln was leaving for Georgetown and decided to join her.

There was singing before the circle, one of the songs being *Bonnie Doon*, a Presidential favourite. Then Belle sat at the piano which beat time. The President was invited by Belle to inspect the instrument, and underneath it for any mechanism. As he was searching, the instrument rose but he could detect no machinery.

A Colonel Kase (sometimes spelled Case and who some have identified as the pseudonym for Judge Salmon P. Chase, United States Supreme Court Chief Justice. He was also alleged to have been present at Nettie's earlier séance), who was also present, requested Belle to make it rise again while he was sitting on it. She agreed to this and suggested other men join him to add their weight. There are two accounts as to what happened next, one supplied by Nettie and the other by Colonel Kase.[6] Both agree that four men sat on the piano while it levitated and Nettie has one of these as the President himself. The Colonel, however, does not recollect the President and replaces him with a bodyguard.

It is strange that Mrs Lincoln, who had virtually the entire psychic world at her disposal, should not have sought guidance from the Foxes, but she never appears to have done so.

Some twenty years after Lincoln's death, speculation arose as to whether or not he had been a Spiritualist. A debate was conducted in the pages of *The Religio-Philosophical Journal* (later collated and annotated by Professor John Buescher at www.spirithistory.com). Belle's brother Jack, who had been 15 at the time, recalled to writer Cyrus Poole, that Mr and Mrs Lincoln had visited his home for séances with his parents, Belle and Nettie Colburn.

Lincoln was a lawyer and his partner in practice, William Herndon, wrote that he could neither confirm nor deny that Lincoln had been a Spiritualist adding, 'Mr Lincoln was in some phases of his nature very, very superstitious; and it may be – it is quite probable that he in his gloom, sadness, fear and despair, invoked the spirits of the dead to reveal to him the cause of his states of gloom, sadness, fear and despair.'[7]

Another lawyer, Professor W.H. Chaney, added to the debate. He had had dealings with both Belle and her husband, Colonel James J. Miller, inventor of Miller's Steam Condenser, after they had divorced and Belle, twenty-five years the Colonel's junior, had fallen on lean times and was seeking maintenance. The Colonel had told him Lincoln had become a Spiritualist after attending Belle's séances.

Having heard of Belle's 'waltzing piano', the Professor asked her, on one occasion as they were sitting in a hotel foyer, if she could demonstrate on the grand piano there. After some persuasion she reluctantly agreed and 'began playing a march, and instantly the piano tipped, keeping time with the music. In a moment all gathered about, crowding close to the instrument and vainly trying to discover the cause of the tipping.'[8]

Guests tried to raise the piano but it would not budge, the Professor estimated its weight at half a ton. Perhaps a steam condenser, and Belle was married to the inventor of such a contraption, could raise a grand piano in a private home, but how could that affect the levitation of a piano in a hotel foyer?

Belle went on to marry a soldier, Theophilus Youngs, who had been imprisoned for desertion and accused of bigamy and who abandoned her when he found himself facing a fraud charge. Two years later a drowned corpse was found which Belle, and a colleague of hers, identified as Youngs. Belle sued his brother, Henry, for Youngs' estate that she considered was rightfully hers as his widow.

There was drama in court when Youngs' solicitor produced a man whom Henry identified as his brother and Belle's husband. Belle denied this and demanded the man be arrested for imposture. The case dragged on but Belle died before it was resolved, still fighting.

A lock of Lincoln's blood-clotted hair reposes in The Chicago Historical Society archives which, it is claimed, was cut from his head after his assassination. A note of provenance is attached signed jointly by Mrs M. Laurie and Belle C. Youngs; Margaret Laurie was Belle's mother, and C was Belle's middle initial. It was uncertain as to who these signatories were, and their connection to the President, until Professor John Buescher solved the mystery.[9]

Mrs Lincoln had requested from the surgeons attending her dead husband a lock of his hair. The Professor suggests that this could have been given to Belle and Mrs Laurie as a link to establish contact with the President. From there it made its way to the Chicago Historical Society.

Mrs Lincoln's grip on reality began, understandably, to fail after John Wilkes Booth put a bullet through her husband's head while he was watching a play at Ford's Theatre, Washington on 14 April 1865. She had already lost two sons and this was just too much. But malignant fate hadn't done with her yet. There was another blow when her third son, Thomas, died of tuberculosis. In 1875 Robert, her remaining son, arranged for a sanity hearing where she was committed to an asylum in Batavia, Illinois, recovering sufficiently to live under the care of her sister Elizabeth. She lived in France for four years but on the return trip to America slipped on the ship and damaged her spine. She was saved by French actress Sarah Bernhardt and when Mme Bernhardt remarked Mrs Lincoln might have died she replied that it was not yet God's will.

After the death of Mrs Lincoln rumours spread that she and the late President were haunting their home in Springfield, Illinois. A piece of music, *The Dark Séance Polka*, was published, its cover derisively depicting Lincoln as a ghost. Ward Hill Lamon, Security Executive at the White House, told how Lincoln had confided a premonition to him that he would be assassinated.[10] Lincoln's corpse was moved several times due to a fear of grave robbers holding it to ransom, and there was a period when no one seemed entirely sure where he was buried. Stories erupted of how he haunted graveyards and mausoleums. They are still circulating.

7

The civil war spluttered to its inglorious end in 1865, the year that Lincoln died. Over half a million had perished in the war and twice as many were seriously injured. More had grievously suffered.

Spiritualism flourished with a renewed and desperate intent but the nature of séances had changed; people now wanted more drama, full-scale materialisations were expected. For her private coterie, Leah had readily shown what she could do, with bugle calls, drum rolls and musket shots not to mention angelic music.

Charles Livermore, that astute businessman, had profited enormously through the war and was now even richer. All through the hostilities he had continued his intimate sittings with Kate.

Both Margaret and John Fox died that year, he before her. Their ends had been fraught with worry about Kate and Maggie as both daughters now drank to excess. In *Time is Kind* Margaret is quoted as telling Dr Edward Bayard that the girls had drunk ever since they had been famous, which had by now been a long time: 'It's been all wrong. I've always felt so, but I never knew what to do about it.' The die was cast.

John had retreated into himself, refusing to talk about it, or anything much, for that matter. He, who had caused so much misery through his own drinking, was now plagued by the alcoholism of his daughters. It was Margaret who found him dead in his chair one morning. An enviably dignified end. After his funeral, which was held at the peppermint farm, Margaret was to stay with Leah, and Kate and Maggie travelled back to New York with them by train. While waiting for connections Kate and

Maggie disappeared and returned the worse for drink. Mercifully, they fell asleep on the train so Leah and Margaret were spared any unseemly behaviour.

Leah and Daniel suggested that Kate and Maggie should go to rehabilitation hospitals, separately as they were lethal together, where there was a chance they might be cured of their hateful addictions. Daniel would meet the expenses. The more pliable Kate saw the sense of this. Maggie refused to be parted from Elisha's shrine. In the end, nothing was done.

Margaret gradually drifted in and out of what today might be described as Alzheimer's disease before catching a severe fever which killed her. Her daughters' fame had brought richness to her life, and she had clung to their skirts, aiding and abetting the breathless ride. Her formerly dull existence had been transformed into a peacock's tail of colour by the spirits. It was a debt of gratitude she could have never repaid.

Preparing for the funeral, Leah had to be restrained from dressing her dead mother in extravagant finery. It was suggested that black might be more dignified but black was a colour for which Leah had little time. Maggie was convinced her mother had believed in the spirits. In her later memoir *The Death-Blow to Spiritualism*[1], which Maggie authorised when she was unbalanced, full of bitterness and hating the world and, above all, Spiritualism, she wrote: 'Mother was a silly woman. She was a fanatic. I call her that because she was honest. She believed in these things.'

After the death of her parents, Kate realised that Livermore had recovered from the heartache of Estelle's death, and he no longer needed her. He, however, retained affection for her. She half-heartedly tried to pick up the pieces of the career she had neglected in favour of the demanding, but satisfying, Livermore sittings.

Maggie was impecunious. Her allowance was erratic and sometimes not paid at all. What she received she spent mostly on drink and was unable and unwilling to give sittings. Leah, who would have helped if civilly asked, washed her hands of her. The last straw came when Leah was told, and she was one of the last to find out, that Maggie claimed to have married Elisha and was now styling herself Mrs Fox Kane. In Leah's eyes this merely rehashed the scandal.

Newspaperman Horace Greeley had, some time ago, come up with an idea to boost Maggie's finances. He told her she must publish Elisha's letters in book form with a linked narrative. The man was an American hero and she one of the most famous women in America. It would be bound to sell. The idea had come to Greeley after he had accidentally met Maggie one snow-drenched midnight in New York. Her cloaked figure had loomed through the blizzard, her breath malodorous, her hair wild. The storm had brought back memories of the time when Elisha had been missing, presumed dead. She thought she was in the Arctic, and she was searching for him, babbling to an alarmed Greeley, whom she did not recognise, that she must find him or he would die. With difficulty Greeley steered her back to her apartment and, dreading scandal if he was seen at that hour with an inebriated woman, hastened her inside. Maggie had no recollection of the event the next day.

Greeley had reported the incident to Margaret who had evinced little surprise and confided to him that Kate was on the same perilous course. Kate had been his special protégé, whom he had virtually nurtured through childhood; he was appalled. There was little he could do for her, but he could lessen Maggie's financial plight.

Maggie was repelled by the thought of publication, not wanting her sacred letters pored over by strangers. They were kept in a beautiful box he had given her, pride of place in her shrine. They were the most important things in her life, her very blood. A patient Greeley pointed out that Elisha had not provided for her, surely an oversight due to his premature death? He would want her to be financially secure. Not really sure to what she was agreeing she had put herself in the hands of a friend, journalist Joseph La Fumee who, sensing a coup, had linked the letters with an explanatory narrative.

She had been uncooperative and difficult from the start. Alternately confiding and furious at his intrusion, refusing to work with him then denying things she had said and withdrawing permission to publish. Sometimes she would rip up his pages. Sometimes she was unfit to work. After much travail, the finished manuscript and letters had been placed in the hands of publishers. But still Maggie did not want it published.

Then the dower rights came to court. Greeley had called a conference with Dr Bayard and others who cared for her, for Maggie had not been totally abandoned by her admirers. They persuaded her to bring a case against Elisha's executors for 'dower on the widow's part' to the Orphan's Court of Philadelphia.

The possibility of Elisha's putative marriage being publicly aired, and news of the intended publication of *The Love-Life of Dr Kane*, which Greeley had leaked, brought a compromise. Maggie accepted a lump sum of $2,000 plus a small annuity, to be regularly paid, provided she did not publish and discontinued her lawsuit. Elisha's letters and the book proofs were to be held in trust by Dr Bayard.

Maggie was not frugal and by 1866 the $2,000 had been squandered and the allowance was sometimes unpaid. Maggie's lawyers deemed the agreement broken. The letters were returned to Maggie and *The Love-Life of Dr Kane*[2] published.

It has been described as a slender volume, which may be the case by the Victorian standard of the three-volume novel, and weighed against such mammoth works as *The Secret Doctrine* and *Art Magic*. By today's standards, though, it is substantial at nearly 300 pages. We are confronted at once by Maggie's brooding, sometimes fierce personality. Although the linkage is ghost written (in the publisher's sense) it's her words that sear the pages.

Elisha is well served by his letters. He can be cruel but he is frequently loving, endearing and often funny. He was a gifted writer and it is easy to see why the ladies loved him. Accusations of editing and fraud have been levelled at the letters. La Fumee was a professional writer and deleted repetitious or irrelevant material, selecting only the most interesting sections. Maggie, too, would have exercised her authority on what was to stay and what was excluded. Some sections were, perhaps, too personal, too indelicate, for public consumption. If the letters are bogus then an expert hand capable of forging two distinct personalities crafted them.

Margaret contributes to the book and there is one distinct misting of the facts. According to her, Maggie was just 13 when Elisha first clapped eyes on her; she had in fact, been 19. When the book was published Maggie was 33, looked older, and had adopted the habit of docking her age.

There are two facsimiles of letters from Elisha, in small neat handwriting. One is addressed to 'Dear Wife', which is the reason for its inclusion. Maggie wants us to know Elisha considered them married. She swears his declaration of vows was 'as firm as if the ceremony took place before a magistrate'. As the author she is credited as Margaret Fox Kane.

Kate missed Livermore terribly. With the death of Margaret, he had withdrawn his support just when she most needed it. She had made him a Spiritualist but he no longer needed contact with Estelle and Kate was redundant. Perhaps he had grown a little bored with Estelle's communications by now, needing something earthier? Perhaps he had grown a little bored with Kate? Perhaps, deep down, he never believed Estelle was as close as Kate said? Kate loved Livermore in her way, and he remained fond of her all his life, and she felt lonely, bereft of their several evenings a week locked in dark ectoplasmic embrace.

Leah repeated her offer for Kate to have treatment, and Dr Bayard and Greeley agreed to contribute, urging her to accept. She decided she had better go through with it as she was in danger of losing her status as a Sybil. An eccentric Sybil is one thing but a drunken one something else. More importantly, there was little else on offer as her clientele was woefully sparse.

Dr Bayard found a place for Maggie at the Swedish Movement Cure, at Sixth Avenue and 38th Street, run by Dr George H. Taylor and his wife Sarah. Dr Bayard believed in homeopathy so the hydropathic cure, with its accent on natural remedies, met his standards. Dr Taylor, him-self with a beard to rival Swedenborg's, seemed the right man for the job. She stayed with them on and off for years even though she tested their patience inordinately. When she was destitute, after the deaths of Dr Bayard and Greeley, they took her in free of charge for Leah, tried beyond endurance, eventually washed her hands of her.

Like Kate, Dr Taylor was a pioneer. Plagued by ill health when young he had attempted to rectify this by studying medicine at Harvard and New York Medical College. He had practised at the New York City Water Cure and, in 1853, established his own practice. His system was based on a Swedish theory of water therapy, and he had invented a steam-driven pelvic massage device for the treatment of ladies. This exposed the insti-tute to comment and a long waiting list.

Kate's recovery was uneven. There were occasions when she dis-appeared for weeks, once for months, when she shared an apartment with Maggie, which they rapidly turned into a drunken slum. On the whole she responded, ate regularly and gained strength. The Taylors had had three children but two had died, their son, Frankie, aged 3 and daughter, Leila, just 18 months. They were devoted to their surviving son, William, but nothing could compensate for the loss of their other children.

Dr Taylor was not too keen on the controversial topic of Spiritualism being discussed among his patients in his early days with Kate. But, despite her husband's reservations, Sarah became interested. Another boarder, a Mrs Lang, was a medium and brought back Sarah's dead mother, Eliza, replete with bed sores and death agonies. Death agonies were a popular part of Spirit repertoire. Kate learned of this and a shower of raps told her she must contact Sarah whose entire dead family were waiting to communicate with her including parents, grandparents, her dead brother Olin and, of course, the children. Soon the Taylors were enjoying regular sittings, most of which Kate conducted through her extraordinary gift of backward automatic writing, her hands, sometimes both at the same time, whirling like dervishes. These mad writings were held up to a mirror and copied by Sarah who kept a record of them. This was later published by her son William[3] who linked them with a narrative.

Leah was relieved Kate was making such a good impression at the Taylors. She herself was on splendid form and had recently received the world famous Norwegian violinist Ole Bull, who was appearing with the American tour of the Ole Bull Concert Combination. Her old friend, violinist Professor J. Jay Watson, who had arranged several of her spirit-inspired melodies, introduced them.

Dr Bull's inspiration was Paganini, rumoured to have sold his soul to the devil in exchange for his dazzling technique. If Dr Bull had struck the same bargain he was not short changed. He became a national hero and his funeral, in 1880, was one of the most spectacular in Norwegian history. He was one of the first to recognise the brilliance of the composer Edvard Grieg.

Professor Watson had been convinced of Leah's abilities after she had rapped a message from his father-in-law. They had had a pact that whomever passed first would contact the other by tugging his hair. His father-in-law had died and, one night on tour in California, the Professor had been jerked violently awake by an unseen hand wrenching his hair. He awoke in time to avoid being murdered by an intruder, an employee whom he had sacked. Leah, who had no prior knowledge of the incident, was able to relate it to the Professor and assure him it had, indeed, been his father-in-law who had saved his life.

Kate's sessions with the Taylors were not morbid. The most popular communicants were, naturally, their children and the parents loved hearing how happy they were in the Summerland, a beautiful place where they now lived. Kate was able to take the sting out of death, make a party of it. Loved ones are near all the time, part of our lives. The spirit children were full of larks, one of their antics, to their father's delight, was to plait his flowing beard as they played around him in the dark. Laughter would ring out during these sessions.

Topsy is a child in *Uncle Tom's Cabin* by Harriet Beecher Stowe, a lady who had an interest in Spiritualism although was never a convert. She was introduced to the subject by Robert Dale Owen, in Naples, when he was ambassador there. They sat in circles ('A perfect Arabian Night's Entertainment', as she put it) and she was impressed by Owen's sincerity, writing to novelist George Eliot: 'I regard Mr Owen as one of the few men who are capable of entering into an enquiry of this kind without an utter drowning of common sense.' Miss Eliot was not impressed, dismissing Spiritualism as the 'lowest charlatanerie'. Mrs Stowe had read Owen's books *The Debatable Land* and *Footfalls on the Boundary of Another World* and urged Miss Eliot to do the same; she promised she would if she could find the time.

The pettiness of some spirit communications did not dampen Mrs Stowe's interest, she wrote to George Eliot: 'I don't know of any reason why there should not be as many foolish virgins in the future state as in this!'[4]

Mrs Stowe and her husband sat a few times with Kate. The authoress was impressed but thought the manifestations might be unexplained laws of nature rather than spirits of the dead. She did not side with Kate's enemies who put it about she cheated.

Mrs Stowe was not deterred by controversy. Back in 1851, outraged by the cruelty of the Fugitive Slave Law, which entitled owners to impose any penalty they chose on a recovered runaway slave, including death by torture, she had written, in serial form, her powerful anti-slave *Uncle Tom's Cabin*, the best-selling novel of the nineteenth century. According to President Lincoln, Mrs Stowe was 'the little lady who wrote the book that made the great war'.

She was no little lady; she was a highly educated, humane and witty woman whose entire history was steeped in clear-sightedness. *Uncle Tom's Cabin* still packs a punch, after which she wrote a book a year and became a leading figure on the international lecture circuit.

Kate herself was about to become international too. Her fame had already spread to Europe and, in 1871, she was about to visit England. It was twenty-three years since the first rappings and she was now 34. The sparkle that could override her mousiness, that Livermore had found so attractive, was not often in evidence and was in danger of fading altogether. Her louche lifestyle was leaving its ugly mark. She had more or less given up on the Taylors and her reputation had deteriorated. Something she did not care about; she cared about nothing very much. There was not much point to anything.

Sarah Taylor's record is a sad diary of Kate's abandonment, full of missed appointments, aborted sittings and accounts of Kate, when she did arrive, reeling in drunk, or staggering in at midnight for an 8pm meeting.

Olin, Sarah's brother, frequently automatically wrote through and about Kate: 'April 17 1870: Katie was on the very step almost of eternity and we know that if she went out the next day, Wednesday, death would have come from the suffering she would have endured.' Kate would sit there, her hands whirring, as the spirits wrote about her: 'If Kate would only abstain for a length of time, she would have health and happiness and sweet flowers, sweet friends, and angels would be her companions instead of those vile roots which grow to weeds. She was so sick when we tried to write on Tuesday night ...'5 Sometimes when Kate was on the razzle, missing her bookings, people swore raps could be heard around her, vainly urging her to return to the Taylors who waited for her in a paroxysm of worry.

> May 7 1870: Katie kept an engagement with a very fashionable family on
> Fifth Avenue. She went well and happy but came back at 10 o'clock sick
> and crazy with brandy ...

So the tragedy went on, endemic of some terrible weakness in her soul that could not be remedied. Both Charles Livermore and Robert Dale Owen begged her to stop drinking. She promised she would, and meant it, for she knew she was on the brink of disaster, but she could not keep her resolve, sometimes not even for a day.

'Curses will follow these people! That give her drink and keep her overnight!' Benjamin Franklin thundered, the pencil almost igniting the paper in his fury: 'I know all! Pity them, I do not! You had better let them know it.'

Even Margaret came through to plead with Sarah to care for her wayward daughter. But, drunk or sober, and it was usually the former, Kate could still produce her magic. Sarah was in awe. Messages were sometimes found that Kate had not written, precipitated from beyond. She added spirit portraits to her armoury – pictures of both Frankie and Leila appeared under pieces of cloth (the confinement was needed for the materialisation process), as did pictures of Sarah's grandmother and Olin, both in fine fettle, despite the less than ideal manners of their passing.

The Taylors were ecstatic one afternoon when Benjamin Franklin announced he would be conducting a new experiment. Their daughter, Leila, would play the harp from Spirit. As her parents listened, spirit fingers could be heard loudly and clearly strumming, neighbours later commented on having also heard it.

Kate showed no pride as wonders exploded about her. All she was interested in was getting to Maggie and their shared debauchery. In the midst of this mayhem, Maggie decided to come out of retirement and give sittings, probably due to the necessity to earn money. The Kane allowance was literally soaked up and the only way Maggie had of earning was the hated circles.

She lurched into public life again and a few clients came. But unlike Kate, booze affected Maggie's performance and most went away disappointed. She was given up for lost. The Taylors, however, cared for Kate. They tried to keep her from Maggie but it was a losing battle, they were too close, loved each other in the way that only blood can love blood. Their only emotional ties were each other. Whenever reason penetrated the morass that was Kate's mind, it was accompanied by desperation to find a husband. She had had wild hopes for Livermore but her lifestyle ensured there was little chance of that. She knew she was well and truly on the shelf. She had given sittings for too many thwarted spinsters in search of romance to expect love for herself, but she needed security and a reason to live. She had none.

Spiritualism had never been a crusade for her, any more than it had been for Maggie, but it had opened doors and was now an unyielding way of life. As Leah grew ever plumper on her island of success, both sisters were lost at sea. Livermore, and his money, came up with a lifeline for Kate. It had been inspired by Leah who, returning from another of her European trips, had mentioned, when bewailing her sisters' shameful fate and how dreadful it all was as Kate had such a formidable reputation in England, how the English would love to see her. Tales of her squalor had not yet penetrated there, and Mrs Underhill would have firmly rebuffed them if they had risen. Kate, abroad, would suit Livermore for two reasons. Firstly he was fond of her and it would be a new start, secondly it could be extremely tiresome when she crashed into his life.

Kate would be sent to England, hopefully to remain there for good. That way she could not further besmirch Leah or Livermore's reputations. Livermore would pay for everything, he owed her that, and arrange for her to be received by Spiritualists who would be delighted to have the legendary pioneer among them. If she were obstreperous while there, the English could sort it out. Hopefully Maggie would disappear back into her shell with Kate gone. Their black spell would be broken. Leah couldn't wait to get Kate on the boat.

Kate would go anywhere she was pointed. Had it been England or Africa it would have been the same. Her world had imploded. For Maggie it was a lethal blow. She had no one apart from Kate. She begged her to stay but the pull of Kate's supporters was stronger. It was also, in the long run, cathartic. Maggie promised to renounce alcohol and was so shaken by her sister's imminent departure that she really made an effort. Occasionally she could now show her face in public and, occasionally, it was sober, if rarely happy.

England was now used to mediums. Since Mrs Hayden, an army of British psychics had mounted the Spiritualist platform, some of whose careers were spectacular. Charles Livermore did not stint on expenses. Kate was to travel first class in her own stateroom. She was fitted out with a new wardrobe, outfits for every conceivable occasion, not that she was interested, and Livermore ensured her cabin was full of flowers and gifts. Really, he was a thoroughly decent man; she had stood by him in his deepest grief and it was now payback time.

The Taylors went to see her off and were amazed at how many turned out on the same mission. Some were Kate's drinking pals and hoping for a good, last session before the off. They were disappointed. Kate had pulled herself together, ready to make a new start. She was elegant in her new wardrobe and composed. Among the seething crowd was a tragic inelegant figure draped in widow's black. In her mind she was a widow, the Widow Kane. She was largely ignored, most had no idea who she was anyway. She hugged her sister and genuinely wished her well then wandered off alone. Maggie had made a terrific effort.

The Taylors saw Kate off with heavy hearts. No one could bring back their children as vividly as Kate. She would be a terrible loss. Dr Taylor's beard would remain unplaited and the harp would no longer sound. They treasured their spirit portraits.

Livermore had thought of everything, including a travelling companion for Kate. Blanche Ogden, a relative of his, turned out to be a godsend. Aware of Kate's illness, she was middle-aged and sensible, she was also good hearted and not averse to adventure, otherwise she would not have agreed to accompany Kate in the first place. England was the salvation of Kate, for a while at least.

Livermore did more than pay for everything; he also took care Kate would be well-treated by the right people. He arranged for prominent English Spiritualists to meet the women in London, and impressed upon Kate that she was to give neither public demonstrations nor dark sittings. She must limit herself to private readings in daylight. His embargo on public demonstrations was obvious: if she was drunk, then a public meeting would be the best way to advertise this to the greatest number of people. The dark sittings were another matter. She had brought him immeasurable comfort through dark sittings, why deny similar comfort to others? Had he, perhaps, taken her comfort at face value, not probing too deeply? Had he perhaps come to certain conclusions he did not wish others to reach? Whatever it was he didn't want it happening in England.

He listed his stipulations to Spiritualist Benjamin Coleman, who met them at Victoria station. Coleman had already met Kate, having had sittings with her in America, and averred she had given him more evidence than any other medium in his seventeen years as a Spiritualist.

Livermore wrote: 'She is a sensitive of the highest order and of child-like simplicity; she feels keenly the atmospheres of everyone with whom she is brought in contact, and to that degree that at times she becomes exceedingly nervous and apparently capricious.'

It was a private letter, just a few tips to make her visit as trouble-free as possible, and it showed how much he still cared for her and knew he was taking a risk presenting her. This was a man prominent in the world of finance. Robert Dale Owen was sure she'd have no trouble in convincing the English of Life Eternal and had written to Coleman, describing her as 'simple-minded', as in, honest to a fault.

Coleman had arranged a welcome reception for Kate. She arrived, with Blanche, wearing one of her new outfits, looking well. She had not enjoyed the Atlantic crossing, during which she had been seasick and unexpectedly lonely. Crossing the Atlantic was a severance of all she knew.

Among those invited to meet her was Henry Dietrich Jencken, a widower of an unhappy marriage, of around 40. Of German extraction, he was a retired lawyer, author of the substantial *A Compendium of Modern Roman Law* and secretary of the Association for the Reform and Codification of the Law of Nations. He was from a wealthy Spiritualist family and eager to meet Kate. He did more than that; he was to marry her and steer her back to the road of normality – or as near normality as she could ever get. On that first evening he escorted her to dinner. There was a plentiful supply of wine waiting to be served. Kate was nervous, this was her first London outing and, it was clear, the metropolis was expecting great things of her.

Champagne was poured and Coleman proposed a toast. *Time is Kind* assures us that raps sounded in response, which delighted the guests; this was, after all, what they had come for. Kate raised her glass politely in acknowledgement then lowered it untasted. Blanche was one side of her and Henry the other. Sense prevailed. Seductive as was the crystal goblet full of sparkling delectation and courage, she declined it. She was on the road to recovery.

But it didn't happen at once. There were several relapses; a spectacular one came one dreadful night when Blanche thought Kate had died. She had left her for a while but returned to their hotel to find her unconscious with empty bottles thrown around the room. On the pretext of a sightseeing tour she hastened Kate off to Paris for a month's treatment for alcohol abuse. London must not discover Kate's secret. They returned to London where Coleman had arranged a welcome-back party, not dreaming his distinguished guest would overturn the table if the mood took her. The strain of her Paris ordeal had left her tense and irritable.

Henry was there and she did not drink, he had never seen her drink, and he must have wondered at her morose temperament. After dinner, however, she held a dark circle of the type that Charles had specifically banned. London was astounded when a luminous hand crossed the ceiling, wandered about the room and then began to write on paper on a nearby table. Kate's hands were held throughout. There were messages for all. Most extraordinary was Henry's, written in German which Kate did not speak any more than she spoke the French or Italian in which Estelle had sometimes written to Charles.

Henry was delighted with her, and awestruck, and they spent much time together, often alone, sometimes on sightseeing trips. It became apparent to all they were stepping out. Luminous hands, spontaneous rapping and the ability to communicate in tongues made Kate utterly desirable to Henry.

Continuing to flout Livermore's wishes, Kate resumed the dark séances. Throwing caution to the wind, she took part in a public double demonstration for *The Times* with the sensational levitating Scottish medium Daniel Dunglas Home. Although despised by Browning, Dickens and Faraday, to name but three, Home was enormously successful and could count among his admirers Mark Twain, Thackeray and Napoleon III. His most memorable achievement had taken place in London on 13 December 1868 at the home of Viscount Adare when, in the presence of the Viscount and others, he had levitated out of a third-floor window and back in again through another.

Henry Jencken was a close friend of Home and had put his legal training to effect in defending the medium on more than one occasion. He had authenticated much of his phenomena, such as his handling of red-hot coals and his ability to alter the shape of his body. On a more prosaic level he had advised him during the notorious Home-Lyon case.

Home was a handsome man whom the ladies adored, particularly those of a certain age. Among these was the wealthy, demanding and probably unbalanced Mrs Lyon. She was so determined to have him that she adopted him, reasoning that as her son, he would have a strong case against her detested relatives should they try to dispute her will, which she would draw up in his favour, after her death. As a condition, she required him to change his name to Lyon, which would blazon their bond to the world. He reasoned he could not do this as he was too well known professionally under his own name, but compromised by calling himself Home-Lyon. Mrs Lyon accepted this and transferred large sums to his account.

She later changed her mind about the whole affair and demanded the return of the cash. He refused. A Chancery Court case resulted during which Mrs Lyon accused Home of fraud, alleging spirit guides that he had manufactured, had urged her to give him the money. He lost the case, to the delight of many a red-blooded man, including Robert Browning, and became the inspiration for Browning's *Mr Sludge the Medium*.

The Times reporter wrote enthusiastically of Kate, the famous American medium, in an article headed 'Spiritualism and Science'. As he was leaving, she took his hands and he was amazed 'when loud thumps seemed to come from panels, as if done with the fist. They were repeated at our request any number of times.'[6]

It was a measure of Kate's distinction that Home had agreed to partner her. He was very much the egoist and always a solo act – excluding the spirits. The two, however, maintained a loose friendship until his death from tuberculosis in 1886. When they first met, he was working on a book of exposure of fraudulent mediums.[7] This sent a shiver through the psychic world, many mediums dreading they might be included: 'I was assailed, both openly and anonymously,' Home noted, 'with slander, lying charges, foul personalities, [and] venomous abuse.'[8]

Kate was not among his traducers, she put pen to paper and told him cosily, referring to the writing of his exposé: 'I was contemplating doing it myself' – she was to do more than contemplate, she and Maggie were to actively plot Spiritualism's downfall, but that would not be until 1888. In the meantime she urged Home to contact her if he needed help, adding winsomely, 'I have never had an unkind thought towards you.'

Home biographer, Elizabeth Jenkins cites an anecdote,[9] based on information from a 1924 book by Henrietta Mary Ada Ward entitled *Memories of Ninety Years*. Mrs Ward recalls that she visited a Home séance where 'a woman used to act as medium at Mr Home's demonstrations. I remember she required two glasses of port and two of some other beverage, before she began her work.'

If she was referring to Kate the anecdote is misremembered. Kate only worked with Home on the one occasion, and would certainly not have been drunk on such an important occasion, particularly when she had made such a success in London and was at pains to conceal her alcoholism from Henry. If she had been drinking to the extent that Mrs Ward describes then the reporter would surely have noticed it; when Kate was drunk there was no possible doubt about it. And there is no way Home would have appeared with a drunk. He didn't need to, he was already Britain's leading medium. Mrs Ward's account appeared some fifty years after the event. Kate was long dead and her alcoholism common knowledge. Perhaps Mrs Ward's recollections were coloured by hearsay.

Kate soon attracted the attention of scientist William Crookes, later to become Sir William Crookes. Born in 1832, a year before Maggie, his achievements were already considerable and he went on to greater things. *The Dictionary of National Biography* lists his career as one of 'unbroken scientific activity'. In 1861, ten years before Kate's visit to England, he had discovered the element thallium. In the 1850s, while Maggie and Kate, via Leah, were introducing rappings to the world, Crookes was at London's Royal College of Chemistry investigating new compounds of the element selenium.

He is still a revered name in Spiritualist and scientific camps but, the *DNB* notes: 'His excursions into psychical research have been strongly criticised, and they certainly led him into some very curious situations, but they show he thought all phenomena worthy of investigation, and refused to be bound by tradition and convention.'

Kate was nervous of meeting him, having consistently suffered at the hands of investigators, both scientific and lay. She still had nightmares about the spiteful hands of the Christian lady 'examiners'. But she could not ignore so eminent a scientist.

The last, squalid days of New York were fading from her memory, as were the few squalid days she'd had in London. She was no longer drinking, Henry Jencken was her constant escort, and she was the toast of London Spiritualists. She had cause to bless Charles Livermore for sending her to London.

She impressed Crookes from the start. At one séance where he was holding both her hands in one of his and a pencil in the other, his feet resting on hers, the luminous hand made its appearance, descended from the ceiling, took the pencil from his hand, wrote on a sheet of paper and rose to the ceiling again, fading away.

He wrote: 'To the touch the hand appears icy cold and dead, at other times warm and lifelike, grasping my own with the firm pressure of an old friend. I have retained one of these hands in my own, firmly resolved not to let it escape. There was no struggle or effort made to get loose, but it gradually seemed to resolve itself into vapour.'[10]

Crookes also noted, as had others, that while Kate was automatically writing one message, the raps were knocking out quite a different one for someone else. Crookes was a trained scientist and his experiments conducted in controlled scientific conditions.

He was impressed by her lack of preparation before producing phenomena. No preamble was necessary; she got straight on with it. She amazed him by rapping on many substances, varying from a tambourine to a theatre floor. He dangled her from the ceiling in a wire cage and stood her on chairs and still the raps sounded. He concluded: 'There has been no escape from the conviction that they were true objective occurrences not produced by trickery or mechanical means.'

Kate's phantom hand was really grabbing London, it had become her calling card. *The Spiritualist* recorded its presence at a circle where it caressed a sitter's face, accompanied by a square of phosphorescence. *Light* Magazine described lights floating about the room. Others told of objects being teleported and of a broken music box being mysteriously repaired, similar to feats later achieved by Uri Geller.

Kate was working well because she was happy. The fear of phenomena, that had never really left her, had diminished and Henry must take credit for this. The closer they became the safer she felt. It had not been a case of love at first sight nor, for that matter of love at all, it was something more durable. And it was a great comfort.

Henry's marriage proposal came during a weekend house party. They were alone in the garden preparatory to dinner when he popped the question under the lilac trees. This was more than a dream come true for Kate, it was salvation. She had received disquieting news of two important men in her life, which had brought back some of her old insecurity. If ever she wanted a drink it was then.

Charles Livermore, to whom she owed so much, and for whom she still carried a torch, had married. The news almost made her swoon. She learned that his bride was young, beautiful and, after marriage, extremely wealthy. How could she not be jealous? She hoped her engagement might wound Livermore but it did the reverse. It relieved him. He cared for her but was not, and never had been, in love with her. He was delighted someone was looking after her.

Her staunch protector, the thoroughly decent Horace Greeley, was now desperately ill. Without him she would feel truly lost; he was to die in the November of 1872, shortly before her marriage. His end was tragic. After a lifetime of fighting good causes, opposition to slavery being one, he had run for President and suffered a humiliating defeat at the hands of Ulysses S. Grant the same year that his wife died. While these dismal events took place he was swindled out of a fortune and lost the *Tribune*, which had done so much to shoot the Foxes to fame. He suffered mental collapse and died in an asylum. Doubts about Spiritualism were seeping in before he died, but these did not lessen his affection for Kate.

Henry's proposal could not have come at a better time and her swift acceptance was one of the smartest moves she ever made. The wedding took place on 14 December 1872 at Marylebone Parish Church. The ceremony was quite small, with the marriage party arriving in three carriages pulled by white horses. Blanche was there, which had been touch and go at one point as she and Kate had had a spat – but who could live with a Fox sister without having a spat? Most of the congregation were colleagues of Henry's with a smattering of minor German royalty. Among the Spiritualists was Henry Cholmondley-Pennell, described by the press as a poet but better remembered today, if remembered at all, as a sometime Inspector of Fisheries and author of *History of the Fish Hook in America*.

The spirits showed their approval by rapping during the toasts, as they had during the actual ceremony. Margaret rapped her congratulations. According to the *New York Herald*, which covered the event, the table at which the newly-weds sat levitated a couple of times, cake and all.

This was exactly the sort of behaviour Henry expected from his bride. It happened after the servants had been dismissed from the room, according to *The Spiritualist*, so as not to excite them too much. The wedding cake was shipped off to America uncut to be divided among Kate's family and friends. Their honeymoon was in pleasant Tunbridge Wells.

The marriage was a success on every level and she did come round to loving Henry. He was caring and considerate. It was no bad thing Livermore had married someone else.

While the table levitated at Kate's prosperous wedding – the papers described Henry as possessing 'a handsome competence' – three thousand miles across the Atlantic, Maggie was still brooding, grief-stricken in her small and increasingly foetid apartment. She hovered in and out of madness and the slice of Kate's wedding cake that arrived bringing news of Kate's happiness only heightened her desperation.

The arrival in 1873 of Madame Blavatsky in New York went unnoticed by Maggie and, indeed, by most of the city. The formidable Russian aristocrat was living anything but aristocratically in a boarding house for ladies, sewing cravats for a living. Before coming to America at her Mahatma's wish, she had been in Egypt and participated in a case of possession. She wrote to her sister, Vera Zhelikovsky, about it from which the following is taken. Near the pyramids, she had joined a party of tourists that included a demure English spinster. The spinster was writing in her diary when Madame, glancing at it, saw the characters merge from English into Russian – which the English lady did not speak. It read: 'Little Miss, help, oh help me, miserable sinner! I suffer: drink, drink, give me drink!' 'Little Miss' or its Russian equivalent, was how servants in Russia had addressed her. She knew, clairvoyantly, that an ancient retainer, an alcoholic, had died.

The Englishwoman threw down her writing and in a rough manner, out of keeping with her usual refined demeanour, demanded drink. Her horrified friends managed to buy some wine, which was gulped before their startled eyes. She drank until falling in convulsions. She was ill for several weeks but, fortunately, Madame was able to pacify the troubled spirit and so free her of possession.

The incident put Madame Blavatsky off alcohol for life, although she had never been keen, having seen its effect on too many debauched Russian aristocrats. An account in an unidentified and undated American newspaper, by a former drunk, tells of an encounter with her in a New

York hotel. He had been behaving abusively and, as he raised his glass to his lips, it shattered. She warned him it would happen again if he did not desist. He ignored her, attributing the breakage to a freak accident. 'So saying,' he continued, 'I half filled the tumbler and prepared to drink it. But no sooner had the glass touched my lips than I felt it shatter between my fingers and my hand bled, wounded by a broken piece. She left the room, laughing in my face most outrageously.'

While in Egypt, in Cairo, she had formed her ill-starred *Société Spirite*, an organisation for the investigation of psychic phenomena according to the theories of Allan Kardec, who advocated Spiritism as a science rather than Spiritualism as a religion. Unfortunately, the mediums she employed were opportunists rather than psychics, ladies who had been attracted to the area by the well-paid navvies who had built the Suez Canal. When the navvies left the ladies had stayed, accepting any chance to earn a living. Genuine phenomena had been unforthcoming so they had stooped to fraud.

Madame left Cairo, urged on her way by a madman brandishing a revolver, 'possessed,' she wrote to her sister 'by some vile spook' who accused her of sending she-demons to haunt him. The police arrived and resolved the situation. She later confessed that the debacle was her fault. Mahatma had warned her the time had not been ripe to form a Society but, in her headstrong way, she had forged ahead.

Madame's hatred of alcohol – and in her opinion it was one of the biggest barriers to psychic development – was possibly why she had not contacted Maggie. It was the reason Maggie's powers had dimmed and sitters were leaving dissatisfied. Even when Blavatsky became world-famous she continued to ignore Maggie. On the other hand, Kate is mentioned admiringly several times in *Isis Unveiled*.

Madame Blavatsky's work for her Mahatma and her meeting with her future lifetime partner, Colonel Olcott, commenced in 'The Green Tavern', Chittenden, Vermont, on 14 October 1874. They were both there, independently of each other, to investigate the Eddy brothers.

'*Permettez moi, Madame*' were the words that brought two of occultism's most famous pioneers together. Colonel Olcott spoke them to Madame Blavatsky as she rolled a cigarette and put it to her lips; she smoked a pound of tobacco a day. The Colonel proffered a match. He'd heard her speaking French with her companion. All noble Russians spoke French – Russian was the language of peasants, a tongue with which to address the servants.

The Colonel had not been so gallant when he had first seen her. 'Good gracious, look at that specimen, will you,' he'd exclaimed to his colleague. Already immensely stout, she had shorn her frizzy hair, contrary to the fashion of the day, a tobacco pouch hung round her neck and she wore a scarlet shirt to express sympathy with Garibaldi. Yet, there was beauty there; she had enormous turquoise eyes and the refined hands of a concert pianist which she had, indeed, once been, having taken part in a performance of a triple concerto with the celebrated Clara Schumann.

The Eddy farm, now renamed 'The Green Tavern' and transformed into a tourist resort, provided a showcase for the talents of William and Horatio Eddy, both of whom had the power of bringing back the dead in physical form. Their fame had spread throughout the world. They were illiterate farmers but born of psychic stock. Their mother took pride in that one of her ancestors was hanged as a witch in the Salem trials. Their father, sadly for them, hated anything to do with Spiritualism, an unloving and sadistic man he had violently ill-treated them. By the time the Colonel came to investigate them they had, understandably, soured into surly middle age. A warm-hearted man himself, the Colonel was astonished at their phenomena but never took to them as people. But then, the Colonel's privileged upbringing had been quite different to the savage dragging up of the Eddys.

Their histories related a childhood of spontaneous levitation and, like the Foxes, uncontrolled raps. Furry elementals manifested in their room and their father, believing this the work of Satan, called on God's blessing as he punched, kicked, burned and scalded them senseless. Since this had no remedial effect on the phenomena he decided to make money out of them and put them on tour.

They went down well. Part of the fun for the audience was that they were allowed to torture the boys at will. Their father encouraged them to be tightly bound; the more brutal the better, from which savagery the boys bore scars all their lives. If the audience decided the boys were working through the devil, they might be attacked. Sometimes they fell into trances and the audience was invited to rouse them by whatever means it chose. They bore no love for humanity, which in no way affected their amazing abilities.

An item in *The Banner of Light*, on the materialisations at Chittenden, had inspired the Colonel to investigate for the *Daily Graphic*, the New York paper for which he wrote. An artist, Alfred Kappes, who would draw the manifested spirits for the *Graphic*, accompanied him. The Colonel was not a Spiritualist, he was a sceptic, and had taken the *Graphic* commission in the hope of an exposé.

Part of the Eddys' repertoire was a talking goose, possessed by the spirit of a murder victim. Possessed animals have cropped up in the psychic field forever; 2,000 years ago St Mark wrote of the Gadarene swine, that Jesus caused to be possessed.[11] Witnesses swore that the Eddy goose had the power of speech. It would mutter 'oh, dear, what shall I do?' and 'God save my goslings' and would startle sitters in the séance room with blood-curdling shrieks of 'Murder!' If the Colonel, however, witnessed the goose he published no notes on it.

Whatever the reality of the goose, the manifestations witnessed by the Colonel gave him pause for thought. He was later to incorporate his reports in *People from the Other World*, his book of psychic research based on the *Graphic* articles, 'mysteries which,' he wrote, 'for many ages, have been confined to the temples and pagodas of Egypt and Hindustan.'[12]

Prior to Madame Blavatsky's arrival at Chittenden, the Colonel had been amazed by the Eddys' spectacular open-air séances. It must be said that whatever the motivation for their demonstrations, it was not financial. A paltry $8 a week was the charge for food and accommodation, basic as it was, and there were no fees for the séances.

William Eddy, the more powerful medium, had a guide in the form of an elderly Native American lady called Honto. Sitters gathered in the moonlight outside 'Honto's Cave' as she appeared in regalia often accompanied by ten or more strapping braves while William sat in a makeshift cabinet under trees.

The common sense deduction would be that the Eddys arranged for actors to play these parts. The Colonel thought so too, but could discover no evidence for this when he examined the site. Neither was there any sign of 'actors' outside the séances, in or near the Tavern, which was situated in the midst of the Green Hills, miles from any habitation. There were also indoor séances, lit by a kerosene lamp, during which William sat in a cabinet on a stage. Materialisations were heralded by music, the instruments, played by luminous hands, floating in the air in front of the audience.

The doughty Colonel, who extended his stay to several weeks, examined both stage and cabinet before and after séances. He also hired a team of carpenters and builders to inspect the restricted backstage area. They concluded it was impossible for anyone to enter or leave undetected by the audience. When Madame Blavatsky arrived, unannounced and unknown, materialisations occurred at an unprecedented rate, most of them centering on her. The audience, including the Colonel, watched in wonder, as the figure of a Russian in national costume, clutching a guitar, built up in front of her. 'Speak to me, my good fellow!' she thundered. The figure seemed cowed and could not utter. In stern tones she bade it, if it could not speak, to play the tune *Lezguinka*. It did this and added a dance to appease her. Madame announced he was a Georgian named Michalko Guegidze who had died five years ago. As the forms appeared, Madame made it clear they should obey her commands and smartly at that, and it seemed, they did. She obviously had a power over them.

She later told the Colonel that she had conjured up the spirits herself and could do so at will, techniques she had learned during her years of study under her Mahatma. She was never controlled, she controlled the spirits. Later, she was to distance herself from Spiritualism in preference to occultism, but she always claimed, and frequently demonstrated, that she could do anything any medium could do. At that time it suited her Mahatma's purpose for her to ally herself to the Spiritualist cause, but her main purpose was to reveal shards of Ancient Wisdom to counteract the waves of materialism that threatened to engulf a dark world.

Still the parade continued. Some spoke in Russian, others in French, an African sorcerer who wore a crown of ringing bells attached to animal horns followed a Kurdish cavalier, armed with swords and pistols. These spoke in their own dialects. The penultimate apparition was Madame's uncle, whom she recognised by the Cross of St Anne he wore and the finale was, as always at the Eddys', Honto, who bared her bosom and invited a certain Mrs Cleveland, from the audience, to feel her beating heart. There was indeed a feeble palpitation. Before departing, Honto twirled her ectoplasmic shawl above her head. (The term 'ectoplasm' was not coined until later, by the French Nobel prize winner Professor Charles Richet, but since the substance has been in use since Spiritualism began, I have used it for convenience.)

Some of Kappes' drawings of these forms are reproduced in *People from the Other World*. They look like extras from a movie set but, the Colonel assures us, according to his extensive research they were not actors. How could a bunch of local actors have spoken to Madame Blavatsky in her native Russian, let alone French and other dialects? The Eddys themselves had trouble assembling a sentence in English; the Colonel had barely been able to comprehend them when he had first arrived.

The Colonel was impressed by the Eddys, but it was his conversations with Madame Blavatsky that converted him from a sceptic to an unshakeable believer in supernatural forces. She told him of her Mahatma, whom he was soon to see for himself and who left an apport – no scrap of filthy, stained ectoplasm this, but an elaborate Sikh turban, still in the possession of the Theosophical Society, an institution later founded by the Colonel and Madame to promote Mahatmic teachings and which thrives today.

The *Daily Graphic* told its intrigued readers of Madame Blavatsky's extraordinary powers. She did not disappoint with investigation and proved her occult strength to many a reporter. She was soon internationally famous. Her fame even eclipsed that of the Foxes. She and the Colonel faced many storms and during one turbulent period she was savaged almost beyond redemption. The scandal reverberated round the world. It almost finished her.

The Eddys, for all their brilliance, never found happiness. They, who had brought so much colour to other lives, were to die reclusive and embittered, loathing humanity. William would never discuss Spiritualism in his old age, let alone demonstrate it. Their sister Mary, who had taken a back seat in the halcyon days, fared best, becoming a professional medium herself although never reaching her brothers' pinnacle of success.

The men survived into the twentieth century. Horatio became a gardener, seemingly gaining comfort, Tolstoy fashion, from the soil and died in 1922. William died in 1932, at the great, but unfulfilled age of 99.

Although there was now no financial necessity for Kate to accept clients, she felt duty-bound to carry on as a medium in a private capacity, rather as Leah was doing. She was, also like Leah, married to a man hooked on her fame.

Another celebrity medium in London, who would have carried on come what may, was Mrs Guppy, named among the guests at Kate's wedding. Mrs Guppy had electrified London by starring in a case of teleportation on 3 June 1871. Teleportation had taken place before, notably in the seventeenth century, when Sister Mary of Agreda claimed to have been transported from Spain to Mexico no fewer than 500 times in just over a decade (nuns are good at teleportation, there are several instances). But that was long ago and far away. Spiritualist London of the 1870s had not witnessed such flamboyance.

Mrs Guppy was a lady of great personality and matching girth. It is important to mark her weight bearing in mind what happened. On the night in question she was at home in Highgate and, preparatory to retiring, going through the household accounts with a servant. She was dressed in nightgown and slippers, sitting in front of a blazing fire, ledger and pen in her hand. She had just written 'Onions' when suddenly she was gone. The house was searched and she was not there. She had disappeared.

Simultaneously, in Lamb's Conduit Street, Holborn, three miles away, a dark circle was being held, consisting of eight sitters. Three of these were Charles Williams and Frank Herne, whose house it was, and William Harrison, editor of *The Spiritualist*. A sitter at the Holborn circle had remarked in jest, bearing in mind Mrs Guppy's weight, how marvellous it would be if she were transported to their séance.

A thud was heard. Lights were put on and Mrs Guppy was discovered in her nightdress, hair dishevelled, ledger in hand, ink still wet from the last entry, standing on the table. She was by no means pleased to be discovered in her state of undress in a strange circle, although she knew the sitters. She stated she had no idea how it had happened but had suddenly found herself there. The naturalist, Dr Alfred Russel Wallace, who had championed Mrs Guppy's early career, later took statements from the sitters, whose honesty he vouched for, concluding: 'The only alternative to a real supernormal phenomenon ... is that there was an elaborate conspiracy of some dozen people, almost all honest, to deceive their fellow workers and the public.'[13] Mrs Guppy specialised in apports and had often been examined, in test conditions, by Dr Wallace, where on one occasion she had materialised a six-foot sunflower attached to a clod of damp earth. Mrs Guppy's apports were frequently damp and dew-bedecked. She boasted she was the first medium in England to produce such effects.

After her teleportation, she was returned in a cab to her home and startled household. Although not as startled as may be expected, as anyone living with Mrs Guppy was accustomed to eccentric behaviour. The incident was written up in *The Spiritualist*, backed up by all eight sitters and a servant.

Teleportation aside, Mrs Guppy's phenomena were astounding and many of the aristocracy, who frequently sat with her, testified to it. Sitters could request items, which she would materialise in circle, and these requests did not have to be uttered – a thought would do. Princess

Marguerite of Naples silently requested a cactus – twenty dropped on the table. The Duchess d'Arpino asked for sand and that, too, cascaded down complete with live starfishes. Eels, lobsters and butterflies were dropped and, most extraordinary of all, three dead ducks, plucked and oven ready. The spirit world was obviously not over-bothered by vegetarianism.

A pile of sugarplums aported in the dark and the spirits were asked whether they could detect colour in a darkened room. When lights were put on they were found sorted into groups of colour. Mrs Guppy produced a heavy slab of ice and, it was pointed out to sceptics, that if this had been hidden before the séance it would have melted. It was already starting to thaw. Her stupendous feats aroused jealously and, as Ronald Pearsall[14] points out, 'There was professional rivalry, professional hatred.' Mrs Guppy was not above such things herself.

Irksome to stout Mrs Guppy was the success of pretty 16-year-old Florence Cook who held materialisation séances in her home in Dalston. Florence had debuted as a 'face medium', producing materialised faces from a window in her cabinet, and some of these had been witnessed by C.M. Davies who noted[15] they 'gave the idea of a mask. I am not saying it was a mask. I am only throwing out a hint that, if the "spirits" wish to convince people they should let the neck be well seen.'

Florence was soon producing full materialisations, the most famous being Katie King, a legendary figure in Spiritualism, and daughter of the famous John King, the bloodthirsty ex-pirate, simultaneously manifesting at Madame Blavatsky's New York séances and the Herne and Williams' séances in London, where he allowed his substantial hand to be shaken by all.

Katie was following in her father's footsteps. Reporters were baffled at her séances, as she left the cabinet where Florence was tied to her chair behind closed doors, and walked the circle, holding the hands of awed sitters. Some suspected the lovely Florence was masquerading as Katie. Others, mostly male, didn't care, it was worth a trip to Dalston just to hold her hand and gaze into her lovely face. Mrs Guppy viewed Katie's success with alarm and perpetrated the masquerade theory. She was joined in her campaign by a married couple, Jenny and Nelson Holmes, residents of Philadelphia although, at that time, practising in London's Old Quebec Street.

Mrs Guppy devised the sinister conspiracy of arranging for a confederate to attend a Katie séance and throw acid in her face. That would certainly decide whether Florence was Katie or not. This was too much for the Holmeses who ordered Mrs Guppy from their house. Having been bilked of the acid test, Mrs Guppy persuaded her husband to attend one of Florence's circles and grab Katie, rather as Helen Duncan's ectoplasm would be grabbed in years to come, and expose her as Florence. He tried, but was prevented from doing this by other sitters. In the midst of the fight, Katie yanked out part of his beard and badly scratched his face before retreating into the cabinet, a very perturbed spirit.

It was some minutes before sitters were allowed to check on Florence. When they were permitted to enter the cabinet, Florence was found still bound to her chair – a minor blip in a career that continued to thrive. Mrs Guppy abandoned Katie but planned revenge on the Holmeses for letting her down. On her instructions, another confederate, James Clark, sat at a Holmes dark séance where musical instruments were playing. He struck a match, which was against the rules, and as the flame flared, the instruments clattered to the ground and Mrs Holmes was seen scampering back to the cabinet. Again, a fight broke out and Clark was nearly thrown from an upstairs window.

Mrs Holmes later explained, through her guide, that her out-of-cabinet appearance was on his instructions. He knew of Clark's intentions and had urged her to take the match from his hand before damage could be done. Why spirits, strong enough to strum instruments, could not have removed the match themselves, he did not explain.

Again, Mrs Guppy was disappointed. She had ordered Clark to shatter the Holmeses elaborate cabinet before leaving and take photographs of anything suspicious, which she would distribute to newspapers. The Holmeses were forced to leave London under a cloud. Before doing so they fired a broadside at Mrs Guppy, accusing her of running a brothel, her séances a cover for prostitutes to fondle elderly clients. That was improbable, Mrs Guppy was rich and there was no need for her to become a Madame. She certainly brightened the shadowy streets of old London.

The Holmeses returned to Philadephia and were soon in trouble again. This time it centred round Robert Dale Owen. Katie King, while still gracing Florence Cook's London séances, when she was not being attacked or subject to acid plots, had, like her father, become transatlantic. She was now a regular visitor at the Holmes' Philadelphia circles. Owen had extended his research to the Holmeses, who introduced him to Katie. It was a fatal meeting.

Katie was considered no less beautiful in America than she was in London. On his own admission, Owen, then 73, became infatuated. Ringing in his ears were the words of Charles Livermore, whose diary Owen had read for *The Debatable Land*. Livermore had gushed, after one of Estelle's appearances: 'No pen can describe the exquisite transcendent beauty of what was this night revealed.' Owen, too, was experiencing nights of exquisite transcendental beauty. Katie had expressed affection for him and, in token, had allowed him to cut off a lock of her beautiful hair. He had left some circles in a heated manner.

Owen bought Katie some nice pieces of jewellery that she promptly dematerialised to take back with her into Spirit. John King also came through and announced that he wanted to dictate his autobiography to another sitter, Dr Henry T. Child, President of the Spiritualist Association of Philadelphia. The doctor accepted this honour with relish.

Owen's dream of love was shattered when he discovered that Katie was no spirit but an earthly employee of the Holmeses, a Mrs Eliza White. She was exposed by another sitter who had called to see the Holmeses not knowing they were away, to find the door answered by Mrs White. Astounded by her likeness to Katie he had questioned her and she had broken down, confessed she had posed as Katie and returned the jewellery, which had not gone to Spirit at all, to Owen.

The Philadelphia newspapers made the most of it. Dr Child resigned as President of the Philadelphia Spiritualists and abandoned King's memoirs for which the world, regrettably, is bereft. The humiliated Owen, honourable man that he was, wrote to *The Banner of Light* confessing he was the victim of fraud. This did not destroy his faith in Spiritualism and not entirely in the Holmeses; he believed that most of their phenomena were genuine. Like many others, they had augmented the real with the false. Mrs White sold her story to the *Philadelphia Enquirer*, thus recompensing herself for the loss of Owen's jewellery.

That was not the end of the matter. Colonel Olcott and Madame Blavatsky read Mrs White's report and were unconvinced. This was an assault on Spiritualism that had to be rectified. Madame Blavatsky declared Dr Child was the devil incarnate for resigning and that he should be horsewhipped. She did not deny that Owen had been duped – she could hardly do so, he had admitted it himself – but resented the imputation that Katie was a fraud. Mrs White's impostures did not invalidate Katie's genuine manifestations.

The Colonel and Madame went to Philadelphia and held a test séance with the Holmeses under the Colonel's strict conditions. Mrs Holmes was placed completely inside a specially made linen bag, confining her arms and legs and the opening of which was sealed with wax, then locked in her cabinet. There was no full-scale materialisation. But a face appeared in one of the cabinet's windows: 'I could not think of anything to compare it with,' wrote the Colonel, 'except the face of a corpse, half-eaten by rats or crabs.'[16] Certainly not the beautiful Katie.

Other séances were held at the Holmeses and at the Colonel's lodgings, Mrs Holmes always in her bag. Robert Dale Owen attended some, hoping desperately his lovely Katie would appear and prove he had not been entirely taken in. John King came through and allowed his beard to be handled, proving he was not an illusion. Katie's face and one hand made some sort of vague appearance through a cabinet window.

Wire mesh was fixed to the inside of the windows, preventing any physical form from stretching from the cabinet and guitars were heard playing inside. This was not good enough for the Colonel who would not rest until he had witnessed the full-scale materialisation of Katie. This was finally achieved. With Mrs Holmes in her bag, a white figure slowly emerged from the cabinet, quite different in form from Mrs Holmes. Unmistakably Katie.

Madame Blavatsky viewed her silently then uttered a mystic word that may have been Arabic; the Colonel does not reveal it[17] and Katie retreated back into the cabinet. Mrs Holmes was found in a cataleptic trance from which it was difficult to wake her. The Colonel considered his job well done. Spiritualism had been vindicated. Katie King was a real spirit. She had appeared before him as he had commanded.

According to Madame Blavatsky, that was not quite the case. She had brought about the materialisation herself which explained Mrs Holmes' catalepsy. The shock of a genuine manifestation of Katie had made her pass out. Madame Blavatsky had materialised Katie for fear further exposure of fraud might fatally damage the Spiritualist cause. She had produced a replica of Katie. As she stated, anything a medium could do, she could do better.

8

There is a not altogether flattering description of the recently married Kate Fox at this time, given by contemporary Spiritualist, the Rev. John Page Hopps: '... a small, thin, very intelligent, but rather simpering little woman, with nice gentle manners and a quiet enjoyment of her experiments which entirely saved her from the slightest touch of self-importance or affectation of mystery.'

Kate's public work was now curtailed but, at her husband's wish, she resumed her experiments with Crookes. The scientist was convinced of her authenticity, as endorsed by his compendious book *Researches in the Phenomena of Spiritualism*. Their work had continued until her marriage, although Kate had had occasional lapses into alcoholism when Henry had been away and this had hampered it. Henry had, in fact, got wind of Kate's problem before they had married and she had, honestly, confessed to him. She was so determined to overcome it, though, and had made such strides to do so, that it had not deterred the infatuated Henry.

Crookes had intended to devote a single month to the examination of psychic phenomena but once he'd started he became addicted. He spent a great deal of time testing Daniel Dunglas Home, particularly his astonishing self-playing accordion, and was similarly fascinated by Kate. He also investigated Florence Cook and Katie King, convinced of the reality of Katie. But it was rumoured that he had succumbed to the charms of Florence, as others had and would, and that her beauty had swayed his objectivity. Some said they were locked in an affair.

Kate called at Crookes' house one evening, by appointment, and he took her straight to the dining room where the séance was to be held. There would be just three sitters – him, a trusted friend and Kate. He locked the door, as always before a séance. It was rapped that a dark séance was required. Crookes held both Kate's hands in his, his feet over hers, and the tinkling of a bell was heard, sounding in the corners of the room and above their heads. After five minutes it thudded to the table, motionless. Crookes remarked that it sounded like his own hand bell but couldn't be, as this was in the library. Lights were put on and it was, indeed, the very bell. He went to the library, where his sons were, and asked if they'd seen the bell. One had, a few moments previously, but it wasn't where he'd seen it. It had, apparently, been transported through a locked door from one room to another and rung over their heads while Kate's hands were held. He could find no explanation other than the supernatural.

Crookes published his experiments with Kate but such was the indignation of scientific opposition that he refused to allow them to be reprinted. He acknowledged, though, that he believed there existed 'invisible and intelligent beings' who claimed to be the spirits of the dead, but he required proof that they were what they claimed to be. Kate had to cease her activities with Crookes shortly after this as she found, to her and her husband's joy, that she was pregnant.

Nothing about Kate Fox was ordinary. Her pregnancy was difficult and her child, Ferdinand, was exceptional. He attracted attention right from the start. Her attitude to this says a great deal about Kate. She couldn't wait to thrust him into the limelight and, by doing so, thrust herself into it as well. There was no way Mrs Fox-Jencken, as she now styled herself, was ever going to be a housewife.

Ferdinand Lowenstein Dietrich, or Ferdie, or Boysie, as he was known, was born in London on 19 September 1873 and was a rapper from birth. Madame Blavatsky tells us in *Isis Unveiled*: 'Rappings occurred on his pillow and cradle, and also on his father's person, when he held the child in his lap and Mrs Jencken was absent from home.' Kate adored Ferdie and wrote to Leah in excitement that he was speaking at 8 weeks old. That may have been parental pride but an article in *Medium and Daybreak* on 8 May 1874, authenticated by a fellow solicitor of Henry's, Mr J. Watson, states that he was automatically writing before he was 6 months old.

The first recorded instance happened in Brighton, where Henry had a cottage, and where he, Kate, the nursemaid and, presumably Mr Watson, were present. A pencil miraculously appeared in Ferdie's hand.

Most mothers would have been alarmed at a baby holding a pointed instrument but, when the maid queried where the pencil had come from, Kate merely remarked that she thought her son wanted to write something. He did indeed, or rather a spirit did. While she held the paper a mature hand wrote that he/she 'loved this little boy'. As Madame Blavatsky noted: 'The professional and scientific rank of Mr Jencken made it in the highest degree improbable that he would lend himself to a deception.' Other reports state that Ferdie wrote in Greek, which translated reads 'Who believes in me shall live', as well as other things in English.

Child prophets were the vogue. Emma Hardinge Britten wrote of 4- and 5-year-old mediums. *Lloyd's Weekly Newspaper* for March 1875, contained an account of the Little Prophet of Saar-Louis: 'The mother had just been confined, the midwife was holding forth garrulously "on the blessed little creature", and the friends were congratulating the father on his luck, when somebody asked what time it was. Judge of the surprise of all, on hearing the new-born babe reply distinctly "Two o'clock!" But this was nothing to what followed. The company were looking on the infant, with speechless wonder and dismay, when it opened its eyes and said: "I have been sent into the world to tell you that 1875 will be a good year, but that 1876 will be a year of blood." Having uttered this prophecy it turned on its side and expired, aged half-an-hour.'

Madame Blavatsky researched this story and wrote in *Isis*: 'The year, 1876, just passed (we write in February 1877) was emphatically, and, from the standpoint of March, 1875, unexpectedly - a year of blood. In the Danubian principalities was written one of the bloodiest chapters of the history of war and rapine – a chapter of outrages of Moslem upon Christian that has scarcely been paralleled since Catholic soldiers butchered the simple natives of North and South America by tens of thousands ... 1875 was a year of plenty, and 1876, to the surprise of everybody, a year of carnage.'

The Victorians were great explorers and tales circulated of the mystical land of Tibet. There were accounts, which delighted London, of how Tibetans selected their Dalai Lama through a series of reincarnation tests. It was said these babes could converse from birth, foresee the future and administer advice. It was believed all High Lamas possessed supernatural ability. The legends still persist and, as recently as 2004, author Mick Brown recorded the belief that, the sixteenth incarnation of the Karmapa Lama (just below the Dalai in rank) spoke even before birth: 'While still in his mother's womb the child could be heard reciting the mantra *Urn Mani Padme Hung*, and immediately before his birth, it is said, he disappeared from the womb altogether, reappearing the following day. No sooner had he been born than the child took seven steps, saying "Mother, mother, I am going away ..."[1]

Ferdie Jencken was retarded compared to those Tibetan aristocrats but, according to contemporaneous accounts, he gave several other demonstrations of his pushchair power and, when this happened at night, his lips and eyes were said to glow in the dark, indicative of the spirit within.

There had been a case of a haunting involving Ferdie; it had happened one evening when his parents had been visiting the new Crystal Palace at Sydenham, leaving him in the care of the servants. When they returned, the frightened staff told of a veiled woman with piercing eyes who had walked through the house, as soon as the Jenckens had left, and gone to Ferdie's room, hovering over his bed. No one recalled having let her in. A policeman had been summoned but could find no trace of her. The cook resigned.

Soon there was another little Jencken. Kate gave birth again in 1875, but this time in America, as she wanted her son to be born on her native soil. The urge overcame her during pregnancy when she suddenly felt homesick for friends and family. Henry and Ferdie were her closest family, of course, and, by her marriage, she was now an Englishwoman, but the ties of blood are strong. Henry, as ever, indulged her. Leah, who had visited England and considered herself quite the cosmopolitan, had been instrumental in urging Kate to go to London but she, too, now missed her sister. Their parting had been fretful, in that Leah had been concerned for Kate's health and the possibility of disgrace, but that had been swept into the past. Kate's drinking days were done.

It was agreed that Kate would stay with Leah in New York; she was, after all, now a member of the English upper classes. Daniel's feelings concerning his house guest may have been muted but, like Henry, he indulged his wife.

Kate, Ferdie and his nursemaid set sail from Southampton in the *Helvetia* in October 1874, and Henry was to join them for Christmas and remain for the birth, expected in February. All seemed set for a rosy future; what a blessing she could not see what was to come. The nursemaid looked after Ferdie, and Henry stayed on board until the last moment when he left by launch, waving his wife a tender goodbye.

England had done well by Kate; it seemed as though America was about to do so, too. Kate was delighted to see Leah and Maggie, who was allowed to meet her at Leah's. Maggie was improved from the time Kate had bid farewell to that lonesome half-mad figure on the quay and, while not one hundred per cent, had pulled herself together. For the first time in years the girls could look at each other eye to sober eye.

Leah adored little Ferdie and was soon relating tales of his genius. He was automatically writing again and did so one evening, as Kate and Leah sat together. He'd been fractious and to keep him quiet Kate gave him a pencil and paper to play with. Leah held a corner of the paper while Ferdie took another and, to her delight, he started writing. It was actually his grandmother, Margaret, who was writing through him, telling how she often watched over them.

Kate caught up with old friends, among them the Taylors who had been so good to her and with whom she stayed for a couple of weeks. They were still running their pelvic massage centre and were delighted with the improvement in her. Henry could not make New York for Christmas, being detained by business worries, more severe than he let on to Kate, and these caused him to miss the birth of Henry Junior who arrived prematurely in January. His birth had none of the complications of Ferdie's, but he was a frail little chap. For all Kate's strong constitution, both her children were weak, possibly as a result of her years of drinking.

The birth of her new son partially compensated for the death of one of Kate's great champions. On 5 April 1874 Judge John Edmonds had died in New York. His belief in Spiritualism had cost him his career but, notwithstanding, he had done much for penal reform, after-prison care of prisoners and the abolition of capital punishment.

Kate was delighted to see Henry when he eventually arrived in May 1875 to take her back to London. He generously agreed to pay for Maggie to visit them in England, which she did several times. It was quite a coup to have both Fox sisters under his roof.

The British National Association of Spiritualists had been founded in 1873, with its headquarters in London, yet neither Kate nor Maggie seems to have made much impression on it. Even so, Maggie attracted quite a following in London. When her sensibilities were not dimmed by alcohol, she was a fine medium. She had by now come to some sort of compromise with her promise to Elisha to renounce Spiritualism as she had had to earn her living by readings; there was nothing else she could do. In the still of the night, though, her terrors returned. She was betraying her church and, more importantly, Elisha. Was he cross with her?

Henry Jr was now showing incipient signs of mediumship. His proud parents gave him all the encouragement they could. Meanwhile, another old stalwart, Robert Dale Owen, died in 1877. His last years had been sad, spent mostly in and out of mental asylums. The wheel of Fortune maliciously creaked round again and, in 1881, just before his 60th birthday, Henry Jencken had a stroke and died. Kate was lost and there was worse to come. A rich sorrow is one thing but a poor one quite another and this was a poor one. Henry's concentration on Spiritualism had made him neglect his business concerns. He had kept his money worries from his wife but Kate found, to her horror, that his fortune amounted to just a few hundred pounds.

She was 44, widowed with two sickly children, with no means of support. Kate tried to keep things going but it was hopeless. English friends did their best, among them the critic Samuel Carter Hall who could see, as could anyone who knew Kate, that she was no organiser, no Leah. She was helpless at caring for herself, let alone her children. He helped her in a practical way by setting up a fund to educate her sons, appointing himself treasurer and sensibly not allowing Kate to touch the money. She repaid his kindness the only way she could.

Hall's beloved wife, writer Anne Maria Hall, had recently died and Kate contacted her. On his birthday, full of expectation, he had a dark session with Kate at his home. As had happened with Crookes, a hand-bell rang all over the room. But this was one Hall had brought with him, on request, and had held in one hand while he held both Kate's hands in the other. He felt the bell gently being taken from him before it started to ring. He had also placed an accordion under the table, and this played tunes, a similar phenomenon to that achieved by Daniel Dunglas Home which had so impressed Crookes. Finally a large bunch of hearts-ease flowers was placed before him and Kate automatically wrote in Mrs Hall's writing: 'I have brought you my token of love.' Hall published an account of the séance in *Light* adding: 'Assuredly Spiritualists owe to this lady a huge debt for the glad tidings she was largely the instrument, selected by Providence, to convey to them.'

Kate tried to maintain herself in the comfortable style to which she had become accustomed but there was no way this could continue. The more her expensive solicitor tried to extract money from Henry's estate the worse matters became. Much of Henry's income had derived from German properties but his interest in them ceased with his death.

The Society for Psychical Research (SPR) was founded in 1882 to investigate psychic phenomena in a 'spirit of unimpassioned enquiry'. Its first President, Henry Sidgwick, Professor of Moral Philosophy at Cambridge, was ably assisted by his formidable wife, Eleanor, future Principal of Newnham College, Cambridge who became the scourge of many a dodgy medium. Mrs Sidgwick had already tested Kate soon after her arrival in England and, although sceptical, had come to no specific conclusion. Under the auspices of the SPR she tested her again. Kate was searched, her ankles tied and placed on glass, nothing new in that, and the raps, indeed, sounded. Mrs Sidgwick was inclined to believe at first they were made by supernatural agency, although she later changed her mind.

These tests did not help Kate financially, but a tour of Russia did. Official censorship frowned on Spiritualism in Russia and, consequently, it had not been embraced with the same fervour as in America and England. But certain members of the aristocracy had travelled, and returned with tales of the fabulous phenomena they had witnessed. Spiritualism held the appeal of the taboo and, in closed groups, mediumship flourished.

An interested party was the Hon. Alexander N. Aksakof, Imperial Councillor of State to the Tsar, who, among much else, had translated Swedenborg's *Heaven and Hell* into German, publishing it in Switzerland. He was to become an advocate of Madame d'Esperance, writing an introduction to her book *Shadow Land* and featuring her in his own work *A Case of Partial Dematerialisation*. The year after Henry's death, Aksakof invited Kate to Russia for a fee of £100. The coronation of Tsar Alexander was to take place and he believed certain officials might benefit from spirit advice. Kate's powers were not unknown to Russian academics; Professor Butlerof of the University of St Petersburg had already investigated her, coming to the favourable conclusion that the raps were independent of 'every such artificial explanation of the phenomena'.[2]

Kate insisted on taking her sons with her. It would be a difficult journey and Aksakof tried to dissuade her but she would not be parted from them. The raps supported her so Aksakof had to agree. The journey would have exhausted anyone, let alone a middle-aged lady with two sickly children. Kate, to her relief, was to give no public demonstrations but concentrate on private sittings. She was an exotic, viewed with the same curiosity as a banana or Bird of Paradise and granted the same

leeway to speak as a Court Jester, and probably less respect. Kate was
an entertainment, a welcome diversion. Tales of her powers spread and
were, doubtless, enhanced. In addition to her fee she was given many
expensive presents, most of which had to be sold when she returned to
London. Impoverishment soon returned.

In New York, Maggie, just about in command of herself but heading
for the skids (she had made a terrific effort to be on form for Kate), was
in the midst of tests by The Seybert Commission. The late Henry Seybert,
a Spiritualist philanthropist, had left a bequest of $60,000 to fund a Chair
of Philosophy at the University of Pennsylvania, providing this involved
an impartial investigation into Spiritualism. She was tested twice and did
not sail through with flying colours on either occasion. The raps were so
faint as to be inaudible. She refused to be tested a third time.

Kate and Maggie corresponded and both were depressed and frightened of poverty. They felt a need for each other. There was no question
of Maggie coming to London, and by now Kate had had enough of
England; it was no longer so marvellous. In the summer of 1885 she
and her sons embarked for New York arriving unannounced at the
Underhills'. A surprised and by no means thrilled Leah took her in. Leah
could tell from one look at Kate's face that her widowed sister was not
doing well.

If Leah had noticed a difference in Kate then Kate noticed a change
in Leah. She and Daniel had grown fond of eating out, in fact aside from
Spiritualism, it had become their main interest in life. The regular carriage trips to restaurants and the years of comfortable living showed in
her figure. With age she had become even stouter and more florid.

Leah did not like a house to be too quiet and most of her nephews
and nieces, who had been frequent visitors, had now grown up. Her
favourite niece Leah, known as Little Leah (David's daughter named in
her honour), had occupied pride of position for a while, but was now
out of favour. Daniel, who had become curmudgeonly, had taken against
her after she had defied him. He, who was her uncle only by marriage,
had decided she must marry a rich friend of his, twenty years her senior.
Taking after Aunt Leah in resolution, Little Leah had shaken her fizzed
head, stamped her high-heeled shoe and balked at this. She had been
ordered from the house until she came to her senses – which she did
shortly after by marrying a handsome young farmer.

Leah missed the limelight and had decided to publish her memoirs.
Every press item, document and pertinent letter had been stored away.

Now was the time to bestow these gifts on humanity. Before Kate had arrived, in the uneasy quietness of her house, between restaurant visits, Leah had turned her attention to sorting out her mountain of memorabilia. A friend was to write the text.

The Missing Link in Modern Spiritualism came out the year Kate had returned from London. As Maggie and Kate's leading roles were kept strictly to a second feature, Kate was not best pleased. It was a rambling collection of essays and letters, with no real shape, but it bristled with Leah's personality. There was humour, too, some intentional some not. It remains an invaluable first-hand account of those gusty early days of Spiritualism, however biased.

The atmosphere at the Underhills' was rendered more strained by Ferdie and Henry. Usually, Leah would have no trouble accommodating children, indeed she had been very fond of Ferdie, but now older and testier, she took against them. Ferdie, whose baby automatic writing she had trumpeted, seemed to have lost his power. Maggie gives a reason for this in *The Death Blow to Spiritualism* where she contemptuously declares his powers fraudulent. She says Kate had written on the paper before giving it to the baby, then let someone else retrieve it, summing up dismissively: 'So much for that and kindred marvels of infant "mediumship".'

Ferdie Jeneken, so far as is known, has never, since that early period of his existence, exhibited any 'mediumistic power'; Maggie had written that for a number of reasons, none of them to do with Christian charity. As Ferdie grew older he became interested in Spiritualism and did give some demonstrations of clairvoyance, but these were poor affairs, unworthy of his Fox lineage and, at the time, he was in financial straits and needed to earn a living. With Kate Fox as his mother what else would he do? Thanks to the Hall trust fund he was sent to school in New York and became quite studious. Henry was more difficult. Diagnosed epileptic his behaviour was erratic and he was deemed too unstable to attend school.

Kate did not move in with Maggie, because Maggie preferred to stay alone. She had been alone for so long she was unable to live with anyone else now. Elisha's lifestyle, the style to which she had once aspired, could not have been further removed from the way she now lived. He would have been mortified had he seen her, something of which she was aware.

Kate went to the peppermint farm and stayed with David and Elizabeth for a while. This, too, was a disaster. Gone were the happy days when the girls returned from tours showering presents on everyone, glowing with success. David was a father several times over but good-natured as he was he too did not take to his nephews. She moved to the Taylors but even they felt the strain. They were delighted to see her and told her how well she looked. They meant it kindly but were lying. Kate was drinking again. It seemed the best friend she had and perhaps it was at that time; it certainly brought her the most comfort.

Sarah Taylor was not keen on the boys. Although a mother herself, with children in spirit and on earth, she yearned for the old days when the only children in Kate's life were those in spirit, mainly hers. And Kate was no longer a workhorse, she was disinclined to give endless circles, she was out of practice and did not want to return to that lifestyle.

Kate moved into an apartment in East 84th Street where she gave sittings and, once a week, a demonstration. She worked merely to pay her way. For Kate and Maggie, life was joyless. Kate would take herself off to the many bars in the city and drink solidly, slumping on the counter, sleeping where she fell or in the houses of companions she'd picked up along the way, whose faces she could not remember next day. Sittings were abandoned without notice and, when they were not abandoned, sometimes it would have been better if they had been. For someone whom the spirits had chosen as their ambassador they did not seem to value her too highly. Perhaps they had washed their hands of her?

She was arrested on charges of disturbing the peace and, more seriously, a charge of child neglect. The boys were confiscated while she was absent and taken into care. Someone, she suspected Leah, had reported her to the New York Society for the Prevention of Cruelty to Children, the 'Gerry Society' as it was known, after its founder Eldridge Thomas Gerry.

It broke her heart for she loved her sons and, however negligent a mother she was, they clearly loved her. The boys, 14 and 12 by then, were, in fact, as healthy, fit and clean as they ever had been. They had no complaints about their mother but plenty against those who had taken them from her. The shame was awful for Kate. She had beaten alcoholism during her marriage but knew the current complaints against her were legitimate. She did not, however, believe the confiscation of her boys was justified. During her absences they were able to take care of themselves. Ferdie was almost a man. Many were working at his age.

Kate could not turn to Maggie for comfort. Maggie was no longer in New York. She had returned to London where, for a while, she contemplated living permanently. She was still a legend in London, albeit one that newer models had eclipsed. She had been invited to tour and, as there was absolutely nothing to stay in New York for, and she badly needed money, she had agreed.

Like Kate, before her move to London, Maggie would have gone where she was pointed. She had no sense of belonging anywhere. London was as good as anywhere and there was also a proposed trip to Paris. Not that that excited her. What's the use of the city of romance when you're alone? Kate cabled news of the boys' seizure to Maggie. Although far away and on another continent, Maggie instantly leapt into action by posing as Edward Jencken, Henry's brother, who was living in London but abroad. In his name she cabled the American authorities that she was the boys' legal guardian and demanded they be returned to Kate, who would bring them to London and his care. The boys were British citizens and hastily released into their mother's keeping, the Gerry Society being quite keen to get them off its hands. This was imposture on a grand scale and matters could have been made worse had it been detected.

Kate had had enough of New York. Back with her sons, she was determined not to let them out of her sight; she sailed to Southampton to join Maggie who met them at the dock where there were mutual congratulations and whoops of delight. Maggie was not among those who took against her nephews, she loved them. Maggie's actions in devising and perpetrating this fraud were not those of an out-of-control drunk. A clear head had been needed. She was relatively sober during her English stay. Reynard the Fox, her close companion all her life, had not deserted her.

During the 1920s, when Houdini was writing his scathing *A Magician Among the Spirits* he interviewed a friend of Maggie's, medium W.S. Davis, who told him: 'She was usually sober. She drank considerably during the later years of her life, and often drank too much, but usually she was sober – she drank because of her hypocrisy.' Singer Rosemary Clooney, talking about Billie Holiday, said much the same thing about her narcotics addiction. Miss Holiday was not out of her mind all the time, there were lengthy periods when she was clean as a whistle. So it was with Maggie.

Maggie had another project that was fermenting in her hurt brain. It had been on her mind long before she'd reached London. Between engagements she wandered alone and unrecognised, a lost soul. She attended a materialisation séance given by a prominent medium and realised at once it was fraudulent. She was disgusted. Elisha was playing on her mind, as were the teachings of Catholicism; the whole Spiritualist field, to her distorted mind, seemed contemptible.

Her resentment was not helped by a scandal in New York. The psychic artiste, Madame Ann O'Delia Diss De Barr had been imprisoned for swindling General Luther Marsh out of a fortune. (Years later, in 1921, her confederate Emma Burkett was also in court accused of fabricating President Roosevelt's signature in an attempt at financial gain.)

Maggie wrote an extraordinary letter to the New York *Herald*. Addressed from her lodgings in Gower Street and dated 14 May 1888, she firstly protests at the treatment of her 'dear sister' and the removal of her 'two beautiful boys' then abruptly changes course to announce 'Spiritualism is a curse. God has set his shield against it'. Mediums are 'glaring humbugs', materialisations are 'nonsense' and, as for believers, 'All they will ever achieve for their foolish fanaticism will be loss of money, softening of the brain, and a lingering death.' The outpouring of a disillusioned practitioner or the sentiments of someone who wants to unburden her conscience? In the midst of this tirade, at its heart, she writes that the raps are 'the only part of the phenomena worthy of notice'.

That is extraordinary. If the raps are worthy of notice then they must bear investigation, as indeed they had done for years. A balanced mind cannot notice something that is not there. But Maggie had never attempted to pass them off as the signals of the dead. She didn't know what they were. Her professional card bore the inscription: 'Mrs Kane does not claim any spirit power: But people must judge for themselves.'

Maggie's depression had not lessened when she left England in June bound for New York on the *Italy*. It was an unhappy trip and she was wandering mentally, imagining she saw Elisha among the passengers. She was sure he was conveying some message to her. She would not let him down this time. She was a troublesome passenger but there was something about her that engendered pity. The ship's crew was kindly and when she arrived in New York she gave them all the English money she had left. She claimed, but for their kindness, she would have jumped overboard. That black madness of depression was taking over again.

Kate and the boys remained in London, where a Mrs Cottell, a Spiritualist who had bought the Chelsea house of the late historian Thomas Carlyle, approached Kate with the proposition she give a public séance in the house and contact Carlyle. This was the sort of thing Kate had done countless times before. It was evidence of her declining powers that she was a spectacular flop. The charming Carlyle is famed for his works on the French Revolution and Oliver Cromwell, he was also a supporter of Governor Eyre of Jamaica who had been dismissed from his post due to his vicious treatment of slaves; after Eyre had brutally quelled an uprising, Carlyle had praised him for 'Saving the West Indies and hanging one incendiary mulatto, well worth the gallows, if I can judge.'[3]

Carlyle had died in 1881 so would have been aware of the Foxes, if not an admirer. Some in the audience who had known him wondered how he would react to being called back. Kate claimed to establish contact but the response was disappointing. Piffle in the opinion of some. *Pall Mall* magazine poured scorn on her. She must have been dire because *Light*, a Spiritualist magazine, virtually agreed. With her tail somewhat between her legs Kate, and her boys, returned to New York, where a Spiritualist volcano was about to erupt.

The Spiritualist movement began in New York in 1848 and the plot to kill it off was hatched in London in 1888. Who better to murder it than the two girls – now degenerating into eccentric, disreputable, old ladies – who had started it? Forty years that had set the Western world alight were about to be explosively terminated.

In 1888 mediumship was thriving, the Western world ablaze with spectacular phenomena, much of it shifty and infiltrated with fraudsters and embezzlers. Mediums were turning circles into circuses with apports of acres of flowers and fruits, not to mention teleportation. Comely young mediums were conjuring up comely young materialisations. So many locks of hair were cut from spirit heads it was a wonder baldness did not become a fashion in the spirit world. The Foxes could not compete with this.

Maggie had concocted the notion of destruction while in London. It was not an abrupt decision but one that had fermented over time. She was genuinely remorseful over what she considered her wicked past, albeit she was still practicing her art over two continents. But the teachings of the Catholic Church had to be appeased, God had to be placated. Elisha's pleas for her to give up mediumship echoed strongly in her head and she kept imagining she was seeing him. She could never forget she had vowed to him, her great love, that she would renounce it. He would surely approve of what she was about to do. Elisha had assumed angelic status in her mind, taken to an early grave as he was too good for this world. Was he shaking his head over her in heaven?

Kate was concerned over her diminishing powers which had so let her down at Carlyle's house. She knew she would need to take a new road to survive. There was also a strong degree of revenge, although revenge on several layers and with a smattering of guilt. Her main target was Leah, who flaunted her wealth in lavish restaurants wearing French gowns, and who had now published her autobiography inflating her role in Spiritualism. She was sure Leah had taken her beloved children from her. Leah would suffer a body blow if Spiritualism were proved to be fraudulent as she, too, would be proved a liar, in front of her society friends. See how the sales of her book prospered then.

Maggie was accustomed to dealing with reporters. She contacted the *Herald* and worked out a plan for which she received a substantial payment. The *Herald's* headline for 24 September 1888 whetted the nation's appetite: 'GOD HAS NOT ORDERED IT', Maggie announced. Captions underneath read: 'A celebrated medium says the Spirits never return … Captain Kane's widow, one of the Fox Sisters promises an interesting exposure of fraud.'

In conjunction with the *Herald*, the Concert Room of the Academy of Music, one of the biggest venues in New York, was hired for 21 October. There, Maggie would denounce Spiritualism and demonstrate how she made the raps, those same raps that had so baffled scientists. She would demonstrate it was all fraud. New York was agog to find out and the Fox Sisters were, once again, at their rightful position, top of the Spiritualist bill. Maggie felt a tremendous surge of relief after she had announced her decision. This was her monument to Elisha. She did it for love of him.

She had moved into a small house on West 44th Street. A *Herald* reporter visited her and met 'a small, magnetic woman of middle age whose face bears the traces of much sorrow and of a world-wide experience.' That was certainly the truth. He could have added that her once lustrous hair, that had delighted Elisha when it had cascaded down his chest, was now streaked with grey. She was nervous during the interview, at times leaving the reporter and rushing to the piano where she 'poured forth fitful floods of wild, incoherent melody', her love songs to Elisha.

It must have been some interview. Between rushing to the piano, holding her head in her hands and telling how she had contemplated suicide, she had cried, 'No one but God can know what sorrows I have had!' Her erratic behaviour was reported in full. But she had enough control to produce the raps for the reporter. 'Is it a trick?' he asked. Raps sounded in confirmation. 'I can always get an affirmative answer to that,' she told him. The full interview is reported in *The Death Blow to Spiritualism*. When someone else questioned her, she rapped out that she was Napoleon Bonaparte. Even in her distress Maggie's dark humour did not desert her.

Kate arrived back in New York on the *Persian Monarch*, looking fit and announcing, as she had before, that she would never drink again; her life from now on would be an unwavering prayer of devotion to her sons. People weren't interested in that, they wanted to know whether she was in with Maggie or not. They did not have to wait long to find out: 'AND KATY FOX NOW', announced the *Herald* of 10 October 1888, followed by 'Spiritualism: a humbug from beginning to end'.

The sisters were delighted to see each other, 'I do not care a fig for Spiritualism,' blithely announced co-founder Kate, shoulder to shoulder with Maggie. The notorious 'apple story' seems to have originated from this time. The girls declared that they had tied an apple to a string and when they were in bed, on that fateful eve of April Fool's Day 1848, under the cover of bedclothes they had dropped the apple to the floor, making it bang and then pulled it along to make it sound like dragging footsteps. The more hysterical their mother became the greater the jape. They continued the ruse when the neighbours were called. Everything had built from that.

That, according to their story, might have well been the end of the matter, a two-week affair confined to their hamlet. But then Leah arrived and all hell broke loose. The girls had confessed their leg-pull to her. Noting the enormous interest, and seeing a chance to make money, she had forbidden them to confess but to continue their duplicity under her instructions. The girls were completely under her control, too frightened to back down. To be the founder of a new religion was the acme of Leah's ambition. She'd given it her all and, in her case, the spirits had reciprocated.

Kate and Maggie went on to affirm that someone else wrote the statement of authentication made by Margaret, and that she just agreed with whatever was said. John had never believed in the spirits, he'd made no secret of this. He had signed his statement under pressure.

The girls had produced the softer raps by clicking their toes, practising until they became expert. Lizzie had been in on things at the start but hated the deception and began to protest. That was why Lizzie had been sent away. Bringing things up to date, Kate snapped, 'every so-called manifestation produced through me in London, or anywhere else, was a fraud.' She said that she'd often cried herself to sleep due to the hypocrisy of her life. Maggie had said the same thing.

Public interest was enormous and Leah, in trepidation, fled, literally, to the hills, taking refuge at David's peppermint farm, praying the aromatic breezes would soothe her vapours. It was a long time before she could be tempted to show her face. 'This old woman made us her tools,' Maggie snarled to the press, knowing how sensitive Leah was about her age; Leah, too, had started docking off the years. 'What did we know?' Kate later asked, sinisterly adding, 'We grew to know too much.'

Maggie's nerve began to quail as the day approached. The sheer volume of interest was terrifying. It was reminiscent of the furore they had created when they'd first started, but then she'd been young. Youth was gone and with it most of her confidence. The Spiritualists were not taking this lying down. She knew many of them would be in her audience. They had received personal proof of the truth of the movement and did not take kindly to usurpers. Neither did charlatans want their livelihoods removed. She had received threatening letters. There was talk of abduction. She was grateful she had hidden the boys with friends.

Over 2,000 people crowded the Concert Room. The atmosphere was tense as the evening kicked off with a dentist, Dr C.M. Richmond, who doubled as a magician, and who had spent over twenty years investigating mediums. He demonstrated how a competent magician could duplicate séance room effects, and wrote with his foot to show how direct writing could be achieved under a table. People grew restless, they wanted she who had promised Eternal Life. A hostile audience waited to hear the raps demolished. Feelings were strong.

Maggie, quivering with nerves, had to deliver. This was not the avenging angel the press had promised, no exotic paramour of the dashing Dr Kane, not even a drunken wreck, this was a frail, grey-haired, bespectacled old lady who unsteadily took her position, fumbling at the lectern and nervously fiddling with her little hat. But she was in command, as W.S. Davis told Houdini: 'She was sober when she made her confession; she was sober when she appeared in the theatre and gave her exposé.'[4]

Her talk was disjointed at times, but its message crystaline, quietly delivered and lethal in its repudiation of all she represented. Kate was in a stage box, dignified and composed as her sister denounced them both as frauds. She nodded her head in agreement. Then came the highlight: the demonstration of the raps. A stool was placed in front of Maggie and, daintily removing her shoe, she placed her right foot upon it. Raps were heard. Nothing spectacular, no thumping, but definite raps.

Three doctors then mounted the stage and, while the raps continued, confirmed these were made by Maggie's toes. Spiritualism was a fraud.

Frauds, too, were Madame Blavatsky and her Mahatmas – at least that's what the public were told by the Society for Psychical Research.

Blavatsky's teachings were rooted in the ancient philosophies of Tibet and India. To be nearer this source, the Colonel and she had moved, in 1879, to India and established their Theosophical Society's international headquarters there, on the lotus-bedecked banks of the Adyar, then a tranquil suburb of Madras. It's still there and the grounds are still lovely but Adyar itself is engulfed by the overcrowded, polluted atmosphere of that great city. (The Theosophical welcome is as warm as ever though. When in Madras I took a chance and called unannounced and unknown at the closed doors of the Society. These opened to me at once and, when I explained I was anxious to see where Madame Blavatsky had lived and worked, I was given an impromptu and friendly guided tour, including the mighty Banyan tree, still standing but very old now, under which she had so often written. Her mighty presence is still palpable there. At any moment I expected to see her substantial form stomping across the lawn.)

India was under the control of the Raj but the Theosophists made their home among the indigenous community supporting local causes and religions. There, Madame Blavatsky produced astounding phenomena, demonstrating her control of the elements by commanding flames to rise and lower, flowers to fall on observers – this in daylight, not the Stygian gloom demanded by Mrs Guppy – and the materialisation of objects as well as forms. Her *pièce de résistance* was a letter from a Mahatma, precipitated from his ashram in Tibet. She was the Mahatmas' sole agent and, at her request, their handwritten letters materialised at destinations all over the world, irrespective of whatever country Madame Blavatsky happened to be in.

To receive a letter was a mark of distinction and great were the demands on Madame Blavatsky to intercede on behalf of earnest believers. She was the psychic post box. Favoured recipients would find letters awaiting them in branches of trees, railway carriages or, sometimes, delivered by hand in remote cols by Eastern strangers. Some communications materialised out of the air, wafting onto the heads of their recipients.

This raised more than an eyebrow. For quick-tempered, gormandising and chain-smoking Madame, the high priestess of these ascetic Mahatmas, appeared to be anything but ascetic herself. She explained this divide in that she was, in reality, two persons combined, the mystic who she referred to as HPB, shackled to a rough old hippopotamus (her words) of a woman known as Madame Blavatsky.

Although she was the first to denigrate Madame Blavatsky (as opposed to HPB), it must be pointed out, her faults were balanced by a generous nature and of all the great mystics she alone possessed a hearty and endearing sense of humour. She was the personification of Zen long before it became fashionable. (The dignified Colonel Olcott, in his advanced years – fully bearded, wall-eyed and with a pince-nez – appeared at her door one day in dhoti, stripped to the waist, to express empathy with his adoptive country; she could not speak for a while for laughter.) She pointed out that the Mahatmas had needed a vehicle for their work and that, although far from perfect, she had been the best available at the time.

Madame's books, teachings and phenomena – and the sheer weight of her personality – attracted literally thousands to the Theosophical Society; writers, politicians and scientists among them. Society was abuzz with people hoping to attain Mahatmic powers themselves or, at least, meet these elevated beings. Many sought them but few were found.

Branches of the TS in Paris, New York and London throbbed to the tales of her powers. In 1884, when Madame and the Colonel were visiting London, executives of the Society for Psychical Research interviewed her and were favourably impressed. But there were enemies in Adyar. One of these was Madame Coulomb, the Judas Iscariot of Theosophy. The Christian missionaries in India and the Theosophists had been at cross swords since day one. Madame Blavatsky, although retaining a sneaking affection for the Russian Orthodox Church, had scant respect for missionaries. During her absence in London she had ill-advisedly left Madame Coulomb in charge in India. Madame Coulomb bore a grudge; Madame Blavatsky had caught her trying to tap Theosophical visitors for a loan and reprimanded her.

Madame Coulomb informed the missionaries that Madame Blavatsky had falsified phenomena and that she had assisted her in this. Furthermore, the Mahatmas did not exist; Madame Blavatsky had written their letters herself and arranged for conspirators to precipitate them. The Ancient Wisdom was only as ancient as Madame Blavatsky's imagination. She produced incriminating letters in Madame Blavatsky's handwriting to back this up. The Christians published these and her accusations and, as a result, the SPR sent researcher, Richard Hodgson, to Adyar to investigate.

Meanwhile, the Mahatmas and Madame had streamlined the letters system. A wooden 'shrine' had been built in which Madame Blavatsky would place letters to be precipitated and in which she would receive replies. The Mahatmas were prolific and there are volumes of their letters in book form still in print.[5] Madame Coulomb stated the shrine was less than sacred, that it backed onto Madame Blavatsky's chamber which had a hole in the wall connected to a sliding back panel in the shrine and that she had inserted and withdrawn items at will.

When Mr Hodgson arrived to inspect this shrine, there was no shrine to inspect. Fearing his desecration the Theosophists had burnt it. He found, however, examples of recent plasterwork in Madame Blavatsky's room which may have been a bricked-up aperture. Handwriting experts later verified that the Mahatma letters could have been written by Madame Blavatsky.

Hodgson interviewed both TS members and Christians, and his damning conclusions were published by the SPR in 1885, including the sentence: 'We regard her neither as the mouthpiece of hidden seers, nor as a mere vulgar adventuress; we think that she has achieved a title to permanent remembrance as one of the most accomplished, ingenious and interesting impostors of history.'

The explosion rocked the psychic world. Theosophists resigned in thousands. Its ramifications are still felt. Like the Fox sisters, Madame Blavatsky was written off as a fraud, but also like the Fox sisters, she was not done yet.

9

Spiritualists were outraged by Maggie's treachery but, by and large, it did not affect the movement. Scoffers had something more to scoff about but believers were unaffected. Spiritualism was too powerful to be demolished by a couple of neurotic women. The sad truth was that the movement no longer needed its founders, particularly founders who had made such vicious fools of themselves. A barrage of hostility was levelled at the girls, which was fair enough, they had attacked first, and many a dodgy medium bristled in outrage at the slight to the profession.

Maggie had agreed to take the exposé on tour. She did not relish this but wearily hit the road again only to find half-full and indifferent houses. It was one thing to turn out for phenomena, quite another to hear it was bogus. Who cared? Not her promoters, that's for sure. This battered and exploited woman was abandoned in Boston, when the tour and her money ran out, to find her own way home. She had not finished with revenge. Leah's success with *The Missing Link*, handsomely bound in scarlet and gilt, rankled with her. Journalist Reuben Briggs Davenport came up with a suggestion. Together with Maggie he would write her side of the story and give fuller details of the exposé.

The aptly named *The Death Blow to Spiritualism: Being the True Story of the Fox Sisters as Revealed by Margaret Fox Kane and Catherine Fox Jencken* tells in detail how their phenomena were a tissue of lies and deception. It forcefully blames Leah for having led two innocent children into fraud. Already in hiding, Leah now had to contend with this. It was smelling salts at the ready. She dreaded every knock at the door.

The book was written in great haste and Davenport's name is kept alive by it; it fetches a high price on the rare books market. He was a vivid writer and, as with *The Love-Life of Dr Kane*, it pelts along at a torrid pace. It is saturated with Maggie's loathing for Leah: 'My damnable enemy. I hate her. My God! I'd poison her!' *The Missing Link* is dismissed as 'this lying book'.

The first part is an energetic confession of fraud; it sags in the middle where space is given to the inconsequential Seybert Commission, but finishes with a flourish with the re-publication of Elisha's letters, containing his pleas for her to discontinue her fraud and admissions from her that it was indeed, a con. Nearly forty years later, Houdini was to pore over the book, quoting its chilling declamation that 'Under the name of this dreadful, this horrible hypocrisy – Spiritualism – everything that is improper, bad and immoral is practised.' She'd said as much to the *Herald*,[1] adding it should be trampled out 'as one would trample out the life of a serpent'.

Years of hurt spill out. Spiritualism had its 'monstrous birth in older heads', a reference to Leah who, for good measure, is likened to Satan. Scorn is poured on those who believed in something devoid of 'a reasonable foundation'. Libel is freely distributed and everyone involved with Spiritualism damned except for Horace Greeley and, of course, Elisha, both of whom tried to 'rescue' the girls. Spiced up by black humour it is a fountain of bile. Compulsive reading.

There are plaintive passages where Maggie tells how she tried, vainly, to discover for herself whether there was survival after death. She tells how she'd sat in graveyards at night trying to communicate with the spirits of corpses, concluding that the dead do not return. Even with Davenport trying to hold the reins it is the ranting of an hysterical woman in the grip of yet another breakdown, possibly a continuation of an earlier one. Her loving nature – and she had loved Elisha unconditionally – had been knocked askew at his death, poisoned by years of loneliness.

Were Maggie's accusations true or just seeping wounds? By denouncing Spiritualism did she believe she was proving her love for Elisha? Did she believe he would be waiting proudly for her when she died? For Maggie, death could not come soon enough. But what about her own admission, in her letter from London to the *Herald*, that the raps were 'the only part of the phenomena worthy of notice'. What was worthy of notice in rapping with her toes and apples? What of the thunderous crashes in front of Robert Dale Owen in Leah's circles – no toe or apple could have done that.

Kate had confessed that she, too, was in on the deception. Had she fooled for years, in test conditions, a worldly newspaper editor like Greeley and eminent scientists like Crookes? And Leah? The number of times she was probed, suspended and tested by scientists? All fooled by her big toe which Maggie assures us she was never that proficient at cracking anyway? What about the dents in the underside of tables?

The Death Blow to Spiritualism leaves much unexplained, as did Maggie's demonstration of rapping with her foot. Because she had rapped with her foot, and undoubtedly had done so many times, did that account for every occasion? When raps were actually felt by people when she was nowhere near?

Once the dreadful deed was done the repercussions set in. They were pariahs among Spiritualists and despised as drunken cheats by the rest of the world. *The New York World* set the tone: 'If spirit rappings find any credence in this community hereafter, it would seem a wise precaution on the part of the authorities to begin the enlargement of the state's insane asylums' (22 October 1888).

The resilient Spiritualists were stirring back into life; the movement had been spawned in controversy. Martyrdom was part of it. The great flower of Spiritualism had been severed at its base but already shoots were springing up. The movement clambered to its knees and stood, shakily at first, then erect again. It was full of charlatans, everyone knew that, but that did not damn genuine phenomena nor assuage the need to believe. 'Remember – and wait for me' had been carved into thousands of gravestones. Well, they would do exactly that.

However wicked fraudulent mediums, Spiritualism had two viler hate objects. Those who had started it, the Fox Sisters. What to do now? They had bitten the hand that had fed them for years. Maggie, in her panic to get even with Leah had given no thought to the future. There was no future now, as far as she was concerned, all that stretched ahead was a mess. Drink helped in that it relieved the strain but she knew something had to be done.

Leah had crept back to New York where a partial recovery had taken place. She had, after all, a loyal husband, friends and money, luxuries not possessed by her sisters. Time would heal. She, who had spent her life working for others.

Kate had a brainwave. She had kept in touch with Mrs Cottell, the occupant of Carlyle's London house. After such a fiasco it might be thought the ladies would have wanted nothing to do with each other, but

Kate was desperate, regretful of having thrown her lot in with Maggie. Her triumph over Leah was short lived.

In a letter dated 17 November 1888[2], twenty-seven days after the denunciation, Kate wrote to Mrs Cottell claiming shock at Maggie's exposé. It had been no shock, of course, Kate had been part of it, and presumably she hoped that Mrs Cottell did not know this.

Referring to the exposé, she came bluntly to the heart of the matter: 'The made $1,500 clear I think now I could make money in proving that the knockings are not made with the toes. So many people come to me to ask me about this exposure of Maggie's that I have to deny myself to them. They are hard at work to expose the whole thing if they can; but they certainly cannot.' She was hoping Mrs Cottell would subsidise an English tour to demonstrate the fraud was not a fraud at all. Possibly bearing in mind the Carlyle séance, Mrs Cottell seems not to have accepted her offer.

The letter shows how much a business transaction the denunciation was. Never mind humiliation, shattered dreams and the stigma of fraud, $1,500 had been made. Kate was offering another business proposal to demonstrate the raps were genuine, convinced they would sound even though her feet and the rest of her body would be examined and restrained before and during the performance. It is a pity Mrs Cottell did not take her up, it would have been interesting to see what happened.

The biting New York Christmas came and went and 1889 arrived to find Kate and Maggie impoverished failures – and they knew it. There were no celebrations and they could expect, and received, no sympathy from the Spiritualists. There were no supporting knocks rapping the way to a brighter future.

Leah gathered her furs about her, ordered a rich meal and put a brave face on things, but Spiritualism would never be the same for any of the Foxes.

Kate joined Maggie and fell off the wagon. What was the point of staying on? It was accepted, even encouraged, for a man to get drunk but for a woman it was shameful. Alcoholism in professional women today is not unusual. There were no higher flying women than Kate and Maggie Fox in their day and they were not the only mediums to stray. Louch behaviour was, and is, regularly found among the profession. Madame Blavatsky questioned why, if spirit guides were so keen to advise others, they did not take better care of their own mediums: 'It is notorious that the best physical mediums are either sickly or, sometimes, what is still worse, inclined to some abnormal vice or other. Why do not these healing "guides", who make their mediums play the therapeutists and thaumaturgists to others, give them the boon of robust physical vigour?'[3]

A good question and as pertinent now as when it was asked over a century ago. Madame Blavatsky herself barely survived sixty years, albeit those were, as Lady Bracknell might have noted, crammed with incident. She picked herself up from the shattering blow of the SPR report and moved from India to Europe, as her disease-ridden body could no longer cope with a sweltering climate. The Indians were never put off by the report, remembering how much the Theosophists had done for them by championing their traditions against the overriding opposition of the Raj. They were indifferent to phenomena, their fakirs were world famous. Madame received a standing ovation before her final departure from India.

Further information came to light regarding the SPR report. The Mahatma letters were examined again, by another expert, who contradicted the original diagnosis by averring the writing was not Madame Blavatsky's. Madame Coulomb's history was found to be steeped in fraud, and her husband was a carpenter and plasterer, employed as a handyman in the Theosophical headquarters, which could explain, as malice, the signs of new plasterwork in Madame Blavatsky's chamber. Colleagues of Madame Blavatsky vouched for the genuineness of her phenomena, including the Countess Wachtmeister[4] with whom she shared lodgings after the SPR report. Piece by piece her reputation recovered, as did that of the Theosophical Society.

She moved to London where she worked on what she intended as an expansion of *Isis Unveiled* but which turned out to be her masterwork, *The Secret Doctrine*, published in 1888 – the manuscript alone stood over three feet high. The Preface contains the lines: 'Abuse she is accustomed to; calumny she is daily acquainted with; at slander she smiles in silent contempt.' Madame Blavatsky was noted for receiving nothing in silent contempt. She erupted like a volcano.

For Theosophical Londoners, her presence in their midst was an inspiration. After her death she assumed God-like status in the eyes of some, one of the reasons, Colonel Olcott assures us, why he wrote *Old Diary Leaves*. He wanted to stabilise this deification, bring her down to earth. In this he failed. He wrote his affectionate, if warts and all, memoir to give us the true picture of this remarkable woman who could, after all, have had the uneventful life of an aristocrat had she so chosen, the highlights of which might have been landscape painting and embroidery enlivened, perhaps, by a spot of archery.

Old Diary Leaves vividly depicts an alluring, mystical world now dead, dominated by Madame Blavatsky. But for the Colonel, we would have had an even less complete record of her life than we now have and he must be thanked for that. *The Secret Doctrine* saw her rise, phoenix-like from the ashes. A whole convoy of the famous and the infamous flocked to her salon in Notting Hill Gate, W.B. Yeats among them. She wrote by day and received by night.

One of her visitors was 42-year-old Annie Besant. Mrs Besant, who had been married to a parson and whose early works include a life of the saints, had rejected Christianity, and her husband, to throw in her lot with atheist Charles Bradlaugh, among whose causes were advocacy of trade unions, women's suffrage and birth control. She'd improved conditions for factory workers, was an outstanding orator and, at that time, in need of another challenge.

Annie was no Theosophist; she had been given *The Secret Doctrine* to review for a newspaper that had previously offered it to her friend George Bernard Shaw; he had rejected it and passed it on to her. She was glued to it and requested, and was granted, an audience with the author. Wearing workman's clothes and a red neckerchief to express her socialist principles, she got off the Tube at Notting Hill Gate and walked in her clogs to the lovely house in Lansdowne Road where Madame Blavatsky lived.

There, in her over-stuffed chair reclined the over-stuffed body of the occultist, turquoise eyes assessing her though the haze of cigarette smoke. Madame was charm itself. 'My dear Mrs Besant,' the socialist was greeted in world-weary, tobacco-husky tones, the accent impossible to pin down. 'I have so long wished to see you.' Annie found her cause. First, she panicked, feeling herself drawn into something that would alter her whole life. Madame put Annie at her ease, charming her with irreverent gossip and blasts of humour, the bejewelled hands that had played the piano professionally deftly rolling her incessant cigarettes.

Only at the end of the interview did Madame Blavatsky bring her mission into play. As Annie was reaching for her shawl to go, she hit her with: 'My dear Mrs Besant, if only you would come among us.' As John Symonds says, 'At that moment the rebel who was Annie Besant died, and the Theosophical movement gained its greatest leader.'[5] Madame

Blavatsky and Mrs Besant became inseparable and her writings and oratory enriched the Theosophical Society. She was as indefatigable as Madame herself.

Madame Blavatsky knew she was nearing the end of her life and needed a successor. She still scuttled about, from time to time, making the occasional sortie to the Café Royal where she would eat large meals and, as often as not, give the staff an earful for their trouble. Driving through Hyde Park in her brougham one day, returning from such an outing, she looked at the crowds and sadly, if cynically, commented to her disciple, Alice Cleather, 'Not a soul among them.'[6]

Then she caught flu. Coupled with the Bright's disease and chronic rheumatism, to which she was already a victim, this brought immense pain. Ignoring instructions to rest she collapsed and was ordered to bed. She liked the handsome young doctor attending her and rolled him cigarettes. He was astounded by her great heart and told her so. 'I do my best,' she answered.

It was not good enough. She continued to deteriorate and, alarmingly, stopped smoking. On 8 May 1891 she died, sitting up in her chair. She had been tapping her foot, something she did when thinking deeply. Disciples were kneeling at her feet. Annie was in New York about Theosophical business and was distraught, the women loved each other.

The crux of Madame Blavatsky's teaching was the Mahatmas. Their existence has been called into question but Annie had no doubts: 'If there are no Mahatmas, the Theosophical Society is an absurdity,' she wrote. She gave the rest of her full life to it. Colonel Olcott witnessed the retrieval, and despatch, of many letters from the shrine. The Colonel was no fool, his rank conferred in recognition of his services to the US Government during the civil war. In *Old Diary Leaves* he tells us that on one occasion he wrote to the Mahatmas via the shrine and almost immediately received an answer: 'It was done while I stood there, and not a half-minute had elapsed. So far as it goes, that pretty effectually disposes of the pretence that these communications were fabricated in advance and passed through a sliding panel at the back of the shrine.' He noted briskly that he was writing history not romance.

The Mahatmas seem, regrettably, to have taken a back seat for the time being. Perhaps they are still precipitating but, if so, the recipients of their letters have not gone public. These days, a Mahatmic email might be more appropriate and technology that can dematerialise, precipitate and re-materialise documents should have no difficulty with that.

Kate and Maggie had no Mahatmas to look out for them and their spirit guides did not seem to be doing much of a job. Having received no inducement to visit England from Mrs Cottell, or anyone else for that matter, Kate was stymied. No one wanted her now; it was a friendless, bitter existence. If she wanted to survive then she had to clamber back on the bandwagon. But she could hardly demonstrate life after death after publicly denying it.

She would have to recant again. The luxury of dignity had long been jettisoned for a need to survive. There were her sons to support, Henry was getting weaker and the worry drove her to desperation. As she had written to Mrs Cottell, Kate was confident she could produce phenomena, and what a coup it would be (she hoped) if she could now expose the exposé and continue to produce the inexplicable. She made it known that Maggie had been wrong in denouncing the spirits and she had only gone along with her through misguided loyalty and bitterly regretted this. She resumed her sittings but there were not many clients.

Maggie also considered her options. Catholicism had not afforded the solace for which she'd hoped and half-empty halls of indifferent audiences brought no comfort. Like Kate, she now had to earn a living. It took her the best part of a year to decide what to do. On 20 November 1889, she called another press conference. The Foxes still sold papers. 'Would to God that I could undo the injustice I did the cause of Spiritualism,' she announced. She blamed the 'strong psychological influence'[7] of persons opposed to the movement and announced, 'I gave expressions to utterances that had no foundation in fact.'

The press, which had paid her to denounce Spiritualism in the first place, was again her mouthpiece. She explained she needed to put the record straight – again – at the express wish of the spirits whom she had so noxiously betrayed. Someone asked if she hoped to make money from this latest venture and she was honest enough to reply that she hoped to earn a living, but purely enough for basic maintenance. She would spend the rest of her life lecturing, trying to put right the wrongs she had caused. The demonstrations were over. She repeated that the charges she had made against Spiritualism were false. She confirmed she was receiving no payment for her retraction, and had only denounced Spirit for money when her 'mental equilibrium' had rendered her not responsible for her actions. From her shaking and tremulous appearance her equilibrium did not seem much improved.

Tellingly she added: 'There is not a human being on earth can produce the 'raps' in the same way as they are through me.' All her life Maggie was consistent that the raps worked independently of her, she never claimed they originated from spirit, just that they were physically independent. Maggie's basic honesty caused her problems. Medium W.S. Davis had told Houdini she drank because of her hypocrisy. Hypocrisy had been necessary because her high-profile clients – presidents' wives, senators, powerful celebrities in all walks – expected great things of her, irrespective of the drain on her not always available resources. She, a working girl, had to get results. She not only had to produce the notoriously unreliable raps but had to ensure their messages were acceptable. That meant bringing back the dead. Maggie was not sure she could bring back the dead.

She was not unscrupulous and far from heartless. She'd had sleepless nights and a breakdown before her denunciation, just how many more sleepless nights had there been before her second recantation? She endured a lifetime's uneasiness about her profession. Kate, the craftier of the two, did not suffer overly from spiritual anguish, but rather the anguish of trying to earn a decent living. Leah, the now wealthy mastermind, who had also been commended for her phenomena, did not have the natural facilities of her sisters. She'd had to work at it, utilising her great nerve and charm. Leah *could* make a silk purse out of a sow's ear. She'd turned a humble music teacher into a high priestess and made her two sisters world famous.

The result was that thousands of decent, devout and lonely people now believed their loved ones were waiting for them beyond the grave. They were treasured recipients of a cosmic truth. Jubilation was great among the faithful at Maggie's retraction. Spiritualism was back on course. 'If ever I heard a woman speak the truth, it was then,' exulted Spiritualist J.L. O'Sullivan, US Minister to Portugal. But the girls were neither forgiven nor welcomed back into the fold. They had undone themselves; they were too dangerous and unpredictable. Discussing phenomena in the 1920s, Conan Doyle wrote, 'It is the same power which is used by the Buddha or by the Woman of Endor.' It is easy to see in which of the two camps the Foxes were.

This time Leah did not take to the hills. She discreetly let it be known that, after Maggie's display of faithlessness, she had now seen the light (again). Leah maintained a supreme public indifference to the doings of her wanton sisters. She had stayed true; after all, she had founded the cause. Leah was getting old, in her seventies, a lot older then than now.

Beneath the aloof façade she, too, was troubled. Blood runs deep. Tales of her sisters drunken carousing had been dutifully, sometimes joyously, relayed to her. For all her protestations of indifference, she cared.

Public contempt had returned the girls to the bottle, that hideous inheritance of their father's. Maggie was now a solitary drinker, Kate more publicly exposed. She had no support, Henry was dying and Ferdie sickly. She was despised, rejected and could not cope. She would disappear for days, leaving Ferdie in charge although both lads often stayed with friends. Ferdie was a caring teenager, a decent lad who looked after his mother and brother as best he could.

Those last, drink-sodden months of Maggie and Kate are untraceable. Wandering the streets at night, Kate might have heard, on a Sunday, the sounds of hymns coming from Spiritualist churches, thanking God for his blessings. Few were extended to her. Those inside turned their backs if they saw her. Most didn't know, or care, who she was.

Leah died from a heart attack on 1 November 1890, most likely triggered by obesity and remorse. She had a new housekeeper, for whom she did not care, and this lady had accidentally shattered an expensive ornament. Empurpled of face, Leah had heaved her bulk from her chair to remonstrate and dropped to the floor, felled by a tantrum brought about by smashed china.

Just before Leah's death Kate returned to the welcoming hearth of Dr Taylor and his wife Sarah, who had been in Europe. The deterioration in her was shocking. Irrespective of this she resumed her automatic writing sessions, her crazy, sprawling hand careering across reams of paper and, as in the old days, sometimes both hands at the same time, the raps usually accompanying her. The betrayal was never mentioned as though the blip had never occurred. She was soon in touch with the Taylor spirit family again, grannies, mothers, uncles and, of course, the children.

Much of the *Fox-Taylor Record*, which Sarah resumed writing, extols the glories of the spirit realm, superior in every way to earth, a veritable heaven. Despite this, Spiritualists were, and are, extremely reluctant to enter it, or for their loved ones to go there. It might be thought death would have warranted a party, as it does in some places. The whole point of Spiritualism is to celebrate eternal life.[8]

Kate retained her apartment, kept in order by Ferdie when he was there and allowed to degenerate into rack and ruin when he wasn't, and gave private sittings, when she remembered to turn up for them. Then she went missing. The Taylors called at her apartment to find no indication of her whereabouts. The boys were with friends but where was Mama? Ferdie and Henry, who may well have seen her on and off, had no idea where she was. No one knew – which was what Kate wanted. When Kate was on a bender she needed no reminders of her past, no witnesses from her Spiritualist life. W.G. Langworthy Taylor, compiler of the *Fox-Taylor Record* assures us that 'Wine was the first and the last weakness of Katie' and that 'No shadow of immorality ever touched her'. By 'immorality' he means sex and, in that department, she seems to have been remarkably uninterested.

Aside from a probable pre-marriage dalliance with Charles Livermore, there are no tales of sexual entanglement. Kate was not capable of loving as passionately as Maggie but, if she had had a love of her life, that was Livermore; she carried a torch for him long after her marriage to Henry. Charles had been fascinated by the extraordinary power wielded by this comely virgin desperate for romance, but that had morphed into grateful affection, exemplified by his support of her even after his second marriage. After that, she had settled down to respectable matrimony and disrespectful widowhood. When she was young she knew the power of her attraction and almost gained the reputation of a flirt but this was always within the limits of propriety; she could never countenance the ribaldry that went with male group sittings.

Kate resurfaced again, unannounced just as she had left, at the Swedish Massage Centre, as the Taylors knew she would – if she were still alive – on 15 February 1892. She had encountered something decent in her wanderings and was full of positive plans; she'd taken a new apartment and planned a new start. It had all been heard before, several times.

However, she brought back the Taylor's myriad relatives, again, and The *Fox-Taylor Record* recommenced for the next three months. Her last recorded sitting with the Taylors was June 1892. Drunk or sober, and she was often drunk, it did not seem to affect her facility. Her power had waned after her husband's death but, in these last months, as sometimes happens with the terminally ill, it seems to have revved up to full strength again. For Kate was seriously ill with kidney failure. The raps and writing, however, were as strong as in her youth.

She disappeared again and was heard of in the maze of bars in lower Manhattan where she hopefully found some happiness or, at least, congeniality with like-minded lost souls. She returned to her apartment and Ferdie did his best to look after her but it was a lost cause. He found her dead in her bed on 2 July 1892. She was 56.

Henry faded away, his sad little candle finally spluttering out the same year as his mother's.

Ferdie became a professional medium but with limited success. But for his mother he would never have been heard of but there was, as there still is, a glamour attached to the Fox name. Happiness was as elusive for him as it was for his Aunt Maggie. He married, became a father but abandoned his wife and children. He had not inherited his mother's psychic gifts, just her alcoholism. The *Fox-Taylor Record* tells us Ferdie died on 22 April 1908 at 34 years of age. A tragic waste of life.

Maggie went to pieces at Kate's death. They had not been close at the end but at least she was her flesh, blood and collaborator. She, who suffered the most intensely of the three sisters, was cursed to die last. Her bouts of drunken insanity grew wilder and, it is said by some, she augmented alcohol with narcotics. She became unable to care for herself and was nursed by a friend. On the icy morning of 8 March 1893, a few months off her 60th birthday, she followed Leah and Kate into that world she had preached about, and promised to others, but never truly believed in herself.

It had all started on an icy March night in 1848 and ended on another icy March night forty-five years later. During that time the daughters of an alcoholic Methodist blacksmith had emblazoned a unique rainbow of exotic promise across the Western world. It is a trail that still shimmers as it perplexes.

EPILOGUE

It would be easy to dismiss the lot of them as frauds – charismatic charlatans in it for what they could get, as are all of us into anything for what we can get. The whole séance procedure lends itself to fraud. Sitters singing in the dark, songs drowning out extraneous noises, spirits using mediums' voices, forms appearing from behind closed cabinets, forms which may not be touched, sitters willing to cling to any shred that will bring back those they loved. What could be easier to fake?

The fakery isn't always intentional. Some mediums truly believe they are in touch with paranormal forces, for whatever reason. The spirits can bring great comfort. Richard Wiseman, Professor in the Public Understanding of Psychology at the University of Hertfordshire, says of the Foxes: 'Based on the evidence as a whole, I think that it is reasonable to come down in favour of a normal, rather than a paranormal, explanation. The girls were tested at a time when scientific research into such alleged phenomena was in its infancy – over the years, more rigorous methods have been developed and evidence for alleged physical mediumship has dwindled to almost nil. Is it possible that these three girls possessed a unique gift that has never been reliably demonstrated by anyone else throughout the whole of history? Yes. Is that likely? No.' (*email to the author*)

Are we expected to believe the odious (but highly entertaining) Mrs Guppy was teleported across London? That flowers with muddy roots attached, not to mention ducks plucked for the oven, were apported to her séance room to impress a handful of people who already believed in the spirits, while those same spirits were unable to deliver so much as a pin in front of objective witnesses? The whole thing is as preposterous as the fact that Mrs Guppy persuaded many of her sitters, and scientists, that she did, indeed, do these things.

Did Katie King make appearances from the spirit world, giving locks of her pretty hair to admirers? Are we to believe ageless souls inhabit ashrams beneath the Himalayas? That they sent letters through The Ether to materialise in Madame Blavatsky's boudoir? Were two adolescent, poorly educated blacksmith's daughers chosen by the ghost of Benjamin Franklin to be his instruments in a fourth-dimensional experiment between this world and the next? That they were chosen as ambassadors above all others?

It's as absurd as the fact that black holes exist, that space is unending and time runs backwards or, indeed, the whole conception of Professor Stephen Hawking's *A Brief History of Time.*[1] Next thing, physicists will be telling us there are parallel universes. So how come so many of us believe in spirits?

Colin Wilson has written: 'I never cease to be amazed by the gall of scientists who declare they have now proved the non-existence of spirits or the soul or second sight or telepathy, when thousands of ordinary people can contradict them from their own experience.'[2] He also wrote in *The Occult,*[3] concerning the Fox phenomena: 'Undoubtedly much of it was fraudulent. Equally certainly, much was genuine.' If a single phenomenon was genuine it would prove their case.

That extraordinary medium, the late Jessie Nason, was living proof to the author that mediums can read the past and the future. People whom she had never met were stunned at her accuracy as, often from a public platform, she relayed personal details of their lives. She fired off names, addresses and dates like a machine gun, no fishing for information. Many recipients, in addition to the writer, confirmed she had accurately predicted the future for them.

Jessie believed the spirits told her these things. Something or someone had done so because she knew them. There were too many for them to be lucky guesses. But if she could foresee the future then it must already be there: otherwise what's to see? We must already have lived it. What about free choice? It introduces questions outside the scope of this book and the intellect of its writer.

The Foxes depended on their clientele for their living. Like any professional, in any field, they had a bag of tricks they could call upon to see them through barren patches. In any other profession it is called technique. Years of practice had taught them to read the slightest change of expression in face or voice. Titbits of information were seized on and amplified. But artifice is no substitute for raw talent.

Maggie's denunciation, made in spite towards Leah and as an attempt to redeem herself in Elisha's dead eyes, came when she was mentally ill and does not invalidate her previous record when she left audiences astounded by her accuracy. She sat for some of the highest in the land, those who were accustomed to facing deceivers and seeing through frauds.

Neither of the Foxes attempted to explain the process of communication. They were examined by the keenest intellects of their time, none of whom detected fraud. What an irony if spirit messengers turn out to exist? If those little home circles, many of which thrive today, contain the nucleus of a universal truth?

According to the *Fox-Taylor Record* the spirit world is in parallel evolution to ours. Maybe Franklin, or whoever may have superseded him, is summoning resources for another breakthrough? The author, for one, is ready to turn out the lights and start singing.

NOTES

1

1 Accounts of what happened that night are included in the signed
   statements of various neighbours, and of John and Margaret Fox, the
   latter two made on 11 April 1848. They are included in *The History
   of Spiritualism* by Sir Arthur Conan Doyle, originally published 1926
   and reprinted 2001 by The Spiritual Truth Press.
2 By Leah Underhill (Thomas R. Knox, 1885).
3 *Time is Kind*, published in Britian as *The Unwilling Martyrs* (Centennial
   Press, 1947).

2

1 Including the author, *Madame Blavatsky* (Regency Press, 1976).
   One of the most comprehensive biographies is *Madame Blavatsky*
   by Marion Meade (G.P. Putnam's Sons, 1980), another, rather older
   but strongly recommended, is *Madame Blavatsky* by John Symonds
   (Odhams Press Ltd, 1959).
2 *Voices from the Spirit World, Being Communications from Many Spirits* By
   the Hand of Isaac Post, Medium (Chas H. McDonnell, 1852). This
   contains, he believed, written communications from, among others,
   Benjamin Franklin, Voltaire and William Penn.
3 *The Missing Link in Modern Spiritualism.*

4   Originally published by J. W. Boulton, 1877, republished several times by The Theosophical Publishing House and still in print. Since the original publication it has never been out of print.

5   By H.S. Olcott, pub. Theosophical Publishing House, 1895 and still in print.

6   *The Debatable Land Between this World and the Next* (Carleton, 1872).

7   *Modern American Spiritualism* by Emma Hardinge, first published by the author in 1870, republished by SNU Publications, 1999.

8   *Time Is Kind.*

9   Published by Bela Marsh, 1855.

10 *Modern American Spiritualism.*

11 *Ibid.*

12 *The History of Spiritualism.*

13 *Modern American Spiritualism.*

14 *The History of Spiritualism.*

15 *Modern American Spiritualism.*

3

1   *Light,* 9 August 1884.

2   *Old Diary Leaves.*

3   *Spiritualism: Its Facts and Fanaticisms* by Eliab Capron (Bela Marsh, 1855).

4   *Modern American Spiritualism.*

5   Published 1853 by Partridge and Brittan.

6   *Mrs Lynn Linton* by G.S. Layard (Methuen, 1901), quoted in *The Shadow and the Light* by Elizabeth Jenkins (Hamish Hamilton, 1982).

4

1   *Jenny Lind* by Joan Bulman (James Barrie, 1956).

2   *Seven Daughters of the Theatre* by Edward Wagenknecht (Da Capo, 1964).

3   *Jenny Lind.*

4   Unidentified and undated press report.

5   *The Leader,* 15 March 1853.

6   *The Love-Life of Dr Kane* by Margaret Fox Kane (Carleton, 1866, and elsewhere).

7   *The Love-Life of Dr Kane.*

8 Published 1875 by Theosophical Press.
9 Full letter contained in *Modern American Spiritualism* from which some of the substance of this account is taken.
10 *Voices From the Spirit World, Being Communications from Many Spirits* By the Hand of Isaac Post, Medium (Chas H. McDonnell, 1852).
11 *They Paved the Way: A History of NH Women* by Jane Appleton Pierce (Heritage Books, 1980).
12 Olive Tardiff.
13 *Autobiography of Emma Hardinge Britten* (SNU Publications, published in 1900 and republished in 1996).
14 I am indebted for this quote to Earle E. Spamer, Asst. Reference Librarian, The American Philosophical Society.
15 24 Feb 1857, carried on website of Elisha Kent Kane Historical Society.

5

1 *Katie Fox, Epoch Making Medium and The Making of the Fox-Taylor Record* by W. Langworthy Taylor (G.P. Putnam's Sons, 1933).
2 The writer was present at a transfiguration circle in London in the 1970s, where the medium, a Mr Christmas, transfigured thirty times under the light of a red lamp.
3 *Voices in the Dark* by Leslie Flint (MacMillan, 1971).
4 *Dark Lover* by Emily W. Leider (Faber and Faber, 2003).
5 *Madam Valentino* by Michael Morris (Abbeville Press, 1991).
6 *Ibid.*
7 *Ibid.*
8 Still in print, published in 1993 by Point Loma Publications, Inc.
9 *Hellish Nell* by Malcolm Gaskill (Fourth Estate, 2001).
10 *Ethereal Body: The Quest for Ectoplasm* (Internet).
11 Journal for the SPR, June 1886.
12 *The Table Rappers* (Book Club Associates, 1973).
13 *A Biography of the Brothers Davenport*, published in 1867.
14 Letters of M. Faraday by Bence Jones, 1870, reproduced in *The Table Rappers*.

6

1   *One Hundred Years of Spiritualism* by Roy Stemman (Spiritualist Association of Great Britain, 1972).

2   Information taken from *The Debatable Land*, other publications also include accounts but Owen was the first to log the phenomena.

3   Reported by Robert Dale Owen in *The Debatable Land* from notes Livermore had made after each séance.

4   The French illusionist Jean Eugene Robert-Houdin was the inspiration for the younger Houdini. Houdin astounded the Victorians with his stage feats of levitation, during which he would appear to soar above the heads of his audience.

5   Published by R.C. Hartranft, 1891.

6   *The Emancipation Proclamation, How and by whom it was given to Abraham Lincoln in 1861.* Although sections of this are quoted the actual document is elusive. Among various sources, information on the Colonel is given on website Best Kept Psychic Secrets by Kathlyne.

7   *Religio-Philosophical Journal*, 12 Dec 1885.

8   *Religio-Philosophical Journal*, 16 Jan 1886.

9   *Unlocking the Mystery of a Lincoln Relic*, www.spirithistory.com.

10 *Lincoln* by Thomas Keneally (Phoenix, 2005).

7

1   By Reuben Briggs Davenport (G.W. Dillingham, 1888).

2   Published by Carleton, 1866.

3   *Katie Fox, Epoch Making Medium and The Making of the Fox-Taylor Record* by W.G. Langworthy Taylor (G.P. Putnam's Sons, 1933).

4   Letter to George Eliot of 8 Feb 1872 contained in Literature Network site 'The Life of Harriet Beecher Stowe'.

5   This, and excerpts below, from *Katie Fox, Epoch Making Medium and The Making of the Fox-Taylor Record* by W.G. Langworthy Taylor (G.P. Putnam's Sons, 1933).

6   November 1871.

7   *Lights and Shadows of Spiritualism* (Virtue and Co., 1877).

8   *The First Psychic* by Peter Lamont (Little, Brown, 2005).

9   *The Shadow and the Light* (Hamish Hamilton, 1982).

10 *Quarterly Journal of Science*, 1874, Vol. IV.

11 Mark 5, 2–22.
12 *People from the Other World* by Henry Steel Olcott, (American Pub. Co., 1875). The account of the Olcott/Blavatsky first meeting, and subsequent séances, taken from this and the Colonel's memoir, *Old Diary Leaves*.
13 *The Theory of the Double, Light* Magazine, 22 Feb 1896, reproduced on survivalafterdeath.org.
14 *The Table Rappers.*
15 *Mystic London*, published in 1875, and cited in *The Spiritualists* by Ruth Brandon (Weidenfeld and Nicolson, 1983).
16 *People From The Other World.*
17 Account included in *Old Diary Leaves*.

8

1 *The Dance of 17 Lives* by Mick Brown (Bloomsbury, 2004).
2 *The Spiritualist*, 4 Feb 1876.
3 *Encyclopaedia Britannica.*
4 *A Magician Among the Spirits.*
5 On sale at the Theosophical Society.

9

1 11 October 1888.
2 Reprinted in *Light* Magazine.
3 *Isis Unveiled.*
4 *Reminiscences of HP Blavatsky* (Theosophical Publishing House, 1976).
5 *Madame Blavatsky* by John Symonds (Odhams Press Ltd, 1959).
6 *H.P. Blavatsky, As I Knew Her* by Alice Cleather (Thacker, Spink and Co., 1922).
7 *New York Press.*
8 I remember an occasion at a *Psychic News* dinner/dance when a celebrated elderly medium dropped dead during the Gay Gordons, in which she was enthusiastically participating. For some reason this inspired outrage by other mediums and groans of horror. It seemed to me an enviable end. The late Maurice Barbanell, then editor of

Psychic News, brought things back to an even keel in the paper with the headline 'Medium Dances into the Spirit World'. (*Note by the author*)

Epilogue

1   Bantam Press, 1988.
2   *Daily Mail*, 22 May 2003.
3   Mayflower Books Ltd, 1973.

BIBLIOGRAPHY

Andersen, Jens, *Hans Christian Andersen* (Duckworth, 2005)

Blavatsky, H.P., *Isis Unveiled* (J.W. Bouton, 1877, currently available Theosophical Publishing House)

———, *The Secret Doctrine* (Theosophical Publishing House, 1888)

Brandon, Ruth, *The Spiritualists*, (Weidenfeld and Nicholson)

Britten, Emma Hardinge, *Autobiography* (Wilkinson, 1900, reprinted SNU, 1999)

Brown, Mick, *The Dance of 17 Lives* (Bloomsbury, 2004)

Bulman, Joan, *Jenny Lind* (James Barrie, 1956)

Capron, Eliab, *Modern Spiritualism* (Bela Marsh, 1885, reprinted Amos Press, 1976)

Cleather, Alice, *H.P. Blavatsky, As I Knew Her* (Thacker, Spink & Co. 1922)

Davenport, Reuben Briggs, *The Death-Blow To Spiritualism* (Dillingham, 1888, reprinted Arno Press, 1976)

Davies, C.M., *Mystic London*, (London, 1875)

Doyle, Sir Arthur Conan, *The History Of Spiritualism* (reprinted The Spiritual Truth Press)

Edmonds, John W., and Dexter, George T., *Spiritualism* (1853)

d'Esperance Elizabeth, *Shadow Land* (1897)

Flint, Leslie, *Voices in the Dark*, (Macmillan, 1971)

Gaskill, Malcolm, *Hellish Nell* (Fourth Estate, 2001)

Hardinge, Emma, *Modern American Spiritualism* (1870, reprinted SNU, 1999)

Home, D.D., *Lights and Shadows of Spiritualism* (Virtue & Co., 1877)

Houdini, H., *A Magician Among the Spirits* (Harper & Bros., 1924)

Jenkins, Elizabeth, *The Shadow and the Light* (Hamish Hamilton, 1982)

Kalush, W.M., & Sloman, Larry, *The Secret Life of Houdini* (Simon & Schuster, 2006)

Kane, Margaret Fox, *The Love-Life of Dr Kane* (Carleton, 1866)

Keneally, Thomas, *Lincoln* (Phoenix, 2005)

Lamont, Peter, *The First Psychic* (Little, Brown, 2005)

Leider, Emily W., *Dark Lover* (Faber and Faber, 2003)

Leonard, Maurice, *Madame Blavatsky* (Regency Press, 1976)

Lycett, Andrew, *The Man Who Created Sherlock Holmes* (Weidenfeld, 2007)

Maynard, Nettie Colman, *Was Abraham Lincoln a Spiritualist?* (R.C. Hartranft, 1891)

Meade, Marion, *Madame Blavatsky*, (G.P. Putnam's Sons, 1980)

Morris, Michael, *Madam Valentino* (Abbeville Press, 1991)

Nichols, Thomas Low, *A Biography of the Brothers Davenport* (Saunders, Otley & Co., 1864)

Olcott, Henry S., *Old Diary Leaves* (Theosophical Publishing House, 1895. Currently available)

———, *People From The Other World* (American Publishing Co., 1875)

Owen, Robert Dale, *Footfalls On The Boundary Of Another World* (Lippincott, 1860)

———, *The Debatable Land*, (Carleton, 1872)

Pearsall, Ronald, *The Table Rappers* (Book Club Associates, 1973)

Pond, Miriam Buckner, *Time Is Kind,* published in Britain as *The Unwilling Martyrs* (Centennial Press, 1947)

Post, Isaac, *Voices From The Spirit World*, (Charles H. McDonnell, 1852)

Stemman, Roy, *One Hundred Years of Spiritualism* (The Spiritualist Association of Great Britain, 1972)

Stuart, Nancy Rubin, *The Reluctant Spiritualist*, (Harcourt Inc., 2005)

Symonds, John, *Madame Blavatsky* (Odhams Press, 1959)

Tardiff, Olive, *They Paved The Way* (Heritage Books, 1980)

Taylor, W.G. Langworthy, *Katie Fox, Epoch Making Medium and The Making of the Fox-Taylor Record* (G.P. Putnam's Sons 1933)

Tingley, Katherine, *The Wine of Life* (Woman's International Theosophical League, 1926)

Underhill, A. Leah, *The Missing Link In Modern Spiritualism* (Thomas R. Knox, 1885. Reprinted Arno Press, 1976)

Wachtmeister, Constance, *Reminiscences of H.P. Blavatsky* (Theosophical Publishing House, 1976)

Wagenknecht, Edward, *Seven Daughters of the Theatre* (Da Capo, 1964)
Ward, Hentietta Mary Ada, *Memories of 90 Years* (Hutchinson, 1924)
Wehner, George, *A Curious Life* (Horace Liveright, 1930)
Weisberg, Barbara, *Talking To the Dead* (Harpercollins Publishers, Inc., 2004)

INDEX

Adare, Viscount 157

Aksakof, Hon. Alex N. 179

Albert, Prince 132–3

Alexander, Tsar 125, 179

Alfie (Leah`s faithful retainer) 45

Ambler, Rev. R.P. 63

Andersen, Hans Christian 80

Arliss, George 113

d'Arpino, Duchess 168

Ashburner, Dr 82

Asoka, Emperor 118

Bach, J.S. 60

Bacon, Francis 72

Bailey, James A. 64, 79

Barbanell, Maurice 213

Barilli, Caterina 49

Barnum, P.T. 64, 79–80, 95

Barron, Henry D. 63

Baxter, George T. 72

Bayard, Dr Edward 102, 107, 145, 147–9

Beethoven, Ludwig van 60, 62

Bell, John 25, 27–9

Bell, Mrs 28

Belle (Spirit guide) 126

Benedict, Mrs 69–70

Bernhardt, Sarah 144

Besant, Annie 198–9

Besinnet, Ada 126

Black Feather (Spirit guide) 117

Blavatsky, Helena 16, 32, 41–2, 55, 91–2, 96, 115, 117–118, 161–2, 164–6, 168, 170–1, 174–5, 189–91, 196–9, 206, 209, 213, 215–6

Blavatsky, General 55

Blitz, Signor 139

Booth, John Wilkes 144

Boucicault, Dion 124

Bouton family 69, 71

Bradlaugh, Charles 198

Brahms, Johannes 60

Brandon, Ruth 213, 215

Bremer, Frederica 43–4

Brittan, Prof. Samuel B. 96

Brittain, Annie 126

Britten, Emma Hardinge 43, 45–6, 50–1, 53, 58, 65, 69–70, 103, 133, 175, 210–11, 215

Brooks, Miss 91

Brown, Calvin 36–8, 41, 45, 62, 64, 76–8, 83, 95–7, 101

Brown, Mick 175, 213, 215

Brown, Rosemary 59, 60–2, 118

Browning, Elizabeth Barrett 72, 86

Browning, Robert 72, 157

Brunel, Isambard Kingdom 113

Buescher, Prof. John 143

Bull, Ole 150

Bulman, Joan 210, 215

Bunker, Chang and Eng 79

Burns, James Drummond 15

Burr, Rev. Chauncey 75–7

Burr, Heman 76–7

Butlerof, Prof. 179

Byron, Lord 117

Calhoun, John C. 92–4

Capron, Eliab 44–50, 53, 59, 63–4, 66, 74–5, 104, 210, 215

Carlyle, Thomas 184–6, 195–6

Chamberlain, Judge 53

Chandler, Raymond 16

Chaney, Prof. W.H. 143

Cholmondley-Pennell, Henry 160

Chopin, Frederic 60, 80

Christmas, Mr 211

Child, Dr Henry T. 170

Churchill, Winston 120

Clark, Rev. Lemuel 44

Cleaver, Alice 199, 213

Clooney, Rosemary 183

Coleman, Benjamin 155–6

Colley, Archdeacon 123

Coman, D.F. 62–3

Cook, Florence 168–9, 173

Cooper, James Fenimore 66

Cottell, Mrs 184, 195–6, 200

Cottingley fairies 127

Coulomb Madame 190–1, 197

Crawford, Dr. W.J. 122

Crisp, Quentin 16

Cromwell, Oliver 185

Crookes, Sir William 158–9, 173–4, 178, 195

Culver, Ruth 75

Cushman, Charlotte Saunders 86–7, 105

Dalai Lama 175

Darwin, Charles 134

Davenport, Ira 123–5, 211, 216

Davenport, Reubin Briggs 193–4, 212, 215

Davenport, William 123–5, 211, 216

Davies, C.M. 168, 215

Davis, Andrew Jackson 57–8, 96

Davis, W.S. 183, 188, 201

Day, Horace H. 102–4

De Barr, Ann O'Delia Diss 184

Debussy, Claude 60, 62

De Morgan, Pof. 82

Dickens, Charles 72, 156

Dolgorukov, Princess 32

Donne, John 83

Doyle, Sir Arthur Conan 48, 51, 57, 59, 70, 82, 92, 116, 122, 126–7, 132, 201, 209, 215

Doyle, Lady 126–7

Draper, Nathaniel 58

Draper, Rachel 58–9

Duesler, Mr and Mrs 25–6

Du Maurier, George 88

Duncan, Helen 120–1, 123, 126, 169

Eagle, Georgina 132

Eddy, William and Horatio 162–6

Eddy, Mary Baker 118

Edmonds, Judge John Worth 71, 92, 96–7, 113, 133, 177, 215
Edwards, Harry 62
Eglinton, William 119, 122–3
Einstein, Albert 16
Eliot, George 82, 151, 212
Elizabeth I 72
Emmerich, Saint Anne Catherine 38
d'Esperance, Elizabeth 118–9, 126, 179, 215
Eyre, Governor 185

Fagnani, Joseph 99
Faraday, Michael 27, 125, 156, 211
Feda (Spirit guide) 126
Ferguson, Rev. Dr 123, 125
Fish, Bowman 20–1, 33
Fish, Lizzie 19–20, 33–5, 40, 44–5, 75, 83, 91, 95–6, 101, 129, 187
Fisher, Amy 122
Flint, Leslie 7, 13, 113–4, 114–6, 132, 211, 215
Foley, Charles 127
Forrest, Edwin 48
Fox family
    David 20, 22, 26–8, 33–6, 40, 54, 67–9, 75, 96, 129, 180–2, 188
    Elizabeth 20
    Elizabeth (sister-in-law) 68, 181
    Emily 135
    John 18–22, 24–6, 29, 33, 40, 45, 53, 62, 68, 83, 129–31, 136, 145, 187, 209
    Leah (niece) 180
    Maria 20, 27, 33, 40, 76–7
Fox, George 39
Franklin, Benjamin 26, 45, 58–9, 95, 112, 139, 152–3, 206–7, 209
Franklin, Sir John 84, 106
Franklin, Lady 84, 108

Galileo 17
Gaskill, Malcolm 120–1, 211, 215
Geller, Uri 159
Gerry, Eldridge Thomas 182–3
Gibson, Mel 38
Gladstone, Rt Hon. W.E. 122
Gordon, Henry 70
Gould, Dr N.B. 124
Granger, Adelaide 33, 38, 49
Grant, Ulysses 160
Gray, John (editor) 76–7, 81
Gray, Dr John 137, 139
Greeley, Horace 64–5, 67–9, 75–80, 84, 88, 90, 93, 98, 102, 104, 107, 130–1, 133, 146–7, 149, 160, 194–5
Greeley, Pickie 64–5, 69
Grieg, Edvard 150
Grinnell, Cornelius 101, 106, 108
Grinnell, Henry 98–9
Groute, Jacques 139
Grover, Belle 33
Guegidze, Michalko 165
Guppy, Mrs 166–9, 189, 205–6

Hall, Anne Maria 178
Hall, Samuel Carter 178
Hamilton, Duchess of 132
Hamilton, General 94
Harmony (Spirit guide) 126
Harris, Bertha 116
Harrison, William 167
Hascall, Judge A.P. 53–4
Hawking, Prof. Stephen 206
Hayden, Maria 81–2, 85, 154
Hedden, Hon. J. 53
Herman, Felicia 43

Herne, Frank 167–8
Herndon, William 143
Hodgson, Richard 191
Holiday, Billie 183
Holmes, Jenny and Nelson 92,
    168–71
Home, Daniel Dunglas 72, 156–8,
    173, 178
Honto (Spirit guide) 164–5
Hopps, Rev. John Page 173
Horsford, Prof. 124
Houdin, Robert 139, 212
Houdini 125–7, 183, 188, 194, 201,
    212, 215–6
Hunt, Thornton Leigh 82

Iris (Spirit guide) 126

Jefferson, Thomas 95
Jencken, Ferdinand 174–7, 181–2,
    202–4
Jencken, Edward 183
Jencken, Henry Jr 176–8, 181–2,
    202–4, 200
Jencken, Henry Dietrich 155–61,
    173–9, 183, 203
Jenkins, Elizabeth 158, 210, 216
Jervis, Rev. 49, 58
Joan of Arc 38
John, the Divine 70
Jones, Bence 211

Kane, Dr Elisha Kent 84–91, 93,
    96–102, 104–109, 129–31, 136–7,
    146–8, 177, 181, 183–6, 188, 194,
    207, 210–1, 216
Kappes, Alfred 163, 165
Kardec, Allan 175
Karmapa Lama 175

Kase, Colonel 142
Kathlyne 212
Katin, Peter 60–2
Keneally, Thomas 212, 216
Keyes, Jenny 113
King, John 91–2, 136, 168, 170–1
King, Katie 136, 168–71, 173, 206
King, Mackenzie 132
Knef, Hildegarde 88
Koons, Jonathan, and sons 91–2

La Fumee, Joseph 147–8
Lamon, Ward Hill 144
Lamont, Peter 212, 216
Lang, Mrs 149
Laurie, Rev. James 141
Laurie, Margaret 141–2, 144
Lees, Robert James 132
Leider, Emily W. 211, 216
Lellenberg, Jon 127
Lewes, George 82
Lewis, E.E. 29, 33
Lill, John 60
Lincoln family
    Abraham 141–5, 151, 212, 216
    Mary Todd 141–4
    Eddie 141
    Robert 144
    Thomas 144
    Willie 141
Lind, Jenny 79–81, 210, 215
Liszt, Franz 59–61
Livermore, Charles F. 95, 137–9,
    145–6, 148–9, 151–6, 159–61, 170,
    203, 212
Livermore, Estelle 137–9, 146,
    148–9, 156, 170
Loomis, Prof. 67
Lorrimore, Gladys 116

Losey, Aurelia 28
Louis, Chevalier 58
Lycett, Andrew 127, 216
Lyon, Mrs 157

McGeachy, Cora 117
McNaughton, Duncan 53–4
Macready, William 48
Marguerite, Princess 167–8
Marsh, General Luther 184
Marx, Karl 134
Mary, Sister, of Agreda 166
Maskelyne 125
Mayer, Louis B. 80
Maynard, Nettie Colman 141–3,
  216
Meade, Marion 209, 216
Mickey (Spirit control) 113, 115
Miles, A.J. 121
Miller, Belle (aka Youngs) 141–4
Miller, James J. 143
Montenard, Madame 98
Morgan, Sir Henry 92
Moroni 57, 117
Morris, Michael 211, 216
Morrison, Herbert 120
Morse, Samuel 26, 41
Morton (Kane's servant) 100
Mundy, Talbot 117–8

Napoleon, Emperor 125
Natal, Bishop of 134
Negri, Pola 113
Newton, Isaac 17
Nichols, Dr. Thomas Low 124
Novello, Ivor 113, 116

Ogden, Blanche 154–6, 160
Olcott, Colonel Henry S. 42, 57–8,
  91, 119–20, 162–6, 170–1,
  189–90, 197–9, 210, 213, 216
Olin (Spirit communicant) 150, 152
O'Sullivan J.L. 201
Owen, Robert Dale 42, 134–6,
  138–9, 151–2, 155, 169–71, 178,
  194, 212, 216

Paganini 150
Parrott, Prof. Ian 60
Partridge, Charles 70, 91, 97
Pearsall, Ronald 123 168, 216
Penn, William 209
Pierce, Benjamin 124
Pierce, Benny 100
Pierce, Jane Appleton 99, 211
Pierce, President Franklin 99–100
Poe, Edgar Allen 93
Pond, Miriam Buckner 37, 69, 27, 216
Post, Amy 38–9, 47, 49, 52, 75, 96
Post, Edmund 95
Post, Isaac 38, 40, 43, 47, 52, 54, 75,
  95–6, 211, 216
Pulver, Mrs 27–8
Pulver, Lucretia 28

Rachmaninoff, Sergei 60
Rains, Major George W. 97
Rambova, Natacha 116, 117–8
Redfield, Mr and Mrs 24–6
Richet, Prof. Charles 165
Richmond, Dr C.M. 188
Roosevelt, Theodore 184
Rosna, Charles 17, 25, 27, 29, 34–5,
  37, 42, 58, 132

Saar-Louis, Little prophet of 175
Sand, George 117
Schubert, Franz 60–2

Scott, Ivy 15
Scott, James D. 70
Seybert, Henry 180, 194
Seymour, Mrs 104
Shaw, George Bernard 198
Sheldon, Henry 112
Sidgwick, Prof. Henry and Mrs 123, 179
Sloman, Larry 126, 216
Smith, Joseph 57, 117
Spamer, Earle E. 105, 211
Stashower, Daniel 127
Stebbins, Emma 86–7
Stemman, Roy 212, 216
Stowe, Harriet Beecher 151, 212
Summefield, Judge 53
Swedenborg, Emanuel 57, 72, 149, 179
Symonds, John 216

Tallmadge Hon. Nathaniel P. 92–4, 103, 133
Tallmadge, William 94
Tamlin, Sarah 59, 91
Tardiff, Olive 100, 216
Taylor family
  George and Sarah 111, 149, 150–4, 177, 182, 202–4, 207
  Eliza 149
  Frankie 149, 152
  Leila 153
  William Langworthy 203, 211–2, 216
Thackeray, William M. 157
Thompson, General Waddy 92
Tiffany, Joel 76
Tingley, Katherine 118, 216
Tolstoy, Leo 166

Turner family 98–9, 101–2, 105
Twain, Mark 157

Underhill, Daniel 112, 129–31, 134–5, 176, 180, 146

Valentino, Rudolph 113–4, 116–8, 211, 216
Varley, Cromwell Fleetwood 140–1
Victoria, Queen 132–3
Vick, Mrs 38, 40
Voltaire 95, 209

Wachtmeister, Countess 197, 216
Wagenknecht, Edward 210, 217
Wallace, Dr Alfred Russel 167
Walter, Ellen 102, 105, 106–7
Ward, Henrietta Mary Ada 158
Washington, George 79, 95
Watson, Prof. J. Jay 150
Weekman, Michael and Hannah 27–9, 34
Wehner, George 117, 217
Wheaton, Blanche 117–8
Whitman, Walt 86, 117
Whittlesey, Hon. Frederick 51
Willets, George 46, 52–3, 58–9
Wilson, Dr 111
Wiseman, Prof. Richard 205
Wolfit, Sir Donald 88
Wriedt, Etta 132

Yolande (Spirit guide) 119, 126
Yolande, Madame 13
Youngs, Henry and Belle 143–4
Youngs, Theophilus 143–4

Zhelikovsky, Vera 31, 161